AN ATHEIST'S V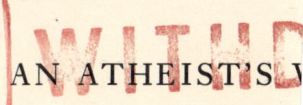

UNIVERSITY OF SURREY LIBRARY

BOOK NUMBER......**7701486**

Please return this book on or before the last date stamped below. Fines are charged on overdue books (see Library Guide). Books may be renewed by phone, letter, or in person provided they are not requested by another reader.

24 FEB 1978

28 NOV 1979

27 SEP 1983

11 SEP 1991

10 FEB 1994

AN ATHEIST'S VALUES

BY

RICHARD ROBINSON

*Fellow of Oriel College
Oxford*

BASIL BLACKWELL
OXFORD

1975

© RICHARD ROBINSON 1964

FIRST PUBLISHED BY OXFORD UNIVERSITY PRESS
AND REISSUED BY BASIL BLACKWELL, OXFORD
AS A BLACKWELL PAPERBACK, 1975

ISBN 0 631 15970 3

SET AT THE UNIVERSITY PRESS, OXFORD
BY VIVIAN RIDLER
PRINTER TO THE UNIVERSITY
AND REPRINTED LITHOGRAPHICALLY
IN GREAT BRITAIN
BY CAMELOT PRESS LTD, SOUTHAMPTON

AUTHOR'S NOTE

This book arose as a course of lectures; and no attempt has been made to remove the lecturing style

CONTENTS

1. **THE NATURE OF THE QUESTION** — 9
   - 1.1. INTRODUCTION — 9
   - 1.2. THE SEARCH FOR THE GOOD — 14
   - 1.3. THE SEARCH FOR THE PROPERTY GOODNESS — 18
   - 1.4. THE CHOICE OF GOODS — 24
   - 1.5. MEANS AND ENDS — 29
   - 1.6. WISE AND FOOLISH CHOICE — 35
   - 1.7. JUDGEMENT — 41
   - 1.8. OBJECTIONS TO THE ENTERPRISE — 43

2. **PERSONAL GOODS** — 48
   - 2.1. PRINCIPLES OF CHOICE — 48
   - 2.2. LIFE — 54
   - 2.3. BEAUTY — 57
     - 2.31. The word 'beauty' — 57
     - 2.32. Beauty is a great good — 59
     - 2.33. Art and sex — 61
   - 2.4. TRUTH — 65
     - 2.41. The ideal of Truth — 65
     - 2.42. Truth is a great good — 67
   - 2.5. REASON — 70
     - 2.501. Virtue — 70
     - 2.502. The word 'reason' — 72
     - 2.503. The love of truth — 73
     - 2.504. Respect for reasons — 74
     - 2.505. The love of consistency — 77
     - 2.506. Deductiveness — 80
     - 2.507. The pursuit of certainty — 81
     - 2.508. The pursuit of probability — 84
     - 2.509. Respect for evidence — 88
     - 2.510. Tentativeness — 94
     - 2.511. The submission of reason — 96
     - 2.512. Practical reason — 98
     - 2.513. Depreciations of reason — 100
   - 2.6. LOVE — 105
   - 2.7. CONSCIENTIOUSNESS — 108

2.8. RELIGION 113
    2.81. Religion and reason 113
    2.82. Faith 118
    2.83. There is no god or after-life 123
    2.84. Religion and reasons for morality 130
    2.85. Religion and causes of morality 133
    2.86. The ethics of the synoptic gospels 140
    2.87. Criticism of the synoptic gospels 150
    2.88. The human situation 155

3. POLITICAL GOODS 158

3.1. THE STATE 158
    3.11. Political goods 158
    3.12. Is the State a great good? 160
    3.13. No State should be worshipped 161
    3.14. States are moral agents 168

3.2. EQUALITY 173
    3.21. Equality in political power 173
    3.22. Equality before the law 176
    3.23. Equality in wealth 178
    3.24. Equality in respect 181
    3.25. The basis of equality 184

3.3. FREEDOM 187
    3.31. Freedom is a good 187
    3.32. Muddles about freedom 194

3.4. TOLERANCE 198
    3.41. The principle of tolerance 198
    3.42. Free speech 203
    3.43. All men are fallible 207
    3.44. The limits of tolerance 214

3.5. PEACE AND JUSTICE 219
    3.51. The uses of government 219
    3.52. Socialism 222
    3.53. The prime ends of government 224

3.6. DEMOCRACY 228
    3.61. The word 'democracy' 228
    3.62. Democracy is a great good 235
    3.63. Plato's argument against democracy 243
    3.64. The maintenance of democracy 248

INDEX 254

1

THE NATURE OF THE QUESTION

1.1.	Introduction	9
1.2.	The Search for the Good	14
1.3.	The Search for the Property Goodness	18
1.4.	The Choice of Goods	24
1.5.	Means and Ends	29
1.6.	Wise and Foolish Choice	35
1.7.	Judgement	41
1.8.	Objections to the Enterprise	43

1.1. INTRODUCTION

WE often hear talk of 'Christian values'. Those who use this phrase are confident that everybody knows what the Christian values are. But I do not know what they are. For example, I am puzzled whether thrift is a Christian value in view of the fact that, whereas thrift is often praised by people calling themselves Christian, it is rejected by Jesus in the gospels.

We often hear talk of 'Western values', as if we knew quite well what they are. I find this puzzling too. Do they include capitalism? Do they include promise-keeping? If so, is promise-keeping therefore not an Eastern value?

The *Cambridge Journal*, iii. 368, wrote of 'the very real conviction of Spaniards that human, and not mechanical, values alone really count'. What is this distinction between human and mechanical values? If you love your mother that is a human value, but if you love your car that is a mechanical value? In that case the *Journal* was saying that according to the Spaniards your love of your car does not 'really count', and hence may be overridden and disregarded.

In the *Sunday Times* of 27 July 1958 someone wrote of the 'unshaken belief that values just cannot be the products of evolution'. This also seems mysterious. I value birds, and I believe that birds are products of evolution. I also believe that I the valuer am myself a product of evolution, and that, until the higher animals were evolved, no valuing was done on this earth and nothing was considered a value. These seem to be platitudes which only the rare fundamentalists deny; but I cannot imagine what else the writer can have meant to deny.

Mr. Gollancz wrote and published a book which he called *Our Threatened Values*. But I could not make out what these values were, nor whether the threat consisted in people's ceasing to value them or in their ceasing to be able to realize them.

Joyce Cary in a broadcast (*The Listener*, 17 January 1952) spoke of 'the feeling that values are not secure'; but it was impossible to tell whether he meant the feeling that people are changing their valuations, or that they cannot be sure of preserving the things they value, or that they do not know what to value.

The view that people do not know what to value is expressed in *The Rationalist Annual* for 1960, p. 78: 'There has perhaps never before been a time when people in the world, and especially in this country, have found it so difficult to know what to believe in and what to value.' This view also seems to lie behind much of the objection taken by some laymen to present Oxford philosophy. They seem to be upbraiding Oxford philosophers for not telling them what to value.

Yet it is very strange if the layman needs Oxford philosophers to tell him that milk and cheese are good, that flowers and butterflies and children dancing in the sun are good, that love and joy and companionship and laughter are good. Is there really anyone who is in the unpleasant condition of not caring about anything and wishing he did care about something?

Well, perhaps there is. After all, we know that small isolated cultures sometimes die when their bearers become aware of European culture, and that this appears to be because they cease to value anything when they see that Europeans, who are much more powerful than they are, do not share their valuations. And nowadays there is something like a quick and never-ending succession of culture-clashes within Europe itself, because of the frequency of communications and the flood of new ideas and inventions and situations. Some people are perhaps rendered very downcast, and dubious about their own valuations, by the discovery that these valuations are not universally shared. And some others, perhaps, who have been shocked by the atomic bomb into belated recognition that we are always liable to lose what we hold dear, have drawn the unwarranted conclusion that what we have held dear is not really dear at all.

With anyone who is in such a position one ought to sympathize, and I do. And he is welcome to listen to me affirming my beliefs as to what is good and what is bad. At the same time I must warn him against some likely disappointments.

First, there is no guarantee that the values I shall defend are precisely those he would like to see defended. The layman who thinks that he wants some authority to tell him the objective truth about good and evil, to provide him with a purpose and a creed, is liable to find, if someone takes him at his word, that he already has very strong valuations of his own, and that they clash with those he is offered. From being an earnest pupil he is liable to become an infuriated teacher. He discovers that he already possesses that 'faith to live by' which he thought he was seeking, and that the man who was to give it to him is really a wicked underminer thereof. Thus he is cured of asking philosophers to give a lead, and comes to see that every man must decide for himself what is good. Perhaps also he comes to see that what he really wanted from philosophers was not that they should lead *him*, but that they should lead *others* to adopt *his* convictions.

The second disappointment that such a layman is likely to suffer is similar to the disappointment that many have felt on reading Euclid's geometry. Euclid at first seems to prove his propositions in a gloriously scientific way; but, when we examine one of his proofs minutely, we find that it rests on certain assumptions which he says he proved earlier. If we turn back to examine this earlier proof, we find that it, too, rests on certain assumptions, for which we are referred still further back. Then the disappointing truth dawns on us that the whole book rests on five original assumptions for which Euclid offers no reason whatever. Now this is not a personal defect of Euclid's. It is part of the nature of proof. It therefore applies equally to the recommendation of propositions about good and bad. And in ethics, unfortunately, we come to these first unproved assumptions much sooner than we do in geometry.

The layman tends still to regard philosophy as our founder Plato regarded it, that is, as the enterprise of discovering, with scientific certainty and objectivity, the real natures of good and evil, which, he thinks, are wholly independent of man, and thus fixing good and evil and right and wrong for all time. This enterprise, however,

I think we now know to be impossible, because good and ill are not wholly independent of man. Philosophy must therefore abate some of the claims which Plato made for it and the layman still makes for it. It remains, however, still very Platonic and very important after having done so.

Another feature of these lectures that may disappoint a layman is their analytical attention to words. That is and always has been characteristic of philosophy, and I cannot help it. Those who believe that the serious discussion of great questions of good and evil can and should proceed without any criticism of language, are certainly wrong, and certainly not philosophers. Philosophy is essentially a hairsplitting form of religion; and this will always alienate people who dislike finding split hairs in their religion.

The most serious disappointment these lectures may give is that the valuations I express may be found not nearly optimistic enough. My views are, in fact, sometimes bitter medicine, depressing and amazing to many young people brought up in the ordinary English way. One of my former listeners was so amazed that he asked me if I really believed what I said. It may easily be that you are not strong enough to bear what I have to say, and therefore should not come. Perhaps you can judge this from the following summary of what I shall say.

Part I. The Nature of the Question. 1.2: The great question, What is the good?, is an error because there is no such thing as *the* good (pp. 14-18). 1.3: We must ask instead, What things are good? And we must interpret this not as a search for the property of goodness (pp. 18-24), but (1.4) as an invitation to make our own choice (pp. 24-29), which (1.5) is not the same as a search for ends (pp. 29-35). 1.6: Choice can be wise or foolish (pp. 35-41). 1.7: The process of making wise choices is judgement (pp. 41-43). 1.8: All good things are harmful sometimes; yet it is worth while to make ourselves a list of goods (pp. 43-47).

Part II. Personal Goods. 2.1: The test of goodness and badness is happiness and misery (pp. 48-53). 2.2: Life is a great good (pp. 54-57). 2.31: The word 'beauty' means that which is good in its sensuous aspects (pp. 57-59). 2.32: Beauty is a great good (pp. 59-61), closely related both to art and to sex (pp. 61-65). 2.41: Truth, which is a matter of statements (pp. 65-67), is (2.42) a great good (pp. 67-70).

2.501: Virtue is a great good, and the greatest virtue is reason (pp. 70–72). 2.502: The word 'reason' means the good employment of man's capacity to think (pp. 72–73). 2.503: Reason commands that we love truth (pp. 73–74), that (2.504) we believe or disbelieve or doubt in accordance with the balance of the reasons available (pp. 74–77), that (2.505) we seek consistency (pp. 77–80), that (2.506) we note the consequences of our beliefs (pp. 80–81), that (2.507) we distinguish between analytic and synthetic statements, pursuing certainty about the former (pp. 81–84) and (2.508) probability about the latter (pp. 84–87), that (2.509) we respect the weight of the evidence (pp. 88–94), that (2.510) we hold our views tentatively (pp. 94–96), and (2.511) submit them to criticism (pp. 96–98). 2.512: Reason is practical (pp. 98–100). 2.513: Depreciations of reason often arise from thinking that the mind is a toolbox and reason is one of the tools (pp. 100–5). 2.6: The greatest good but one is love (pp. 105–8). 2.7: Conscientiousness must be subordinated to reason and love, but it is a great good (pp. 108–13).

2.81: Religion is more of an evil than a good because it is gravely inimical to truth and reason (pp. 113–18). 2.82: Faith is a vice (pp. 118–23). 2.83: There is no god or afterlife (pp. 123–30). 2.84: Religion provides no good reason for behaving morally (pp. 130–3) and (2.85) is not the only cause which in fact makes people behave morally when they do (pp. 133–40). 2.86: To discover what the Christian values are is a matter for study and interpretation (pp. 140–9). 2.87: The main precepts of Jesus according to the synoptic gospels were: love God, believe in Jesus, love man, be pure in heart, and be humble (pp. 149–50). The first two of these are to be rejected; the third is to be accepted; the fourth and fifth are doubtful (pp. 150–5). 2.88: The human race is alone and insecure and doomed. Let us meet this situation with cheerfulness, courage, love, and the affirmation and pursuit of our ideals (pp. 155–7).

Part III. Political Goods. 3.11: Political goods are goods arising out of the existence of governments, and they are genuine goods (pp. 158–60).

3.12: The State is often regarded as a god (pp. 160–1). 3.13: But no State should be worshipped (pp. 161–8). 3.14: States are, however, moral agents (pp. 168–73).

3.21: Equality in political power is impossible, but we should approach it (pp. 173–5). 3.22: Equality before the law is impossible, but we should approach it (pp. 176–8). 3.23: Equality in wealth is a bad ideal (pp. 178–81). 3.24: Equality in dignity is profoundly good, but hardly a political matter (pp. 181-4). 3.25: The basis for equalization in dignity is equality in suffering, and therefore it should be extended to the beasts (pp. 184-7).

3.31: Freedom is a great good (pp. 188-94). 3.32: The concept of freedom is very liable to muddles (pp. 194-8).

3.41: We must not suppress the evil behaviour of other men until reasonable examination has made it very probable that trying to suppress the evil would greatly lessen human misery upon the whole (pp. 198-202). 3.42: Free speech is far more likely to produce a general spread of true opinion than is any suppression of it (pp. 203-6), because (3.43) all men are fallible (pp. 207-13). 3.44: In certain departments the limits of tolerance come sooner than liberals have been inclined to think (pp. 214-19).

3.51: There is no single right purpose of all government at all time (pp. 219-22). 3.52: There is no single right answer to the question what common enterprises a government should undertake (pp. 222-4). 3.53: But the primary ends of all States should be peace and justice (pp. 224-8).

3.61: Democracy is the constitution in which the people can at regular intervals constitutionally dismiss the governors if they so choose (pp. 228-35). 3.62: It is on the whole a great good (pp. 235-43). 3.63: Plato's argument against it fails because government is not a science (pp. 243-8). 3.64: We need to remind ourselves of our duties concerning the maintenance of democracy (pp. 248-53).

1.2. THE SEARCH FOR THE GOOD

Plato propounded the great question: What is the good? The good, he made his 'Socrates' say in the *Republic*, is the greatest study. We do not know what it is, and yet without this knowledge no other knowledge is of any use. Some think it is pleasure; some think it is knowledge; but it cannot be either. It is the only thing of which we are never content with a mere seeming. Every soul pursues it, and does everything it does for the sake of it, divining that it is something, but doubting and being unable to find out for certain *what* it is. In his *Philebus* Plato added that the good is perfect and sufficient and capable of making happy the life of man.

Aristotle said: 'They did well who represented the good as What everything aims at. There must be some end of our actions which we

THE NATURE OF THE QUESTION

desire for its own sake, while we desire other things for the sake of this end. It cannot be that we desire everything for the sake of something else; for that would give an unending process, so that our impulse would be empty and vain. There must be therefore an end which we desire for its own sake, and this is clearly the good and the best.' (A paraphrase of parts of the first page of the *Nicomachean Ethics*.)

The followers of Plato and Aristotle have ever since been trying to answer this great question, What is the good?, or else to rewrite it first and then answer it in its rewritten form. These lectures are my attempt to do so.

It is not the question what men actually think good or actually pursue. Perhaps most men actually aim at money or sex or power. Perhaps they do not aim at anything of a general nature, but merely pursue some particular aim today and another tomorrow. This is a question for statistical psychology, or some such observational science. But evidently the question Plato propounded is not a request for statistics.

Is it the question How to be happy? That seems harder to decide. On the one hand, it seems that the good must have some connexion with happiness. Plato said that it is capable of making happy the life of man. We can hardly imagine that the good could possibly be inimical to man's happiness, or even indifferent to it. It seems inconceivable that anyone who had offered an account of the good should then add: 'but we shall be happier if we avoid it.' Aristotle concluded that the good *is* precisely happiness.

On the other hand, the question how to be happy seems another of these scientific questions, to be answered by observation or experiment. Does regular physical exercise tend to make us happy or not? That seems very little to do with Plato's question What is the good? Anyhow, the question How to be happy? is a question of means, of what means of making ourselves happy are in our power; but the question What is the good? is clearly not a question of means. It appears then that the two questions, What is the good? and How can we make ourselves happy?, are related but distinct.

Now a consideration arises which threatens to put an end to the whole enterprise of discovering what the good is before it can begin. This is that What is the good? is a false question.

A false question is one that implies a falsehood. For example, Why are you twenty feet tall? is an obviously false question. Every question implies some statement or other. People sometimes complain of examiners for asking questions which imply a statement that may not be true; but it is impossible to invent a question that does not do this, as you will find if you try. Hence we may reasonably ask about every question what statements it implies, and whether these implied statements are true or false.

The question What is the good? implies the statement that there is such a thing as *the* good, and this implies that there is one and only one thing that is good. To talk of *the* good implies that there is one and only one good thing.

To understand this it is necessary to examine a little the meaning of the word 'the'. It is all right to say that 'the Provost of Oriel spoke' because there is one and only one Provost of Oriel. But it is wrong to say 'the Archbishop of Oriel spoke' because there is no Archbishop of Oriel; and it is wrong to say 'the undergraduate of Oriel spoke', because there is more than one undergraduate of Oriel. It would be correct to say 'the undergraduate of Oriel spoke' if you were describing a group in which there was one and only one Oriel undergraduate.

This is not to say that the word 'the' always means one and only one. It evidently does not mean that in the phrase 'the kings of England', or in any phrase where it is followed by a noun in the plural. Nor does it always mean that when followed by a noun in the singular. The statement that 'the robin is a pugnacious bird' does not imply that there is only one robin, but is a way of saying something about robins in general.

Sometimes, however, the word 'the' does mean one and only one; and it means that in the question What is the good?

But it is obvious that there is more than one good thing in the world. Westminster Abbey is good, and so is Beethoven's Fifth Symphony. Or, if we turn to generalities, truth is good and so is love. Hence the question, What is the good?, is false. Instead of being answered, it requires to be rejected: many things are good. Thus our enterprise seems to end before it begins, and Plato's question seems a mistake. There is no such thing as *the* good.

If you find this difficult to believe, and think there must be something wrong with the argument, consider the following supporting evidence.

No one has ever given a satisfactory answer to the question What is the good? Plato in the *Republic* made his 'Socrates' disclaim knowledge of the answer, and content himself with a comparison of the good to the sun. In the *Philebus* he seems to be preparing himself to give the answer, and does at the end say something that looks as if it might be meant to be the answer; but it is completely unsatisfactory. The good, we seem to be told, is in the first place measure, secondly symmetry, thirdly mind, fourthly knowledge, and fifthly pure pleasures. I have not yet heard of anyone who felt enlightened by this. No subsequent writer has redeemed the master's failure. The suspicion arises that the question is unanswerable because wrongly put.

Aristotle's argument that the good must exist is a mistake. He shows that there must be *at least* one thing that we desire for its own sake, and assumes that he has thereby shown that there is *only* one thing that we desire for its own sake.

It is a very common error to use the word 'the' so as to imply that there is only one thing of a certain kind when in fact there are many. People are always asking What was *the* cause of the collision? as if it had only one. People are always talking about *the* aim of education as if all teachers had one and the same aim, or ought to have.

Fairly common also is the opposite error of implying that there is more than one when there is only one by using 'a' when you should use 'the'. People write of 'keeping vibration to *a* minimum', whereas there is only one minimum of vibration, namely no vibration. A British Labour Party pamphlet of August 1951 said that 'the maintenance of the social services is *a* first charge on the resources of the country'. There can be only one first; so it should have been 'the'. But it is politically convenient to say both that one is putting the social services first and that one is putting some other things equally high.

Such an elementary error maintains itself easily enough if it serves a great human need, and this particular error does so. No good thing or combination of good things is perfectly satisfying to us. In spite of enjoying them all we are often dissatisfied and sad. So we come to hope for a panacea, something that will permanently remove all misery for ever. The doctrine of *the* good is in a form that makes it possible, for some of us some of the time, to believe that there is such a panacea. *The* good, then, is that which cures all misery always, that which 'can give all men a happy life'.

Alas! There is no such panacea. Or, rather, there is, but it is death. Death is the only permanent cure for dissatisfaction and misery. While we live we are liable to them.

The idea of *the* good is among other things a way of shutting one's eyes to the inevitable conflicts of goods, and pretending that they do not exist or need not exist. *The* good is conceived as being a good that never conflicts with any other good and never has any kind of ill effect. But there cannot be such a good. Nothing is guaranteed never to have any bad effects, and never to interfere with anything desirable. If a man has more than one interest in life (and we all inevitably have) it is always possible for circumstances to arise in which he cannot satisfy one interest without disappointing another. Those who think there is a god may *believe* that he never has any ill effects, but they cannot *show* it. On the contrary, it certainly looks as if, if there is a god, he has done and is doing terrible things. When people use the undesirable phrase 'there are no absolute values', this is perhaps one of the things they confusedly mean, namely that everything has some bad effects; and in that sense the phrase is true.

I conclude that the question What is the good? is false, and must be not answered but rewritten.

1.3. THE SEARCH FOR THE PROPERTY GOODNESS

How can we rewrite Plato's question so as to eliminate the falsehood it implied, while retaining as much as possible of its spirit and intention?

The first rewriting that comes to mind is: What is the supreme good?, or What is the best thing? The opening of John Stuart Mill's *Utilitarianism* suggests that he thought that this was what had always really been meant: 'From the dawn of philosophy, the question concerning the *summum bonum*, or, what is the same thing, concerning the foundation of morality, has been accounted the main problem in speculative thought. . . . And after more than two thousand years the same discussions continue, philosophers are still ranged under the same contending banners, and neither thinkers nor mankind at large seem nearer to being unanimous on the subject.'

This rewriting will not do any better than the original question. Though it no longer implies the obvious falsehood that there is only one good thing, it now implies something not at all obviously true, namely that there is some one thing that is better than all other things. This is not necessarily so. There may be no best thing, either because three things are all equally good and each better than any fourth thing, or because what is best in the universe changes from time to time. Even if there is a best thing, it may be so little better than a host of other good things as to deserve no more attention than any of them. The phrases *summum bonum* and 'supreme good' are dubious in the same way as the recent phrase 'maximizing total welfare'. It seems probable that there always could be a higher degree of welfare than there is, and always could be a greater good than there is. Anyhow, we hope and believe that it is always possible to have greater goods than we have; and we want *all* goods, not merely one of them even if it is the best.

It may be that Plato regarded his question, at least in part, as being the search for a standard. *The* good, he perhaps thought, is that good which is the standard for all other goods. So arises the idea that we might rewrite his question as: What is the standard good?

However, this second rewriting will not do either. It is good to have particular standards for particular purposes. For example, it is a good thing to have standards for eating-apples. But it would not do to take the standard for eating-apples and turn it into a standard for apples in general. We may reject an apple for eating and yet accept it as good for cooking. We insist on using both standards—the eating standard and the cooking standard. Nor can one say that, if we put the two together, the eating plus the cooking standard, then we have *the* standard for apples; because we also insist on keeping always open the possibility of adopting yet more standards in the future, perhaps one for cider apples and another one for apples to decorate the house, and always the possibility of yet another some day.

But if *the* good were a standard it would be a standard for everything. That is what would be meant by calling it *the* standard. Hence it would involve rejecting now for all time to come everything that did not conform to itself. To answer the question what the good is, in this sense, would be to legislate now for every valuation we are ever to make. That would be foolish, and we intend not to do it. We intend to leave ourselves free to adopt new standards of goodness in the future as events suggest them to us. If we adopted a standard good, we should be rejecting all future novelty and creativeness of the highest sort. We have seen too much already of new kinds of good thing being despised because they did not conform to adopted standards, and we want no more of it. Thus we cannot accept Plato's question in this form either, though I shall later adopt another sort of standard.

Nor can we accept, thirdly, the religious version of Plato's question, as meaning What is the end for man? or What is the purpose of life? There is no one purpose that all of us ought to adopt. A multiplicity of different ways of living may be good, some of them not yet imagined by anybody. People who tell us that the end of human life is so and so are in effect commanding us to do that, choosing our ends for us. But they have no right to do so.

Most of them, of course, would reply to me here that they are not issuing their own orders to us but reporting God's orders to us. This reply fails twice, however, once because they have no respectable evidence that there is a god and these are his orders, and once because if there were a god he would have no right to give such orders. It would be wrong for a father to say to his child: 'I begot you in order to have support when I am past work; therefore you ought to support me.' It would be equally wrong for a god to say to his creature: 'I created you in order to do so and so; therefore you ought to do so and so.' If you procreate a child to get a nurse for your old age, or a plaything, or a defender of the State, your intention does not oblige your child to seek the end you had in mind. Similarly, if a god created us human beings for some end which he had in mind, his act does not morally oblige us to pursue that end. No person, human or divine, has a right to prescribe another person's ends.

I come now to a fourth rewriting of Plato's question, namely: What things are good?

In this form the question at last seems to presuppose nothing false. It presupposes now only that there are some things and that some of them might possibly be good; and this we are confident enough is true.

On the other hand, this is a disappointing change at first, because the question in losing its falsehood seems also to have lost its thrill. The mystery and holiness of *the* good have vanished.

Yes, they have vanished, like other imaginary delights. And it is our task to cease regretting them, and to come to take an interest in the true question that has replaced them. We can help ourselves to do so by noticing that this new question, What things are good?, is not, as we may for the first minute suppose, pedestrian or obvious or unimportant. We are often in doubt whether a thing is good; and, when we are sure that it is good, we can often find somebody else who is sure that it is not; and disagreements about whether a thing is good often seem desperately important.

One way to come to take an interest in this question is to observe that there seems to be no good way to answer it. This was first clearly brought out, I believe, by G. E. Moore in his famous *Principia Ethica*. He wrote that 'no relevant evidence whatever can be adduced' (*P.E.* viii). He was referring to the question, What kind of things ought to exist for their own sakes?; but he regarded that as equivalent to the question, What kind of things are good in themselves? He held that there can be evidence that a thing is good as a means to something else, because there can be evidence whether it does produce that other thing; but there can be no evidence that it is good in itself. And this certainly seems to be correct. You cannot infer the goodness of a thing from laws of nature, because laws of nature do not mention goodness. Goodness is not a property that we see or hear or smell or taste in the course of observing the world and acquiring evidence.

Although Moore held that there cannot be *evidence* whether a thing is intrinsically good, he did not think that there was no *method* whatever of determining whether a thing is intrinsically good. On the contrary, he possessed and practised what he called 'the method of isolation'. 'It is absolutely essential', he wrote, 'to consider each distinguishable quality, *in isolation*, in order to decide what value it possesses' (§ 55). And again: 'In order to arrive at a correct decision on the ⟨question what things have intrinsic value⟩, it is necessary to consider what things are such that, if they existed *by themselves*, in absolute isolation, we should yet judge their existence to be good; and, in order to decide upon the relative *degrees* of value of different things, we must similarly consider what comparative value seems to attach to the isolated existence of each' (§ 112, p. 187).

The method of isolation is thus a sort of experiment in imagination. In order to test whether a thing is intrinsically good, one imagines the universe as consisting in nothing but that thing, existing quite alone, and then asks oneself whether it is good. In order to test whether one thing is intrinsically better than another, one imagines first a universe consisting solely of the one, and then a universe consisting solely of the other, and compares them. Moore's famous comparison of the two worlds, one very beautiful and one very ugly, and neither of them containing any sentient being, is, I suppose, an example of the method, though it occurs before he has described it (pp. 83-84). Thus the method can tell us, he thought, whether beauty is good in itself.

It is clearly a method for obtaining reliable intuitions, intuition being knowledge obtained without inference. It is not a way of *inferring* that a thing is good in itself, but a way of getting oneself into a position to *see* that it is good in itself. It is a method for producing sharp mental vision, just as opening one's eyes and adjusting the light are methods for producing sharp physical vision.

But have you any confidence in this method of isolation, or in the intuition that is supposed to result? For my part, I have none; and I find it very odd that Moore writes as if, when he employed this method of determining whether anything is intrinsically good, he usually became confident what the true answer was. When I place myself in one of these imaginary situations, I find that all my confidence evaporates, and I no longer seem to have any intuition whatever as to what things are good in themselves. I feel rather as if I were being asked to keep quite still while somebody removed the floor on which I was standing.

In order to see better the true colour of a patch, it is sometimes useful to isolate the patch from surrounding patches. For this purpose people take a neutral grey card with a little window cut in it, and hold it so that the patch they wish to see better shows through the window and nothing else does. Thus a certain method of isolation really is useful in examining colours. It seems to me, however, that there is no corresponding useful method in the non-physical examination of a thing as to its goodness. Goodness seems rather to be something that cannot appear by itself as yellow can. The physical isolation of a patch of colour makes *more* clear whether it is yellow; but the mental isolation of anything makes *less* clear whether it is good.

Moore does not suggest that there is any other method of discovering what things are good in themselves. If, therefore, the method he offers is a failure, and if he is right in thinking there can be no evidence that a thing is good in itself, the conclusion seems to be that the question What things are good? is no more answerable than the previous questions which we have rejected. Whereas, however, the previous questions were unanswerable because they implied falsehoods, this one seems to be unanswerable because we have no means of finding the answer.

I wish now to suggest that the unanswerability of Moore's question is really of the same kind as before, that is, due to its implying a falsehood, only in this case the question does not necessarily imply a falsehood but was merely misinterpreted by Moore to do so. Moore regarded the question What things are good? as being the question what things possess a certain property. He thought of goodness as a property which certain things possessed. Furthermore, he thought that a thing's possession or non-possession of the property goodness was quite independent of its relations to everything else and intrinsic to itself. (For this see also his essay on *The Conception of Intrinsic Value*.) It was precisely this independence and intrinsicality of the property that made it impossible to discover a reliable method of determining its presence. If the property is independent of all else, there is no law governing its presence or absence; but inference and evidence work by means of laws. Since the property was also insensible, there remained nothing but a supposed inner intuition as a means of detecting it.

Interpreted in this way, the question What things are good? is false. Since there is no means of reliably deciding what things possess the property goodness, it is highly probable that the property does not exist. Anyhow, we have no good reason to suppose the occurrence of a property which we can never detect.

Furthermore, the presence or absence of such an independent property would be of no practical interest to us. Since it was completely independent, it could make no difference to any of our concerns. If the decision that a thing was good were the decision that it possessed this inert property, it could not reasonably affect our actions. Or at any rate we should still have to choose either to pursue or not to pursue this inert property. No matter how much we might believe a thing to possess the independent property of goodness, the question whether to aim at that thing would still be another question, a question of choice. And if someone says that the only rational action then would be to aim at the thing, we can properly ask him why it would be rational, and point out that he can give no reason why we ought to pursue a thing discovered to possess the property of independent goodness. He may think that no reason is required, that it is selfevident that we ought to pursue what is good. I answer that perhaps it *is* selfevident if the statement that the thing is good is rightly understood, for to decide that a thing is good is something very like deciding that, other things being equal, we will pursue it; but it is not selfevident if the statement that the thing is good is understood as a factual report that the thing has a certain property which, since there can be no evidence for it, can have no regular connexion with anything else, and therefore must be inert and unimportant. To choose goods for whose warrant we had only the method of isolation would be unreasonable. There is nothing to prevent it from pronouncing good something that we all abhor.

1.4. THE CHOICE OF GOODS

This shows that we have been misinterpreting the question What things are good? For we know very well that it *is* a practical question, that answers to it make a difference to actions.

What sort of question is it, then? We have already given the reply. The answer lies in the word 'practical'. It is a practical question, that is, a question of practice, of action, of what to do. To wonder whether a thing is good is to wonder what to do with regard to it, as whether to pursue it, to praise it, to preserve it. To conclude that it is good is not to reach a belief as to its qualities and peculiarities, but rather to reach an attitude towards it, an evaluation of it, and a decision how to behave with regard to it. It is to choose it.

The question What things are good? is not scientific; and no science gives a true answer to it; and no study that offers to tell us what things are good is properly called a science. For science is the reasonable and methodical attempt to give general descriptions of the world. But calling things good is not describing the world; it is judging the world. In this inquiry we are not scientists but judges, because we are choosing what is to be done rather than discovering what is the nature of the world. Goods exist by choice rather than by nature, and we are our own architects of the end, as Aristotle implies (*Nicomachean Ethics* 1152^{b}2, cf. 1094^{b}16).

Making such a choice is different from reporting other people's choices, and also from reporting one's own choices. It is not reporting at all. It is a kind of generalized action or preparation for action; and it is possible only for beings who have the instrument of generality, which is language.

This observation helps very much to restore the interest and importance of the question, which seemed to disappear when we were obliged to abandon the original form, What is the good? Anyone who tries to answer the question What things are good? is doing something of great importance and interest, namely appreciating the actualities and possibilities of life and taking general decisions about his future actions.

That our question What things are good? is a search for evaluations and not for facts, has a linguistic side, and may be truly represented as a fact about language. It is one of the essential jobs of language to formulate and express our general evaluations; and in discharging this job language often uses words that are designed precisely or mainly for this purpose. Such words may fairly be called evaluative words in contrast to descriptive words whose main task is to help us in describing the world and reporting facts. One such evaluative word is 'good'. To call a thing good is not to describe it, or register it as possessing a certain property, but to appraise it, or reaffirm one's appraisal of it.

This character of the word 'good' is the cause of its sounding very odd to say that a thing's being good is no reason why we should pursue it. To say that a thing is good is in fact very like deciding to pursue it, other things being equal; and therefore it is something very like a selfcontradiction to say that a thing's being good is no reason why we should pursue it. But if, as Moore thought, to say that a thing is good were to describe it as possessing a certain property, then a thing's being good *would* be no reason why we should pursue it; and so it was fair of me to use this as an argument against Moore's view.

It is not the case that 'good' is a purely evaluative word, and never has any descriptive function at all. Its uses vary all the way from pure evaluation to pure description, and include every proportion of mixture. Thus, if you ask 'Is that a wormy apple or a good one?', you are clearly using the word 'good' mainly in order to describe an apple as not wormy. On the other hand, if, after listening to a piece of music of an utterly new kind, you say you think it is good, you are almost solely evaluating it. For the only properties or descriptions that a hearer can reasonably infer from your statement are descriptions of somebody's actual or possible evaluations, as that future critics will judge it good.

This evaluative, non-descriptive business of language is very important. To overlook it, and assume that all statements are descriptive, is a big mistake, and one that breeds many other mistakes. It is a mistake that is often made, and has been made in some very high quarters. For example, Bertrand Russell wrote in his introduction to Wittgenstein's *Tractatus* that 'the essential business of language is to assert or deny facts'.

The view, that the question What things are good? is one of choice rather than one of objective fact, arouses various objections, among which are the following.

1. It is sometimes objected that the view is wicked. To hold it, and to deny that there is such a thing as an objective property of goodness, is thought to be wrong in itself. Thus Professor H. J. Paton defined the good man precisely as 'one who acts on the supposition that there is an unconditioned and objective moral standard holding for all men in virtue of their rationality as human beings' (*The Moral Law*, p. 7). From this it follows that he who does not act on the supposition of an objective standard is by definition not a good man.

2. Secondly, it is often felt that the subjective view is intensely depressing. If there is no objective good to pursue, then, some people think, all our choices are pointless and futile, and therefore life itself is futile. Whatever we choose, we might just as well have chosen something else.

3. Thirdly, it is often thought that the subjective view has the depressing consequence that we shall never reach agreement about the good and the bad, because there is no objective fact to control our thoughts and bring them into agreement, while there is a strong force tending to make us disagree, namely the private and exclusive interest of each one of us. The prospect of eternal disagreement is depressing in itself; and it is likely to lead to desperate and endless fighting, because men feel so strongly about the good and the bad.

Let us consider these three objections. The first of them, namely that the subjective view is as such wicked, is to be rejected as false. The good man is not to be defined as he who believes some complicated and learned proposition, whether this is Professor Paton's Kantian proposition, or the Athanasian creed, or any other. It has been a recurring temptation of theologians and moralists to place human goodness in the act of believing some sophisticated proposition beyond the comprehension of most people. Yet it has always been obvious that a good person may be incapable even of understanding these creeds, while, on the other hand, some who believed them have been wicked men and acted horribly. It is perfectly plain that the good man is not this. The good man is he who displays the virtues. That is to say, the good man is he who is brave, temperate, just, wise, benevolent, and so on. Of course! What could be more obvious?

The other two objections are both to be dismissed as irrelevant. They both urge that the subjective view is depressing, as if that were relevant to the question whether it is true. But whether a view is depressing or not has, evidently, nothing to do with whether it is true. And that is the end of that.

The points raised by these objections are, however, interesting for their own sakes. Let us consider them a little.

People are often alarmed when they begin to entertain the idea that they might some day have to adopt the subjective view. And, if they do come to adopt it, they are sometimes depressed by it at first. Life in general, and their choices in particular, do often seem to them at first quite futile. A man's zest for life is often connected with certain beliefs that he holds. It may mean a lot to him, for example, to believe that his wife is a fine woman, or that his country is the best country. Above all, it means a great deal to many a man to believe that he himself is a decent and successful person; and the loss of this particular belief is probably the most depressing loss of belief there can be.

Yet I hardly think there can be a law of human nature that people *must* believe certain things in order to be happy. Even the most desirable belief of all, namely that oneself is decent and successful, is probably dispensed with by certain happy tramps and scamps. As to a general proposition expressing a learned opinion, such as our proposition that there is no objective property of goodness, we can always learn to dispense with it, and attach our happiness to other propositions, or, better, not attach it to belief in any particular proposition at all. Though it may take us some time to get used to some particular changes of belief, there is one consolation that we can have immediately, namely the thought that we are reverencing the ideal of truth, in that we are trying to hold the more probable opinion, and sacrificing some happiness to that end.

Depression caused by adopting a subjectivist doctrine of goodness is sometimes partly due to false views about its consequences. This brings us to the last objection, for it rests on a false view about the consequences of the view that the question what things are good is a matter of choice. The prospect of our agreeing with each other as to what things are good is better if this is believed to be a question of choice than if it is believed to be a question of fact, and not the reverse as is sometimes held. It is common experience that in deliberative bodies, where practical choices have to be made, those who see the matter as one of objective right and wrong are much more likely to remain in disagreement with each other than those who see it as a question of compromising between different people's wishes. As Professor Nowell Smith has written, it is no accident that all the great persecutors have been objectivists. Furthermore, the general proposition that goodness is an objective fact does nothing to settle any of the infinite particular questions whether so and so is good. It remains perfectly possible for two persons to agree in holding that goodness is objective, and yet to disagree as to which things are good; and if they disagree they have no method of convincing each other, no reasons to give.

The greatest measure of agreement as to what things are good is likely to be found among those who both believe that this is a question rather of choice than of fact and also desire to be in agreement with other men. If we wish men to agree on what is good and what is bad, what we can do about it is to train them to wish to agree with each other and to teach them that it is a question of choice rather than of fact.

It does not follow from this subjectivist view that the statement that something is good is neither true nor false. On the contrary, the statement that this thing is good is exactly like the statement that this thing is round in that it calls for general acceptance or rejection. Every statement by its nature invites general acceptance or rejection. If we declare it false, we imply that all men should reject it. If we declare it true, we imply that all men should accept it. That is the primary function of the words 'true' and 'false'. They indicate the adoption and rejection of statements.

Statements differ from each other in the criteria by which the reasonable man decides whether to accept or to reject them. For statements about nature the main criterion is, of course, nature herself, as observed in our best efforts of observation and experiment. For statements about value the criterion is unfortunately not universally agreed. But, whatever the criterion by which we decide that a certain sort of thing is good or bad, and however different this criterion may be from that of scientific statements, the fundamental meaning of the words 'true' and 'false' is the same when they are applied to statements of value as when they are applied to those of science, namely that the statement should be generally accepted or rejected. Every man who calls a statement true thereby implicitly calls on all men to adopt it; and that is what I am doing when in what follows I call a statement of value true.

1.5. MEANS AND ENDS

In pursuing the question What is the good?, or What things are good?, thinkers have often brought in the ideas of means and ends, and interpreted the question thereby.

Plato in his *Republic* made his speakers divide goods into those that we welcome only for their consequences, those that we welcome only for themselves, and those that we welcome both for their consequences and for themselves; and declare that the third kind is the best. He made his 'Adimantus' urge 'Socrates' to show that justice is good in itself, apart from the question whether its consequences are good.

Aristotle in his *Nicomachean Ethics* wrote of the good as that which is the end of all things, and as something that is a pure end, and not also a means. There must be such a pure end, he argued; for, if everything were desired for the sake of something else, desire would be empty and vain. This pure end is happiness, which in fact is sought always for its own sake and never as a means.

John Dewey, in his interesting book *Human Nature and Conduct*, sets himself to oppose Aristotle on this matter, to depreciate ends and praise means. Ends, he says, are only points of redirection. With this may be compared Mr. Harrod's statement that the plain man applies the word 'good' to means only, never to ends (*Mind*, 1936, pp. 141-2).

Moore in *Principia Ethica* adopted the distinction between being good in itself and being good as a means to something else, and expressed it as the distinction between intrinsic and extrinsic goodness (pp. 21-27). He regarded the search for the good as the search for intrinsic goodness only. It is an error, he wrote, p. 187, to suppose that 'what seems absolutely necessary here and now, for the existence of anything good . . . is therefore good in itself'.

All of these views are fundamentally mistaken in the same way, however they differ from each other. Neither the question What is the good? nor the question What things are good? is a search for either ends or means or both. The question cannot be accurately expressed with these words. 'Good' is an evaluative word; but 'ends' and 'means' are not evaluative words, or not nearly to the same extent as 'good'. Hence to rewrite the question by omitting 'good' and introducing 'end' is to ask a different question. Even if, like Moore, you retain the word 'good', but covertly introduce the notion of an end by talking of 'intrinsic good', you are still changing the question; for in calling a thing good, or wondering whether it is good, we are not thinking either of ends or of means or of their difference. To say positively what we *are* doing, the only accurate expression is just this, that we are judging it good, but more loosely we can also say that we are evaluating it, appraising it, giving ourselves the principle of furthering its existence, contemplating it with satisfaction, or deciding to recommend it.

The following consideration helps to show that the distinction between means and end is irrelevant to the question what things are good. It could logically happen, and probably does happen, that two persons agree that a certain thing is good, while one of them regards it purely as a means and the other purely as an end. For example, perhaps there are two men who both think that equality is a great good; but one of them regards it merely as an end; he is passionately attached to equality as such, and does not care what the consequences are; while the other has no love for equality as such, but thinks it a very necessary and efficacious means to various highly important results. It would be a mistake to belittle the agreement existing between these two men. Each of them will say that equality is a great good. Each of them will work hard for equality. They may both be earnest members of the British Labour Party for life and never come to any disagreement with the Party or each other on the matter of equality.

The relation of means to end is the relation of cause to effect regarded by someone who intends the effect. It entails both causation and intention, and is non-existent when either of them is absent. A match is a means of lighting a fire only if both a match causes the fire to light and somebody intends the fire to light. If the match by some strange accident lights the fire without anyone's intending to light the fire, it is not a means to the lighting but merely a cause thereof. The cause of an effect becomes the means to it when it is intended by somebody to cause it. The effect becomes an end when someone introduces the cause with the intention of producing that effect.

Thus an end is an effect which somebody intends to produce by means of some cause. But this is not the same as a good. In thinking that something is good, we do not necessarily have the notion of cause and effect in our minds. It may be a good effect, or a good cause, but more often it is just a good. If we rephrase the question what things are good as something about ends, we introduce the notion of causation, which was not there before, and thus alter the question.

There is, however, another and wider sense of the word 'end' to which the argument does not apply. An end is not always something which we intend to effect by means of some cause. It can be anything which we intend, whether we require some means in order to produce it, or can produce it directly without any means. Your intention and end may be to light a fire, in which case you will have to look for some means, such as a match. But it may also be to sing, in which case you will not have to look for any means; you will just sing. Thus ends and means are not correlative. Every means is the means to some end; but not every end is the effect of some means.

In this wider sense of 'end', however, it is still true that you alter the question if you use it to explain what you mean by What things are good? Although you no longer have the inappropriate notion of cause and effect, you still have something inappropriate, namely a much too direct and specific purposiveness. To call a thing an end is to imply that you, or somebody else, is going after it, or ought to go after it, in a very definite and particular way; but to call it good is far more indefinite. To call it good implies that one *would* or *should* go after it under certain circumstances, but not that the circumstances are present, or ever will be present. Hence even in this wider sense it is a mistake to use the word 'end' to express our question; and, of course, there is always the danger of falling back into the still less appropriate narrow sense.

Men value means as well as ends, and call both of them good. Not merely does the blazing fire seem a good thing to them, but also the match that is a means thereto.

Men come to value things as ends just because they recognize them as effective means. This has often been insisted on; and may be summed in the phrase that means often become ends. If you ask a man to give you a reason why a thing is good, or to justify his praise of it, nine times out of ten his reason consists in representing the thing as a means to something else. Democracy, he may say, is good because it makes the government look sharp to remedy the people's miseries. Nine times out of ten there is nothing that you *can* say, to bring a man to value something which he does not yet value, except that it is a means to something. A famous example of this is the discussion of the goodness of justice in Plato's *Republic*. 'Adimantus' proposes, and 'Socrates' undertakes, the task of showing that justice is good in itself, regardless of its consequences. Yet in the very act of proposing this task 'Adimantus', without realizing that he is doing so, also represents it as the task of showing that being just has good consequences in a man's soul; and it is this latter task that 'Socrates' actually fulfils.

If you are asked to show that justice possesses some intrinsic property wholly independent of man, whose name is 'goodness', it is futile for you to argue that justice is a means to a desirable state of the soul; your premiss would be quite irrelevant to your conclusion. It is absurd to try to prove that justice is good in itself from the premiss that it is a good means to something.

On the other hand, it is sensible to try to get a man to love justice by showing him that justice is a means to a happy state of the soul. If someone says to you 'Make me love justice, make me value it highly and be sure that it is good', then it is very useful to point out to him that justice is a means to something he already loves. And the question, Is justice good?, is in fact far more like the request, 'Make me love justice!', than it is like the question, Does justice possess a certain property?

For this reason, if we represent the question What things are good? as a search for ends rather than means, or for intrinsic rather than extrinsic goodness, we cut ourselves off from the chief way of answering it. We have satisfactorily answered the question What things are good? when and only when we have achieved stable and confident valuations of things. But the main way to achieve stable and confident valuations of things is to discover their consequences; and we discourage ourselves from doing this if we say we are looking for ends. For an end, as an end, is something with whose consequences if any we are not concerned.

Since nine tenths of our actual reasons for thinking a thing good are its consequences, those who say they are looking for ends, and decline to consider consequences, find very few things good. They impoverish the world. They come out with a disappointingly small set of things worth having or doing. Thus G. E. Moore, who is perhaps the most resolute excluder of all consequences and all 'extrinsic' goodness, comes to the strange conclusions that virtue is not much of a good, and that in fact only two things are very good, the perception of beauty and personal affection. To insist on the distinction between intrinsic and extrinsic is to be in danger of emptying life of interest and satisfaction. It is a great pity to be reduced to saying that, for example, 'the individual personality of man alone has intrinsic and ultimate worth' (Ernest Barker, *Reflections on Government*, pp. 15-16). It is a great pity to say of anything that it is the only ultimate good.

If you go as far as Aristotle, and demand a good that is a pure end and in no way also a means, you are demanding an impossibility, and will be left with no good at all. Aristotle thought he was left with happiness, which, he said, is sought always for its own sake and never as a means to something else. But happiness is often sought as a means to something else. The manager of a factory tries to make the workers happy in order to get greater production. The politician tries to make the voters happy in order to stay in power. A man may try to make himself happy in order to make himself more efficient, or more conscientious, or in order to make his family happier. Everything whatever logically could be sought by someone as a means to something else. And it seems very probable that everything that is sought by anybody is sought by somebody as a means to something else. And, if that is so, Aristotle's good is non-existent.

To recommend anything as the sole end must be ineffective in so far as it is selfconsistently done. For we can get a man to adopt an end only by starting from other ends which he already has, and we must therefore acknowledge those other ends in order to move him.

Most persons assume that every good is a means to some other good, and derives at least part of its goodness from its being a means to other goods. The common man is accustomed to ask about any proposed good: What is the use of it? And this is equivalent to asking what it is a means to. He is disconcerted or sceptical if he is told that some goods are useless and not means to any other good.

There is nothing selfcontradictory in the common man's opinion, though followers of Aristotle sometimes think that there is. It is perhaps selfstultifying to say that every good thing derives *all* of its goodness from being a means to some other good; for from this it perhaps follows that there are no goods at all. But there is nothing foolish about saying that every good derives *at least part* of its own goodness from being a means to some other good. And it is probably true; for it is probably true that every good may lead to some further good, and if it does so it is a better good in virtue of that. Plato's characters were right when they agreed that the best kind of good is that which we welcome both for itself and for its consequences; and Aristotle was completely wrong in arguing that there must be a good which is to no degree good in its consequences, because otherwise all desire would be empty and vain.

It is a great mistake to say 'So and so is merely a means; therefore it has no fundamental value'. We do, in fact, value profoundly a number of things which, when we examine them, we seem to be valuing purely for their results. Political goods like democracy are notable examples. Our whole recommendation of them may consist in pointing out that they are means to other goods. Yet we consider them also very great goods in themselves. They engage our emotions profoundly. And it is sometimes good that they should do so. It is sometimes an error to try to loosen our affection for them by saying that they are mere means, or merely extrinsic goods. In my recital of goods I shall therefore not reject anything on the ground that it is merely extrinsic, and I shall frequently recommend things by their consequences.

It is also a great pity to make the opposite error, the error of declaring that only means are good and ends are worthless, as Dewey appears to have done and as the common man tends to do. This mistake often lurks in the gospel of progress; the present is considered to be good only so far as it is leading to some better future, and so on for ever; the jam is always for tomorrow. The beginning of wisdom is to recognize and embrace the possibility of finding good things here and now. It is a mistake to value literature only as a means to political improvements, or to value knowledge only as a means to the prevention of disease, or to value music only as a means to the glory of one's State. It is better to love them all for themselves.

The beginning of wisdom is to value something for itself. (And the second step in wisdom is to value a second thing for itself.) This first step is hard for the simple-minded. They go wrong from the beginning by looking for 'the ultimate purpose of existence', an enterprise destructive of happiness and integrity. We must say to them: 'You love some things. Keep on loving them. Approve of your loving them. It is a good thing that you love them. Do not let the indifference or the disapproval of others weaken your love or your approval of your love. Nothing should weaken it except the discovery that one of your loves is on the whole harmful to you or others. Add to your loves.'

To this discussion of ends and means I will append some comment on the common phrase 'the end justifies the means'. It is a common gambit in argument to suggest that your opponent is implying the doctrine that the end justifies the means, and to infer from this that he is wrong, because this doctrine is odious.

This gambit is always bad and should never be used. The doctrine that the end justifies the means is not odious; it is meaningless. What end? And what means? It is obviously true that *some* ends justify *some* means; for example, if you want to smoke a cigarette, that justifies you in making a spill out of yesterday's newspaper and setting it alight. It is obviously false that *all* ends justify *all* means; for example, if you want to smoke a cigarette, that does not justify you in making a spill out of a five-pound note and setting it alight. Sometimes the proposed means is justified and sometimes it is not. We have to judge separately for each given case whether it is justified. The blanket condemnation of an opponent, on the ground that he has allowed the end to justify the means, is therefore absurd. One might as well issue a blanket condemnation of eating, because people sometimes eat when they ought not to.

1.6. WISE AND FOOLISH CHOICE

What kind of a choice is it to ask in general what things are good? For evidently it is not what we most commonly call choice, such as choosing between two plays after deciding to go to a theatre. I proceed to characterize the kind of choice or evaluation expressed in an answer to the question What things are good?

In the first place, it is a pure choice. The word 'good' is being used here purely evaluatively, without any descriptive dimension at all. We are simply trying to decide where to put our love and praise.

In the second place, choices may be particular or general. We may choose to put this particular yellow flower in just here, or we may choose to put some kind of yellow flower somewhere about here. Our question, What things are good?, is an invitation to general, not to particular, choice. It is not like saying 'What shall I do now?' but more like saying 'What shall be my general line of action in a certain sphere?' It is a choice, but a choice that does not lead to any particular action without some further choice and some particular occasion. It is a general decision that will influence a great many particular decisions but not suffice to determine any. Or, if the notion of a general decision is objectionable, we may say that it is an evaluation rather than a decision.

In the third place, this kind of general choice, this activity of answering the question What things are good? is one that goes on throughout our lives. The child tries to learn from its elders what to approve and what to disapprove. That is the point of the recurrent joke in *1066 And All That*: 'He was a good king' and 'He was a bad king'. We want so much to judge each king. When we grow up we do not abandon this childish activity; nor do we think that we have completed it. We do it continually, but more complicatedly and critically and generally. It is one of our main interests in life. Or perhaps I should say: it *is* our interest in life. We long to be confident and abiding in our valuations instead of uncertain and bewildered.

Thus our question What things are good? is an expression of one of the most pervasive and important aspects of our life, our evaluating activities. But it is not merely an expression of this. It is also, in the fourth place, a criticism of this.

For, strange as it seems, we often evaluate our own evaluations, and approve or disapprove our own tastes. Many men are proud of themselves for disliking milk, or approve of themselves for thinking their country better than other countries, or thank God that they value Beethoven and not jazz. The exhortation to 'lay not up for yourselves treasures ... where moth and rust doth corrupt' is an evaluation of an evaluation. One can have a sneaking approval of something, that is, approve of it and disapprove of oneself for approving of it. We wish to approve of our own approvals, and to be pleased with ourselves as appraisers of the world. We thus become critical of our own evaluations, and interested in putting the question what things are good although we already have a set of answers to it. We distinguish what we do value from what we will try to value, because we recognize the truth of Bosanquet's opinion that 'to like and dislike rightly is the goal of all culture worthy of the name' (*Three Lectures on Aesthetics*. I recommend this little book to you).

While we have all already made many valuations which we are never going to change, yet we are also all engaged all the time in making further evaluations and in reconsidering those we have made. A general choice can always be reconsidered just because it is general. A particular choice, such as to go to a theatre this evening, can no longer be reconsidered when this evening is passed. We can, of course, condemn or approve ourselves for having gone to the theatre yesterday; but the decision itself is completely exhausted; the actions which it potentially contained are all done. A general choice, on the other hand, may always bear on further possible actions, so long as the chooser lives. The opinion, for example, that Bach is a good composer, bears on all future occasions when I might hear or avoid hearing Bach. At all times of my life, therefore, this opinion retains some practical force. At all times of my life, therefore, the reconsideration of this opinion will itself be a practical matter.

General choices which can be reconsidered will be reconsidered from time to time. A man will sometimes reconsider his evaluations if they are challenged, or if unpleasant consequences of them force themselves upon his notice more strongly than before, or if his tastes change, or simply because he has the habit of evaluating his own evaluations.

Choice can be wise or foolish. We desire to answer the question What things are good? wisely rather than foolishly.

Wise choice proceeds upon principles. Placing an action under a principle relates it to all the other possible actions flowing from that principle. Practical principles include moral laws, maxims of prudence, statements of standards, and the individual's private rules. Practical principles are themselves choices. That is, to have one and act on it is to have adopted and be carrying out a general choice.

Our practical principles often take the form of setting up standards. And whether a certain thing meets a certain standard is a question of fact, not of choice. This point was very illuminatingly made by Mr. Urmson in his article 'On Grading' in *Mind* for 1950. It was also made by a number of other writers during the years 1949-52, usually with the intention of rebutting the subjectivism of Professor C. L. Stevenson's *Ethics and Language*. But these writers all failed to mention that a standard becomes *your* standard only when *you* adopt it, and an adoption is a choice. Before you can answer the question of fact, whether the thing meets your standard, you must answer the question of choice, what standard you adopt.

It is a fact, perhaps, that the motor-cars of 1960 satisfy most people's standards better than the motor-cars of 1930. But that does not make everyone call the motor-cars of 1960 better, because not everyone adopts the standards by which they are better. There are some oldfashioned codgers who cling to other standards, and by those standards correctly call the motor-cars of 1930 better than those of 1960. The man who calls those of 1930 better, and the man who calls those of 1960 better, may both be quite correct on their respective questions of fact, namely Which car meets my standard better?, and may be differing merely in their choice of standard. It is important neither to represent the question whether a thing is good as a mere question of choice, by suppressing the question whether it in fact meets your standard, nor to represent it as a mere question of fact, by suppressing the question what standard you have chosen.

The rebutters of Professor Stevenson round the year 1950 made the mistake of softpedalling the question of the choice of standard. For example, Professor Toulmin, in his *The Place of Reason in Ethics*, 1950, can be seen on close inspection to be adopting some kind of vaguely utilitarian standard of right and wrong, but drawing no attention to the fact, and concentrating interest on the derivation of particular duties from the standard. One of these writers, Mr. Tomas (*Mind*, 1951), actually shows, though it is contrary to his intention to do so, that the element of choice is far more pervasive even than Stevenson said.

There are good reasons for adopting one standard to the exclusion of another. Certain choices of standard may properly be called wise. Others may properly be called foolish, or even insane. Wise men look for standards, perhaps, that correspond to our natural propensities, or help us to achieve our purposes, or tend to make us happy rather than unhappy, or are likely to be generally adopted. All that is true and should not be overlooked. Nor should it cause us to overlook the fact that the wise man is still adopting a standard, however wisely; he is not just reading off a fact.

Ultimate choices must occur, in one sense of the phrase. That is, at any given time any given person must have principles which he is not deducing from any ulterior principle. Even if there could be an infinite regress of practical principles, none of us could actually have the whole infinite series in mind. We all inevitably have, at every moment, some principles behind which we have not gone; and those are our ultimates for the moment.

Each of us naturally tends to find other people's ultimate principles highly arbitrary and insecure. A few of us find all ultimate principles as such highly arbitrary and insecure, and wish there were some way of avoiding them. But, since we cannot hold in mind or run through an infinite deduction of principles, the only way to avoid having a first principle is to have no principle at all, like a lizard perhaps.

If we conclude that we must have at least one underived principle, we next hope that at any rate it may be selfevident and certain. But even that is too much to hope; for a practical principle cannot be selfevident. There are only two kinds of selfevidence, the perceived truth and the analytic truth; and neither of these can be a practical principle. That I am now talking, which is a truth I now perceive, is not a practical principle but a description of fact. And no analytic truth is a practical principle because analytic truths are compatible with any and every state of affairs. The command, 'Thou shalt do no evil', sounds like an analytic but practical precept; but it is not practical, for it does not tell us what is evil. 'Thou shalt do no murder' is selfevident but analytic. 'Thou shalt not kill' is practical but dubious.

It is inevitable, then, to have at every moment practical principles which for the moment are neither derived nor selfevident. But it is not inevitable to be uneasy and insecure about this, nor is it necessarily an unreasonable state of mind. The way to ease and reasonableness lies in the examination of consequences.

It is wise to choose in view of probable consequences, and foolish to choose without considering consequences. In order to decide whether a thing is good, the wise man ascertains the facts of its nature, connexions, conditions, and effects. He does not call democracy good, or television bad, without having reached firm views as to their consequences. He differs from the fool in paying more attention to facts before he makes his choices, in being more of a scientist in his practice. Thus the question What things are good?, though not a question of fact, yet ought to be decided by reference to facts.

This characteristic of the wise chooser, that he ascertains facts more than does the fool, helps to make many people believe that the question What things are good? is itself a question of fact. And, when they hear someone say it is not a question of fact, they tend to infer wrongly that he means that no attention need be paid to facts in answering it. They tend to assume wrongly that to deny that it is a question of fact is to recommend that it should be decided carelessly and irresponsibly. On the other hand, people who see clearly the element of choice or decision in the question What things are good? occasionally assume that therefore the question may be or even must be answered without consulting the facts. The double truth is that What things are good? both is a question of choice and ought to be answered only after careful examination of facts. We wish to make our decisions and evaluations in view of the world as it is, not in view of some imaginary world which we erroneously suppose to be the real world, nor in view of nothing at all.

The wise man's particular choices are guided both from below by the consequences which he expects and from above by his principles or general choices. The reasons for a choice are both the consequences which it would produce and the principles under which it can be placed. The higher and nearer to ultimacy the choice is, the fewer principles it can be placed under, but also, in compensation, the more consequences it involves. Ultimate choices can be recommended only by their consequences, but their consequences are enormous. Thus no choice of any importance need be without its reasons; for either it falls under principles, or it involves grave consequences, or it is unimportant. A good paradigm of ultimate choosing, where everything depends on the consequences because there are no ulterior principles to appeal to, is the choice which, in Aldous Huxley's *Brave New World*, the controller sets before the savage.

Ultimate principles are no more undiscussable than ultimate laws of nature or axioms in geometry. They are endlessly discussable. They merely have the peculiarity that the discussion of them consists entirely in the consideration of their consequences. They can be discussed and they ought to be discussed. We ought to criticize them. We ought to make ourselves conscious of their existence, their natures, and their bearings.

In another sense of the phrase 'ultimate principle' there are no ultimate principles. For every man can always reconsider tomorrow the principle which he takes as ultimate today. Tomorrow he may decide to drop the principle, or he may deduce it from an ulterior principle. In either case it will no longer be an ultimate principle.

1.7. JUDGEMENT

The process of making a wise choice, in view of principles and consequences, is judgement rather than deduction or induction or inference or intuition. Deduction plays a part in it, for example in seeing what a given principle implies in a given situation. But deduction never forms the whole of deliberation and judgement. There is in addition at least the choice to apply this principle to this situation. Induction also plays a part; for in predicting the consequences of a proposal we must use our inferences as to what the laws of nature are. But induction, too, never forms the whole of deliberation and judgement, because prediction is not choice. Both deduction and induction are radically distinct from judgement in that they are abstractive, separative, analytical, whereas judgement is concretive and synthetical. We judge what is best to do in this whole concrete situation. The wise man tries to see all the relevant principles and all the important consequences, and then to make a judgement on the whole.

Thus an important choice has far more grounds than an inference has. In an inference you can say quite shortly what the whole of your reason is for your conclusion. But in a wise judgement it is a very long business to give your reason, because your reason ought to be nothing less than the whole of the principles relevant to your choice and the whole of the consequences of your choice, and the whole situation in which it occurs. Hence in practice people sometimes renounce the effort to give a reason for their choice. They feel that they could only say part of it, and that to represent a part of it as *the* reason would be to misrepresent the choice. Hence choice often looks like intuition, that is, like something totally unreasoned. It often looks like intuition even to the wise chooser himself, who has really reviewed a great deal of matter in making it. Good choice is all-considering; and the all-considering sometimes looks like the nothing-considering.

The all-consideringness of wise choice is not well brought out in ordinary speech. We tend to speak of deliberation on the model of deduction, where the conclusion is drawn from quite a small number of quite abstract premises. Thus a minister of the Crown, when declining to do something suggested by a member of parliament, will often say that he sees no reason for it. This is nearly always absurd. There is some reason for almost every possible line of action; and the fact that a member of parliament wants it done is quite a strong reason for doing it. The truth is that the minister has judged that upon the whole the reasons for not doing it are much stronger than the reasons for doing it; but we are reluctant, I do not know why, to talk like that.

Similarly, we are prone to ask 'What is your reason for that decision?', as if he had only one. It seems that the best answer would be: 'If I made this decision for only one reason I should be injudicious. I have made it, I hope, in view of the whole situation and the whole of my general principles, since that is the judicious way to reach a decision. If so, my reason for it is my view of the whole situation plus all my relevant principles.'

The worst of defending your abstention from something by saying that you see *no* reason for it is that you make some people think that, if there is *some* reason for doing it, it should be done; and that is folly.

The final judgement, after we have made our review of all the relevant considerations, is always a risk and often feels like a risk. Judgement is riskier than either deduction or induction. Deduction is safe and sure, a pleasant occupation for the timorous, because the premisses entail the conclusion. Induction is unsure, because the premisses do not entail the conclusion; but still it is theoretical; we are risking only a theory. Judgement is neither sure nor theoretical. It is risking our lives.

Though I have here discussed judgement in reference to choice, and contrasted it with induction, judgement is often required not merely for deciding what to do but also for deciding what the particular facts of the world are. It is a matter of judgement whether you can safely overtake another car or not, a question of deciding what emerges from the whole concrete situation which you perceive. Induction is more our process of adopting abstract and general statements about the world, than our process of deciding the nature and course of any concrete event. Whether there is a god, for example, a particular concrete question about the world, is a matter for judgement rather than for induction or deduction.

Judgement is not the same as skill or cleverness; and little skill or cleverness is required in order to make judicious choices. In card-games the great superiority of poker over bridge lies largely in the fact that poker requires little cleverness and much judgement; whereas bridge requires little judgement and much cleverness.

What Wittgenstein says about learning to judge the genuineness of an expression of feeling will do very well as a statement about acquiring good judgement in general. It runs as follows in Miss Anscombe's translation of *Philosophical Investigations*, p. 227: 'Can one learn this knowledge? Yes; some can. Not, however, by taking a course in it, but through *"experience"*.—Can someone else be a man's teacher in this? Certainly. From time to time he gives him the right *tip*.—This is what "learning" and "teaching" are like here.—What one acquires here is not a technique; one learns correct judgements. There are also rules, but they do not form a system, and only experienced people can apply them right. Unlike calculation rules.'

I believe that to be correct. I will add only that there is one sort of experience that is common to all judgement, in whatever sphere, and important for all good judgement; and that is simply the experience of seeing the need for judgement, and wanting to judge well, and forcing oneself to make a judgement. I believe that most people come to make fairly good judgements in every sphere with which they are acquainted, if they force themselves to judge and want to judge prudently and well. What makes us judge badly is rarely a lack of the capacity to judge well. It is usually a lack of strong desire to judge well, or the presence and triumph of some partial emotion.

1.8. OBJECTIONS TO THE ENTERPRISE

What is it that makes judgement essential to practice and choice? What is it that makes the abstract reasoner and inferrer a dangerous politician? It is, of course, that all things are connected together by cause and effect, and therefore every good thing is connected to many bad things.

Every good thing is connected to many bad things. There hardly is such a thing as an 'innocent' pleasure. There hardly is a pain unrelated to any good. At any rate all great goods, all goods that count a lot in men's lives, are great evils too. What do you consider a great good? Religion? Political equality? Love? The good will? Each of these has done terrible harm. Any person who sets up some one good as a perfectly safe end, who thinks that this end justifies *any* means and *any* consequences, like Madame de Maintenon thinking that religion justifies the killing of Protestant Christians, is a grave danger to the world.

How then can it be wise to set up any goods for oneself at all if they are all evils too? How can it be prudent to offer any answer to the question What things are good? if all things do harm? Since all great goods are greatly harmful sometimes, it seems foolish to affirm them and set them up as objects of enthusiasm and pursuit.

Furthermore, there seems to be something wrong about the very idea of a list of goods. Such a list must, it seems, be endless, and it must co-ordinate things that are not on the same level. Freedom, equality, reason, beauty, love, truth, morality, worship, justice, life, pleasure, happiness, democracy, virtue, power, progress, art, importance—it seems that this can never come to an end, and that anyhow it destroys a certain differentiation and articulation of factors and aspects in the good.

We must admit, I think, that there is something essentially inadequate about a list or creed of great goods. We must admit that there can be no systematic list, because goods are on different levels and in different dimensions, and no complete list, because we do not want our ideal to be finished. A list of great goods, therefore, can only be a list of those things which at the time seem most important or specially engage the author's devotion; and such is the present course.

We must admit too, I think, that all good things are harmful sometimes. But, if so, we are compelled to choose between affirming goods that are sometimes harmful, and not affirming any general goods at all; and the former is clearly the better. It is foolish to decline ever to love a dog because dogs have some nasty habits. It is foolish never to love a cat or a woman because they sometimes scratch. It is foolish to deny the goodness of wine because of the terrible evils of alcoholism.

We might say that man needs slogans. This is a low and inaccurate way of putting it, but has its value. Slogans like 'liberty, equality, fraternity', or 'truth, beauty, goodness', can give life enormously greater interest and elevation. It is a question of choosing them

THE NATURE OF THE QUESTION

rightly, and of deepening as much as possible our understanding of what they involve. An answer to the question What things are good? is, from this point of view, a choice of slogans for living, and an attempt to see far into the consequences of these slogans, their harm as well as their benefit.

Or we might say that man needs ideals. This also is a useful way of putting it, and higher than the former. But it is still inaccurate. For the word 'ideal' suggests something never yet realized, whereas beauty and truth and other great goods are often realized around us. We need goods that are always realized in part and unrealized in part, goods that both confirm the worth of some things that have already happened and guide us for the future.

Such goods, or such slogan-words, are to be found; and it is good that they should be from time to time examined and rejected or affirmed. It is good that we should start at once to value according to some general conceptions the actualities and possibilities of our existence. Though we shall never know enough to do so with final rightness, we ought to begin doing so at once. The enterprise helps to unify and give significance to all our petty evaluations of every day, and to make our lives as a whole firmer and better.

'But is it proper to conduct this enterprise in public? Why should I, or any man, publish his choices in a course of lectures and invite others to listen to them? A man's personal evaluations of life seem to be a private matter, not suitable for a public lecture. The question What things are good? was suitable for public discussion so long as it was thought to be a fact-finding or scientific question. But now that we see it to be a question of choice, it appears no more suitable for public discussion than the question whether to make or accept a proposal of marriage. It seems that the public inquiry should end with the discovery that Plato and his successors have been regarding as a public and scientific question what is really a matter of private choice.'

This reflection overlooks the social setting of our evaluations. Most of us desire to be in agreement with our fellows as to what is good and what is bad. To find good what everyone else finds bad is apt to be uncomfortable or worse. Most of us welcome the evaluations of others as a means of forming our own. Even when a man offers no reason in support of his opinion, we may still welcome it as giving us a new idea, or enlarging our conception of the possibilities. For example, suppose a man to say that flowers are out of place in a garden, which should contain only trees and grass. Even if he gives no reason for this judgement we may be glad to hear it. It may strike us as a novelty and worth considering. We may like to imagine ourselves maintaining such a garden and rejecting flowers, and to ask ourselves whether that would be a change for the better. Therefore it may be reasonable to publish personal evaluations as a service to others.

Furthermore, when we have achieved any stable and general evaluations, we desire to convert others to them; and it is permissible and reasonable to recommend them publicly.

Thus we may meet the difficulty by saying that, while the question what things are good is personal, it is not *purely* personal. The point of the word 'purely' is to suggest that each man ought to keep to himself his personal decision as to what things are good. And that suggestion is wrong. He will help both himself and others to decide better if he communicates his decisions and gets them criticized. Our choices can be wise or foolish; and they have more chance of being wise if they submit to criticism from others, and use the choices of others as a means of criticizing themselves.

When the question What things are good? is regarded as a mere question of objective fact, like What metals are lighter than iron?, personal preferences are disguised as objective facts, and private valuations are imposed on other persons by being represented as objective facts. We can now see that to do this is to be inadequately sincere. We must be as honest as possible; and it is no longer possible honestly to present our answers to the question What things are good? as scientific statements of independent facts which the uninstructed hearer ought to believe. Instead we must confess that they are private valuations and recommend them as such.

The answers which I shall give, to the question What things are good?, are my personal choices and evaluations. But they are also invitations to you. I try to find reasons to recommend them to you, and I try to carry you along with me in my choices, or at least to stimulate you into making your own.

You can find other lecturers on the question What things are good?, particularly in churches, who will assure you that they are not giving you their subjective opinions, but objective truths about good and evil independent of man, something much better, therefore, than the private and unauthorized opinions of an impudent individual. If you think they are right, it is wise for you to go to them and leave me. But I think, you see, that the difference is that from them you get unconfessed choices instead of confessed ones, choices pretending to be scientific discoveries instead of admitting their nature. I believe myself to be doing consciously, and to that extent better, what some other people do under the false impression that they are not choosing policies but ascertaining facts.

2

PERSONAL GOODS

2.1.	Principles of Choice	48
2.2.	Life	54
2.3.	Beauty	57
2.4.	Truth	65
2.5.	Reason	70
2.6.	Love	105
2.7.	Conscientiousness	108
2.8.	Religion	113

2.1. PRINCIPLES OF CHOICE

Misery is an evil and happiness is a good. If anyone denies this, there is nothing to say to him. If he contemplates happy children without any satisfaction, if he calls to mind the vast array of miseries in the world, such as wounded stags eaten alive by ants, oiled birds battered on the rocks, men and women with arthritis or insane depression, and feels no pity or disturbance, there is nothing to say to him. We choose to lessen misery and he does not. We choose to promote happiness and he does not.

Some men, while not denying that misery is an evil and happiness is a good, doubt whether this is a significant proposition, or whether the words 'happy' and 'miserable' convey clear and applicable notions. But this doubt is an intellectual's selfobfuscation, produced by too much thinking and too little observation. Let anyone take to observing children, in the school yard or elsewhere, and try to recognize those who are miserable and those who are happy. He will find himself doubtful about some of the children, naturally; but he will find himself certain about others. We can usually know when Jack and Jill are miserable and when they are not.

Some men have thought that misery was the only evil, and happiness the only good. But this is clearly false. It is utterly obvious that vice as well as misery is an evil, and that knowledge as well as happiness is a good. The world is full of a great many sorts of bad thing and a great many sorts of good thing.

The notion that happiness is the only good is in part a bad result of the intellectual desire to simplify and summarize. But it is also in part the result of a dim perception of a great truth, namely that happiness and misery provide the most important *test* of all goodness and badness, as follows.

Any kind of thing is bad if it, or the pursuit of it, increases the misery of living things upon the whole. Nothing is good if it, or the pursuit of it, leads on the whole to very much more misery than contentment. Unease is a criterion. *Inquietum est cor nostrum donec.* . . .

These sentences express an enormously general choice which I find myself strongly inclined to make. If I ask myself about anything considered good, Would you still call it good if you were convinced that the pursuit of it probably increased misery?, I think I find myself determined to answer: 'No, I should call it bad.'

This principle provides a negative test of goods. It does not determine that anything *is* good; but it determines that some things are *not* good, namely those whose pursuit probably increases misery. It is not a standard, by adopting which we can decide in every case whether a thing is good or bad or indifferent; but it is a criterion that applies to any choice or kind of choice, and either condemns the choice or does not condemn it.

The adoption of this principle is a supreme or ultimate choice, not in the strong sense that it entails every other choice, but in the weak sense that it tests all other choices and condemns some of them. It is also ultimate, in me, in the sense that I have no higher choice under which for me it falls, and I defend it only by referring to its consequences, not at all by referring to higher principles. Its consequences concern all that part of the misery of living things which can be caused or prevented by the action of man. This is not the whole of misery; but it is a great ocean of misery nevertheless.

This 'principle of counter-misery', as it might be called, is often rejected, sometimes explicitly but more often by implication. In these days of rabid nationalism it is often rejected on behalf of some State. One can easily imagine Hitler saying: 'I prefer the misery of every living thing, including every German, to the humiliation of the German State.' Resistance movements look like an affirmation that the sovereignty of some State, say France or Greece or Cyprus, is worth any amount of misery. Most of us cherish at least one good which we are strongly inclined to pursue no matter what the consequences in misery to the human race. With many people this reckless good is the reign of certain moral laws which they have adopted. (That is the spirit of 'let justice be done though the heavens fall'.) With me it is the spread of knowledge and truth.

On the other hand, the principle of counter-misery is a hard one to reject when you are explicitly faced with it. Probably very few people feel quite easy about subordinating it to their favourite good. It seems likely that the more it is brought to people's attention the more widely and effectively it will be adopted. Thus it seems to be a principle on which there is some faint hope that the human race may some day agree; and that will recommend it to people who want agreement on practical principles.

This principle of counter-misery has some resemblance to utilitarianism; and people who like 'ism' words may wish to label it 'utilitarianism'. But we should avoid label-thought; and anyhow this principle differs from Mill's in at least four important ways.

In the first place, J. S. Mill regarded his principle as determining all rightness and wrongness. This principle, however, merely determines that certain things are bad. It is a principle for the rejection of goods, not for the adoption of them. It says where we should not lay our treasure up, not where we should. It leaves us free to adopt and proclaim any goods we choose; and it gives us no orders or guidance in doing so, except only that our goods must not increase misery.

In the second place, Mill regarded happiness or pleasure as in an important sense the only good, and may therefore fairly well be called a 'hedonist'. But this principle does not say, or entail, that happiness is any kind of a good at all. It only says that misery or unhappiness is a negative test of goods. Happiness *is* a good and misery is an evil; but this principle does not say so.

Thirdly and very importantly, this principle substitutes the conception of misery for Mill's conception of pleasure. Instead of setting up pleasure as the sole end, it sets up the non-increase of misery as a requisite of all ends. Instead of saying that the only thing worth aiming at is happiness, it says that nothing is worth aiming at if its pursuit increases unhappiness. It is 'antilypism' rather than 'hedonism'! This is a profound difference, as Dr. Popper points out when he writes:

> There is, from the ethical point of view, no symmetry between suffering and happiness, or between pleasure and pain. . . . Human suffering makes

a direct moral appeal, namely, the appeal for help, while there is no similar call to increase the happiness of a man who is doing well anyway.... Pain cannot be outweighed by pleasure, and especially not one man's pain by another man's pleasure. Instead of the greatest happiness for the greatest number, one should demand, more modestly, the least amount of avoidable suffering for all; and further, that unavoidable suffering ... should be distributed as equally as possible. (K. R. Popper, *The Open Society*, U.S. edition, p. 571.)

Fourthly and lastly, I put forward this principle as a choice to be made; but Mill was not clear whether he was putting forward utilitarianism as a choice or as a fact, as a proposal or as a proposition. He often seems to be on the brink of saying that it is a proposal, for example when he disputes the Kantian view of morality. His queer chapter on the possible 'sanctions' of the doctrine is really there to avoid the reproach that he is wasting our time by proposing that we should adopt a decision which there is no hope of our adopting. It would be irrelevant if utilitarianism were an assertion of fact; for whether people will believe an assertion of fact is not evidence whether it is true. Yet Mill never becomes quite clear that what he is giving us is really not a proposition but a proposal; and that is the main cause of the unfortunate illogicality of the essay, which has often been gloated over.

To adopt the principle of counter-misery is not to love the human race. Most of us find it impossible to love the human race after we are forty; but we can still adopt this principle.

I am inclined to go further and adopt a second principle concerning misery as follows: *No kind of act may be forbidden unless its discontinuance would lessen misery upon the whole.*

This is a principle of right and wrong, whereas the other was a principle of good and bad. It is a principle concerning laws, their making, enforcement, and unmaking, whether laws of the State or laws of morality or custom. It entails that every State law is unjustifiable unless its enforcement lessens misery upon the whole, and that nothing is a true moral law unless general obedience to it would lessen misery upon the whole. These consequences are acceptable to me. All laws are limitations of freedom and to that extent bad. What can justify us in imposing limits on freedom? Only, it seems, an important decrease in misery obtainable in that way and that way only. I reject all legislators who claim to impose on us a law for any reason but that it decreases our misery. I reject all preachers who lay down moral laws for any reason but that their reign would decrease our misery.

We have now two very general principles for the guidance of evaluation and legislation, and hence for the guidance of action; (1) *Any kind of thing is bad if it, or the pursuit of it, increases the misery of living things upon the whole*, and (2) *no kind of act may be forbidden unless its discontinuance would lessen misery upon the whole*. From the point of view of a search for great goods, each of these principles is negative. The first indicates that certain kinds of thing are not good to pursue, and the second indicates that certain kinds of law are not good to have. Neither indicates that any kind of thing is positively good. Can we find any positive principle for telling what kinds of thing are good?

A positive principle is liable to say or imply that only one kind of thing is good; and any principle that does that must be rejected. It would be foolish to forbid ourselves to value any new kind of thing in the future. In the past we have sometimes come to value a new kind of thing. For example, mountain scenery was not valued before the eighteenth century. It is an obvious point of prudence to leave ourselves free to do the same again. That is why we must not say of pleasure, or of happiness, or of anything else, that it is the only good.

There is, however, a way of introducing pleasure into a positive principle of choice which does not restrict the number of good things, but on the contrary makes it indefinitely large. That is to say that (3) *Anything is good if the pursuit of it pleases somebody and does not increase misery*; or, in A. E. Housman's words, that 'whatever is pleasant is good, unless it can be shown that in the long run it is harmful, or, in other words, not pleasant but unpleasant' (*Introductory Lecture 1892*, p. 33); or, in the words of Plato defending nakedness (*Rp.* 457 B, cf. 608 E), that 'the useful is fair and the harmful is foul; and this is a most fair saying both now and for ever'.

To adopt this is to acknowledge as so far good whatever anyone values or enjoys, or enjoys the pursuit of, because he does so, provided only that people's valuing it does not on the whole increase misery.

In favour of adopting this principle we may say that it expresses a generous instinct which we wish to realize. Of course a thing is good, we feel inclined to say, if it pleases more than it harms. To be against pleasure is to be against life itself, because successful life is necessarily pleasant, as Aristotle nearly said (*N.E.* x. 4, §§ 10-11). We may also argue that it is by following this principle that a man becomes an objective critic of beauty, as opposed to an expresser of private feelings. The good critic will sometimes pronounce good a work that never gives him any pleasure; and this will not be insincerity; it will be his declaration that the work does give pleasure to some people, which is what we want to know from him as critic.

Yet there is also something to be said against the principle. We distinguish between good and bad novels, and among the bad ones we include many that have given pleasure to many people and done no harm. We wish to affirm aspirations towards something great and high, and this seems to involve denying the goodness of many commonplace pleasures, at least in matters of art and beauty. 'The best is the enemy of the good', as Voltaire expressed it (*Philosophical Dictionary*, article on dramatic art).

But, after all, in saying that the best is the enemy of the good, we admit that the good is good. And that is all that this principle claims. It does not say that anything that pleases anyone is a *great* good. It does not command us to put the novels of Charles Garvice on the same level as those of Tolstoy. It only commands us to recognize that the novels of Charles Garvice are humble goods of a kind. I conclude that the principle is to be adopted.

We need to have room in our hearts for both the best and the merely good. We need both to approve of everybody's petty goods and to seek great goods. The doctrine that the best is the enemy of the good is to be taken as an exhortation to press on from the good to the best. It is not to be taken as a licence to condemn everything but the best. On the contrary, we must allow our fellows to be pleased in their own ways.

I have no fourth general principle of choice to propose as even worth consideration. Quite likely, three such principles are three too many. In the question What things are good? it may be better to proceed like the law, refusing to answer any new question until it becomes practical, and then answering as specifically as possible, though certainly each evaluation should be made in the light of all one's other evaluations.

2.2. LIFE

The word 'life' is often put forward as one of those slogan-words that indicate great goods to which our hearts may thrill.

> How good is man's life, the mere living! how fit to employ
> All the heart and the soul and the senses for ever in joy!

Let us consider this.

It may be said that nothing is good unless life itself is good, for goods exist only for living things, not for the inanimate or the dead. 'There is nothing either good or bad, but ⟨living⟩ makes it so!' This reflection, however, is a mistake; for it rests on the false principle that every condition of a good is a good. Not every condition of a good is a good. Suffering is an evil although it is a condition of pity and pity is a good. Life does not have to be itself good because it is a condition of there being any good. It is consistent to say that something is good and yet life is not a good.

On the other hand, it has been believed that, by the test of misery which I have adopted, life is very much more miserable than happy upon the whole, and therefore not a good but an evil. Life involves death, and death is felt to be a very great evil. Some life lives by killing, and all life dies. To give birth to a child is to prepare another death. Some feel that this cancels all the value of life and makes everything futile. A few feel that it makes life intolerable; these find themselves in the absurd position of seeking death because life is intolerable because it ends in death.

We can, however, reasonably urge that at least the fact of death is not a good argument against life. The ending of an individual life, if we distinguish it from the pain and fear that may accompany it, is no more a bad thing than the ending of a good play. W. P. Ker died in a moment, on a mountain where he was walking gaily with companions, at the end of a great and happy life. In such a death the only evil is the loss to those who remain. But it would have been far worse never to have had the man they lost. This objection about death seems less likely to be valid than the objection that life is essentially miserable on the whole, a blind willing which by its nature must be unsatisfied, as Schopenhauer thought.

It may be said that the proposition, 'Life is a great good', is too vague or general to be argued about, for some individual lives are predominantly good and others predominantly bad. Some men are, alas!, born to trouble as the sparks fly upward; but others find their lives very happy and good.

Or it may be said that the proposition, 'Life is a great good', is to be disregarded for another sort of reason, namely that it professes to give a principle of action but does not. Every proposition of the form 'x is a great good', where x is a general term, claims to provide a very general and important principle of action. But, it may be thought, the only question that could be decided by this proposition is whether to stay alive or to kill oneself. Nearly everyone, however, avoids suicide for a reason quite independent of the question whether life is a great good.

Or it may be thought that life as a great good can only be the sum of the various great goods, if any, that may be realized in living, so that the decision that life is (or is not) a great good must come after the examination of all other proposed goods, and will then be merely the sum of our decisions about them. If it seems to be other than this, it may be thought, that must be because we are really referring by the word 'life' not to all life or to life as a whole, but to some aspect of life, some nameless residue left when we have abstracted from life all those goods that have a name. For instance, perhaps we here mean by 'life' just all the less noticeable and less nameable forms of physical well-being and spiritual contentment, just all indefinite 'feeling good'. There are, indeed, wonderful joys to be had on the purely animal side of life, in feelings and satisfactions accompanying moving and resting, working and playing, eating, drinking, making, doing, and congregating. (John Skeaping was probably referring largely to these when he wrote that 'the purpose of life as I see it is to enjoy being alive'.)

We may combine these last two lines of thought, and say that life is a great good in that it realizes many nameable and well known goods, such as beauty and truth, and also in that it realizes many nameless satisfactions and pleasures.

But does not life realize more evils than goods? Is it not on the whole a bad thing? Must we not, when we contemplate the vast array of sorrows, agonies, losses, brutalities, lonelinesses, terrors, hates, envies, frustrations, and dyings, as Schopenhauer, for instance, invites us to do, conclude that it would be better for us all not to be?

This is not a practical question to most people. In some sense no doubt it is true that, once the possibility of suicide has occurred to a living thing, its ultimate choice is to be for or against life. But most people are determined anyhow to go on living as long as they can.

Whether the question is practical or not, I think that we cannot sum and balance all the goods and evils of life so as to come out with any probable answer to it. I think that reason commands us to suspend judgement permanently on the question what has been, or will be, the balance of advantage between goods and evils in life. And this view deprives the proposition that life is a great good of its last chance of representing an important practical choice. Life, then, let us say, is indeed a great good; but to say this is not to commit oneself as, for instance, to say that knowledge is a great good is to commit oneself. It is rather to summarize commitments already made.

To affirm life is not to say that birth-control is always wrong, or that the best population policy is that we should aim at having ever more persons living ever longer.

To affirm life is not to say that killing is always wrong. That simple universal statement leads to the absurdity of Jainism, of hiring a poor man to sleep in your bed and feed the bugs which you are unwilling to have killed. Every time a man eats, his stomach juices kill living things that have come down in his food. We are confronted with many difficult and doubtful choices about when and what to kill and when and what to make live; and this difficulty increases as our knowledge and power increase concerning the conditions of life and death. For instance, it has recently increased through our acquiring the power of artificial insemination. We are coming more and more to have to choose about the survival not merely of individuals but also of species. We know that we have destroyed whole species in the last 400 years, and we are wondering whether we can stop ourselves from doing so in future.

To affirm life is not to say that suicide is always wrong. I will make a digression on suicide. There is such a strong taboo against it in our society that it is very difficult to think well on the matter. Foolish opinions flourish, and frequent among them is the opinion that suicide is wrong because the suicide is a great nuisance to others. Every death is a great nuisance to others; but we all die, and those of us who die by long distressing illnesses are much more of a nuisance to others than those who die quickly by their own hand.

In Kant's statement, that a system of nature could not subsist if it had the principle that 'I shorten my life if its continuance threatens more evil than it promises pleasure', the odd phrase 'a system of nature' means, I suppose, a community of human beings. But, if it means this, we have here another statement so foolish that only where there was a strong taboo on suicide could it be believed. Whether such a community continues will depend on what proportion of its members kill themselves before they have reared children. The ancient Romans' suicides in old age had no effect on the continuance of the community.

The chief argument for the legitimacy of suicide is that life is a trap. We have not asked for it, and it can be terrible.

But, since I am speaking to an audience of undergraduates, it is important for me to add that the suicide rate is far too high among undergraduates, and that nearly all undergraduate suicides are thoroughly injudicious and undesirable. They arise through the young person's terror or horror at finding himself alone and facing some unimagined and very miserable situation, such as a nervous breakdown, an inability to obtain the honours expected of him, a grave depression, the commission of a shameful crime or what he thinks a shameful crime. None of these justifies suicide in youth. The emotional illnesses can be cured. The imaginary crimes can be disproved. The real crimes can be expiated and forgiven. A long, happy, and useful life can be lived in spite of them. The thing to do, if you are ever inclined to kill yourself during your youth, is at once to communicate your miseries to some discreet and sympathetic elder person and to put yourself in his hands. Here at Oxford you are very lucky in this respect, because each of you lives in a community headed by a score of superior elder persons well disposed towards you. You can certainly find among them someone absolutely safe and unshockable, competent, and determined to help you. Here ends my digression on suicide.

2.3. BEAUTY

2.31. *The word 'Beauty'*

I wish to celebrate two great contemplative goods, namely Beauty and Truth. And first Beauty.

By the word 'Beauty' I mean that which is good in its sensuous aspects, that which is good to the eye or ear or nose or tongue or skin, that which gives us pleasure of sense.

In the pleasures of sense I include the pleasures of imagination. Both when you see rowanberries red against the blue sky, and when you afterwards imagine what you saw, the goodness that you apprehend comes under the head of Beauty. By 'imagination' here I mean that image-maker in the soul of whom Plato speaks in his *Philebus* 39 B. Imagination in this use of the word is conditioned by the experience of the senses, which it in semblance either merely reproduces or remoulds and extends.

I do not include in the beautiful anything non-sensuous, as is often done. That paradoxical eternal Beauty of Plato and his followers, which is described as if sensible and yet said not to be sensible, would be no part of what I am talking about here, even if I believed that it existed. The recommendation that I am here making places me among those whom Plato depreciates as loving the many perishable imitations of Beauty instead of the One Beauty itself.

Plato's language draws some of its persuasiveness from the fact that there are many borderline cases where it is difficult to say whether the goodness that we are enjoying is sensuous or not. The so called elegance of mathematical proofs is an example. We are in doubt whether they are literally or only metaphorically beautiful, because we are in doubt whether or not there is something sensuous in our delight in them. The pleasures of emotion form another kind that is very difficult to classify; for is emotion sensuous or not, or is it partly sensuous and partly not? There is no doubt that the perception of a high degree of sensuous Beauty gives a pleasant emotion, other things being equal; but there is doubt whether feeling an emotion is always a sensuous affair. Certainly one cannot be a good critic of Beauty without distinguishing to some extent between the pleasures of emotion and the pleasures of sense.

It is easy to exaggerate the connexion between Beauty and art. Most art is aimed wholly at utility, not Beauty; for example, the arts of medicine, money-making, and mass production. Even so called fine art is often aimed wholly or largely at utility; for example, architecture, pottery, and the paintings in caves. Fine art is frequently aimed at Truth as much as at Beauty, especially in painting and in serious literature. Sophisticated artists are often annoyed to be told they are aiming at Beauty. It would be less wrong to go to the other extreme, and say that there is no particular connexion between art and Beauty. To Plato it seems never to have occurred that artists aimed at Beauty or that their products were the place to look for it. The majority of beautiful things are not made by art but by nature, and nature is the chief realm in which to look for Beauty.

Beauty is not a quality shared among a number of things. There is no common quality, such as proportionality, or significant form, or organic unity, that makes the Beauty of every beautiful thing. What makes an animal beautiful is not what makes a symphony beautiful. If they are both beautiful it is because each of them, when sensuously contemplated, can give us pleasure; but each does so in virtue of its own peculiar qualities. As Sir David Ross has put it, what is common to all beautiful things is only their power to arouse the aesthetic pleasure. Theorists are always trying to find some objective identity in them all; but this leads to empty formalities, or else to a refusal to see and enjoy the infinite variety of Beauty.

So much for the meaning of the word 'Beauty'.

2.32. *Beauty is a great good*

There is a strong tradition against Beauty. Though the Greeks were generally in favour of it, their greatest writer had ascetic tendencies which worked powerfully against it, and in his *Phaedo* he condemned all the interests of the body. Among the Christians there has long been a powerful tradition against Beauty, though it has not been unopposed. I doubt whether it occurs already in the New Testament. When James wrote that love of the cosmos is hatred of God, he was probably not thinking of Beauty. But certainly no special enthusiasm *for* Beauty occurs in the New Testament; and the Christians soon came to be suspicious of it. Augustine assumed that the love of the cosmos forbidden by John (1 John ii. 15-17) included the love of Beauty; and he struggled to weaken his delight in sex, in food and drink, in smell, in sound, and in sight (*Confessions* x. 30-34). He puts sex first among these forbidden delights. Sex and Beauty are, indeed, closely related, and many Christians have come to be enemies of Beauty from being enemies of sex. In Anglo-Saxon countries today one great threat to Beauty is its connexion with sex and the Anglo-Saxon's adolescent fear of sex.

Certainly Beauty is dangerous. So are all great goods. In every case the dangers ought to be weighed and guarded against. There is no great good, either Beauty or any other, about which it is wise to take the reckless line of insisting on it at all times at any cost to other goods. Art for art's sake, or Beauty for Beauty's sake, are stupid or detestable doctrines if they mean that bad consequences for other interests do not matter, or that there are no bad consequences. Of course the love of Beauty conflicts sometimes with morality; and of course morality matters.

But, equally certainly, danger is not always to be avoided, or we should avoid all great goods. Furthermore, it is not Beauty so much as art that the moralist has to fear. Enjoying the products of nature has bad consequences far less often than enjoying the products of artists. Furthermore, the products of bad art are more dangerous to morality than the products of good art. The good artist's representation of evil prevents rather than encourages evil activity.

I believe that Beauty is a very great good. I believe that all who seek to enjoy it will be rewarded. The contemplation of Beauty, and especially the Beauty of nature, is an immense solace and joy, calming and cheering. It is sharable by all. If you stare at the yellow elmtrees in the autumn sun you hinder nobody else from doing so too. The contemplation of Beauty is a form of living that involves no competition, interference, consumption, or destruction. In it we are released for a while from our treadmill of production and consumption, that is, of earning our living. There are always at hand a thousand forms of Beauty (the stars at night, for example) that cost nothing except the petty courage to stand and look at them. And the cultivation of Beauty encourages, and is closely allied to, the cultivation of another great good, namely Truth.

The contemplation of Beauty sometimes induces ecstasy, and ecstasy is the happiest state, a humming perfection of the whole person. The greatest artcritic of the earlier twentieth century, Bernard Berenson, writes in his *Sketch for a Selfportrait* that at the age of five or six he experienced an ecstasy when out of doors. He continues:

> It has remained for seven decades the goal of my yearning, my longing, my desire. Not always alas! but often enough in moments when passion, or ambition, or selfrighteousness would have had their way with me, the feeling of that moment at the dawn of my conscious life would present itself and like a guardian angel remind me that IT was my goal and that IT was my only real happiness.... IT means taking things as they come ... with grateful recognition of what they offer and an almost holy joy in their being.... From childhood up I have had the dream of a life lived as a sacrament. With the years it merged into the wish that it could be

lived with the significance of a work of art: not imitating any visual, musical or literary masterpieces but an art as independent, as autonomous, as each of the arts should be and like them flowing from the same source in the human spirit.

Let us therefore cultivate our appetite for Beauty, and our habit of attending to it, and our power to see it where it is. Let us not eat good food without tasting it, nor pass a rosemary hedge without drawing a hand through it and sniffing. Let us make our own persons and possessions beautiful rather than ugly, as surely it is our duty to do; our dress, our gestures, the way we keep our hair, the house we build, the word we coin, the sentence we write, the way we write it. Let us try to judge who are the good critics, and to see Beauty where they say it is; but at the same time always sincerely to ask whether we ourselves are actually perceiving it. Let us learn to distinguish Beauty from emotion, from sentiment, from antiquity, from modernity, and from whatever else we may tend to confuse it with. When our little opportunity comes to influence the young, let us spread the view that the contemplation of simple, obvious Beauties is a reasonable and civilized thing to do. Let us avoid whatever may bring ridicule or suspicion on the love of Beauty.

2.33. *Art and sex*

In appendix to this recommendation of Beauty I wish to add a few remarks on art and sex.

Although Beauty is not identical with the product of art, and should be clearly distinguished therefrom, because art aims at much else besides Beauty, yet art is closely related to Beauty, and some of its products are extremely beautiful. The lover of Beauty will seek it among artefacts as well as in nature, even if like Berenson he wonders 'whether art has a higher function than to make us feel, appreciate and enjoy natural objects for their art value'.

The activity of art or making, when successful, is itself one of the great goods of life, whether what is made is Beauty or something else. It is perhaps the greatest good that is almost universally available. It *is* almost universally available, for nearly every human being can learn to make or do something well, and can have daily opportunities for exercising some of his art. It is not, however, available to most young children. The great handicap of the human child is that he can do little or nothing well; and one of the advantages of children's play is probably that it manufactures an opportunity of doing something successfully or seeming to. It is important to give children frequent opportunities for doing something well, and to equip them with powers of art and craft.

Representative art in its higher reaches can be a rich and valuable 'expression of the imaginative life', because it 'is separated from actual life by the absence of responsive action, and hence freed from moral responsibility and the binding necessities of our actual existence'. 'When freed from these necessities we can clarify and cultivate our perceptions. In the imaginative life our emotions are weaker but much more clearly realized; and we can give them a new valuation.' This point was made by Roger Fry, and I have been quoting his words.

Whether representative or not, all art can be an absorbing and glorious occupation for its own sake, well worthy of being pursued without ulterior reference to wealth or honour or other goods. This absorption in art as such is the good meaning of the phrase 'art for art's sake'. And the finest affirmation of it known to me is Gustave Flaubert's letter of 1852 to Maxime du Camp beginning 'Mon cher ami, tu me parais avoir à mon endroit un tic ou vice rédhibitoire'.

One great hindrance to the love of Beauty in Anglo-Saxon countries is that Beauty is closely connected with sex and Anglo-Saxons are afraid of sex. Is sex a good thing? We are not prepared to say no. We are not ascetics with the courage of their ascetic convictions. On the other hand, we are certainly not prepared to say yes. Some of us feel it as just a revolting necessity, like killing animals in order to have food—necessary in order to continue the race, but disgusting because, as Yeats has put it, 'love has pitched his mansion in the place of excrement', and because such a surrender of the person is intolerable anyhow to our pride. Some of us feel it a shameful pleasure, keenly attractive but necessarily furtive. Most of us are in doubt what value to put upon it, and we incline this way and that as the momentary influences move us, never reaching a confident evaluation that we are prepared to defend.

In this atmosphere of vacillation and uncertainty, of shame and desire and disgust and fear to think, we become the prey to various horrors. We behave towards the enemies of sex as pusillanimously as the Germans behaved towards the Nazis. That is, we do not believe them; but we will not fight them; and, whenever they make a move against sex, we submit and pretend we agree. It only takes one citizen to say a book is obscene, and ninety-nine other Anglo-Saxons will bow their heads although they disagree, will withdraw the book from circulation and prosecute the publisher. We display in sex the cowardice which we accuse the Germans of in politics. The cause in both cases is the same, lack of open and thorough contemplation of the issue. The tyranny, against which we are sensitive and vigilant in politics, flourishes unrebuked among us in matters of sex. We cannot think of any piece of sexual behaviour as improper without instantly thinking that there ought to be a law against it. We see nothing odd in invoking the law against a book that encourages the enjoyment of sex, though we never invoke the law against a book that encourages hatred of the Jews. Yet hatred of Jews is bad and enjoyment of sex is good.

And what a dreadful set of laws they are that we invoke against sex! We make male homosexuality illegal and we fix no age of consent for males. Our hypocrisy and timidity allow hateful arguments to be used in court. For example, it is sometimes suggested that a homosexual must be a liar, much as it used to be suggested that an atheist must be a liar. It is sometimes suggested that coition is a filthy business. The disgusting belief that the erotic is necessarily obscene flourishes in our courts, and that is a great shame upon our lawyers.

One effect of our fear and shame is that gross ignorance and gross error about sex are very common. Sexuality is a field where everyone begins by being bewilderingly in the dark; and in our culture his own shame and other people's repression tend to keep him so. The opinion prevails, and is fostered by our horrible lawcourts, that only scientists and medical men have a right to know about sex. But these very doctors themselves have often been afraid to know. When asked by a newly married couple for advice about sexual intercourse, which in my opinion it is eminently their duty to give, some of them have replied that there is nothing to be said. A few have even repulsed their patients with abuse.

Sex is dangerous. Let us begin by admitting and realizing that. There is the obvious danger of producing a child that is not wanted or cannot be cared for. There are several less obvious but grave dangers, including emotional fixations that make for misery, uncontrollable and brutal desires, frustration or starvation leading to emotional illnesses and vulgarization. An hour of sexual intoxication can make a lifetime of misery for more than one person, much as an hour of alcoholic intoxication can make a murder. Hence, indeed, we must all say with the Prayer Book that coition 'is not by any to be enterprised, nor taken in hand, unadvisedly, lightly, or wantonly . . . but reverently, discreetly, advisedly, soberly . . . duly considering' the consequences thereof, and the obligations which they involve. And we must say that to invite another person to sexual activity, and especially to initiate a person into it, is an act involving very great responsibilities.

Next we must say that sex is a great good. The sexual act is the source of every new life. It can be a glorious experience in itself. Its imaginative reverberations can spread joy and energy and beauty far and wide through marriage and life and art. That is a large part of the goodness of sex, the fertility and pleasure of its reverberations through life and art. Because of the vivifying and beautifying effect of these long reverberations, we must reject the idea that sexual thoughts and feelings are to be entirely repressed except where they can at once lead to married coition. Here is the main division of opinion about the censorship of art. Much art contains and arouses these sexual reverberations. Some think that is so dangerous that it should be suppressed. I say it is not very dangerous and it is very good. While the sexual act itself is so consequential that it must be severely limited and controlled, imaginative extensions of it and its accompaniments in life and art are neither dangerous nor criminal and are often very good. The dangerous persons are those who have not read books, not those who have.

Every human being has a perfect right to know *all* that is known about sex, and our culture would be a lot better than it is if most people knew a lot more about sex than they do. This right belongs entire to children as well as to adults, and children in particular have sometimes a grave need to know about sex to help them in understanding and controlling the bewildering things that are happening to them. It is our duty to help them, both by answering their questions informatively and unemotionally, and by leaving informative books where they can read them without embarrassment, and by making such books available in libraries. We must not, however, be angry with librarians who keep these books off the shelves and look searchingly at borrowers who ask for them. We must remember that the poor librarians are at the mercy of Mrs. Grundy (who has no mercy). Mrs. Grundy is waiting to pounce and take away their livelihood if she can. The librarian wants to lend us the books. That is his aim in life. But we must help him by being very discreet in our requests, and letting him see that we are on his side and are not borrowing the book in order to prosecute him.

For the ideal sexual behaviour there exist the words 'purity' and 'chastity'. But on the question what kinds of behaviour deserve these virtue labels, there is probably less agreement than on the question what social arrangements deserve the label 'justice'. In the matter of drink the ideal behaviour is temperance, and there is a strong tendency to the bad idea that temperance is abstinence. Similarly, in sex there is a tendency to the bad idea that chastity and purity consist in total abstinence or virginity. Thus the *S.O.E.D.* defines 'violate' as to destroy a person's chastity by force. But you cannot destroy a person's chastity by force, because chastity being a virtue is a matter of free will. What you can destroy by force is only her virginity. A violated girl is not an unchaste girl.

2.4. TRUTH

2.41. *The ideal of Truth*

There is a great good for which the best one-word name is 'Truth' or 'Knowledge'. Neither name indicates fully what we have in mind, partly because we have not completed our ideal of the good in question, and partly because both these words are used in several ways. The word 'Truth', for instance, is sometimes used to mean a virtue, either the virtue of sincerity or that of loyalty; but the good that I have in mind now is not a virtue. I mean now something to do with man's power of speech, which is the most peculiar power that he has and the seat of his enormous advantage over all other kinds of life. When words take the form of statements they are either true or false, that is either to be accepted or to be rejected. The great good called 'Truth' is something like the accumulation of acceptable statements, the pursuit, formation, and possession, of as many acceptable statements as possible.

Truth is not to be understood as the knowledge of ultimate secrets, and we are not to talk about 'the ultimate structure of the universe', or about *the* Truth (as if there were only one or preeminently one), or about Truth the woman (as if she were one thing). These are all misconceptions. There are no secrets of the universe; for a secret is a truth deliberately withheld from one person by another person; but no one is deliberately withholding from us facts about the universe; we are deliberately constructing statements about the universe, that is all. There is no ultimate Truth; for what could 'ultimate' mean here? If it means that every other Truth follows from this Truth, there is no such Truth. If it means that he who knows this Truth wants to know nothing else, such a person would not be much of a truthlover. The word 'ultimate' suggests the metaphor of climbing to the top of a pyramid. It would probably be truer to say that the pyramid is upside down; we start from the little apex which is at the bottom; and we climb endlessly towards the ever expanding and ever receding top.

Could there be such a thing as 'the ultimate structure of the universe'? Atoms are constructed into molecules, molecules into cells, cells into men, men into societies, and so on. There is no fixed end to this, and so no ultimate structure in this direction. Molecules are constructed out of atoms, atoms out of protons and other particles. We do not know whether there is a fixed end to this; but anyhow such division is an unnatural meaning for the word 'structure'. The phrase seems to refer to nothing possible.

The ideal of Truth is something more catholic than this. Truth is an ever extending pyramid with indefinitely many chambers in it, all worthy of interest and respect. If we do not regard it in this catholic way, we fall into puerile esotericism and mysterymongering, a danger that is always at hand.

There is, however, a distinction between important and petty truths, and we want the important rather than the petty ones. A telephone directory when first published is probably far more true than any history of Athens; but the history can realize something of the ideal of Truth and the directory cannot. We want truths that make us understand the world, rather than merely put us in touch with a number of particular facts.

We want also precise rather than vague truths. For it is easy and useless to make a true statement if you do not care how vague it is. It is true but useless to remark that 'something somehow is', or that 'it will rain sometime'.

The ideal of Truth is sometimes adopted in the half-way form that 'Truth is good for me and my friends, but not for the masses'. 'It is all right for me to read about sex, but not for you.' Plato affirms in noble tones that the philosopher kings of his Callipolis will be passionate lovers of Truth; but examination of other parts of the *Republic* shows that he intends them to be lovers of Truth for themselves only; they are to have no interest in letting the common citizen know the Truth. When we ask ourselves the question, we know that this will not do. The ideal of Truth includes Truth known or at least available to all speaking beings, although we should not force a department of knowledge on those whom it bores, nor press the more terrible Truths on those who are not ready to bear them.

We include in this ideal the pursuit and discovery of acceptable statements, as well as the possession of them. Truth is inquiry at least as much as contemplation. To learn is probably better than to know, contrary to the opinion of Aristotle. The pursuit of Truth is the profession of the scholar or scientist. It would come out more clearly if we had a single word that embraced both scholar and scientist. Julien Benda revived for this purpose an old use of 'clerk', and published a book affirming that the duty of clerks is to show the world an example of disinterested intellectual activity, to set up a corporation whose sole cult is that of justice and truth, to restrain the passions of the layman, to tell the layman truths which are displeasing to him, to quench human pride, and to pay for this with his own peace. (Julien Benda, *The Great Betrayal*, London, 1928, a translation of *La Trahison des clercs*.)

It is a misfortune that a great writer has declared that 'Beauty is Truth, Truth Beauty'. Nothing is gained by this equation except a vague emotion; and an important distinction is lost. Beauty and Truth are, indeed, related to each other more closely than to any other great goods in that they are the two contemplative goods, the two which lie to a large extent in what may be called just looking at the world. But Truth is intellectual, whereas Beauty is sensuous. The enjoyment of Beauty is largely independent of man's power of language, whereas Truth is completely dependent thereon.

Representative art does, indeed, give us the good of Truth as well as that of Beauty; but representative art is only a small part of the domain of Beauty.

2.42. *Truth is a great good*

There are strong arguments against accepting Truth and Knowledge as a great good.

It may well be said that men in general have very little interest in Truth, and therefore it is hopeless to set it up as a great good. Psychologists listing basic drives rarely include curiosity among them. Most people show only a very faint interest in learning anything but what their neighbours are doing. On the other hand, many people have a great love of mystery, that is of *not* knowing but being ignorant; and they complain of those who remove mysteries and make things clearer.

It is quite commonly thought that mere knowledge is bad rather than good. In the Old Testament we read that 'in much wisdom is much grief: and he that increaseth knowledge increaseth sorrow' (Eccles. i. 18). The New Testament mostly passes knowledge by in silence; when it does glance at it the glance is unfavourable. Paul wrote that 'knowledge puffeth up, but charity edifieth' (1 Cor. viii. 1). He was thinking of the particular knowledge that, since there are no gods but God, it is harmless to eat meat that has been offered to idols. But many Christians have taken his words in a far wider sense; and he himself elsewhere says that 'God hath chosen the foolish things of the world to confound the wise' (1 Cor. i. 27). Augustine, when he became a Christian, tried to kill his interest in lizards and spiders (*Confessions* x. 35). Bernard wrote a sonorous passage condemning all knowledge but knowledge for the sake of edification. He stigmatized knowledge for its own sake as 'base curiosity' (*In Cant. Cant. Sermo* 36, Migne clxxxiii. 968). Even Aquinas the Aristotelian was restrained in his praise of knowledge. He did, indeed, assert a virtue of 'studiosity', which was an aspect of temperance, and consisted partly in restraining the appetite for cognition when necessary, partly in urging it on to overcome the labours of learning. But curiosity was vicious to him, too, and so was the disinterested study of sensible things. (*Summa Theologica*, II. ii. 166, 167.) Pascal wrote that 'man's principal disease is restless curiosity about things that he cannot know; and it is less bad for him to be in error than to be in this state of useless curiosity' (vii. 17). John Henry Newman described as a 'temptation' Nicodemus' question How can these things be?, and implied that God does not care for men to have knowledge as such (*Sermon* XVI).

The mantle of Christianity has now fallen to Communism, and Communists have adopted the Christian contempt for the ideal of Truth. The pursuit of knowledge for its own sake, and the doctrine that universities exist to pursue knowledge for its own sake, appear to the Communists as a denial that knowledge has any useful purpose to serve in society, or a refusal to help man in obtaining control over his environment. Pursuing knowledge without reference to its use seems to them identical with pursuing useless knowledge and asserting that knowledge has no use.

There is no doubt that both the pursuit and the possession of Truth often do harm. The agitation against vivisection is an obvious reminder of the harm sometimes done by the pursuit. As to the harm done by the possession of it, the spectacle of the universe as it really is may perfectly well be terrible and depressing.

Against the authority of the Christian tradition about Knowledge, it would be easy to set other authorities in favour of Knowledge. But authority is not much of an argument anyway. And the Christians were obviously interested parties; they feared that the love of Knowledge would turn men away from the exclusive love of a god which they demanded. Their tirades against Knowledge for its own sake are not convincing but rather contemptible, or, in a very great writer like Augustine or Pascal, saddening.

Against a recital of harm done by the pursuit or possession of Truth, it would be easy to set a recital, of any desired length, of the good done thereby. That Truth has an enormous utility is obvious to anyone who believes in history as a guide to our actions now, or in science as a means of ameliorating our physical condition.

And there is an instinct of curiosity, to form a natural basis for the good of Knowledge and Truth. Aristotle declares it: 'All men by nature desire to know.' And Aristotle was a great observer of men and beasts, and the first man to write a methodical and empirical treatise in psychology. The instinct exists also, to a smaller extent, in some other high vertebrates; and is probably connected with the elaborateness of their nerves. Because of it men often find very great joy in discovering facts.

Because of this instinct the pursuit of Truth cannot be completely stopped. It can be discouraged and disapproved and starved, as it often has been. But wherever there are men there is some curiosity; and wherever men have any strength left after getting their food this curiosity flourishes to some extent. It is ineradicable because of man's nature, and because the greatest enemy of Knowledge cannot help seeing the usefulness of some knowledge. So the only choice we have about it is whether to drive it underground and make it furtive and feeble, or, on the other hand, to encourage and develop it. The better by far is to develop and encourage it. We cannot live a rational life except on the basis of knowing the facts; as reasonable persons we must base our actions on the best relevant knowledge we can acquire. Furthermore, nothing else is consistent with our dignity. The ideal of man evidently includes the seeker and the knower, the being who is aware of the world as much as he can be, and who is developing ever farther the great system of statements by which he describes the world and takes up his attitude towards it. The ideal of universal love also demands the pursuit of truth; for we want to love the world that is, not an illusion.

Truth shares with Beauty the great advantage of being a largely non-competitive good. Your learning does not hinder my learning but helps it. Though I cannot be the first to discover what you have discovered, there is more to discover, and always will be. The pursuit of Truth often extends and enhances other goods, which without it would be of shorter duration or intensity. Thus the pleasures of eating are purified and heightened and lengthened by those who pursue knowledge about how food is obtained and prepared and eaten in different parts of the world.

2.5. REASON

2.501. *Virtue*

Although the word 'virtue' is rather out of fashion today, and tends to be written off as one of the more fatuous interests of theologians and philosophers, yet we all still mean by it fairly well one and the same thing, and that a thing which we admit after some reluctance to be very important. A virtue is some valuable aspect of a human being, and to some extent of any living thing so far as it can resemble human beings in this respect. It is not *any* valuable aspect of the person, not, for example, his beauty or intelligence or speed of running. That comes out clearly if we consider the valuable aspects we ascribe to a person in writing a favourable testimonial about him; for we then find that most of the good qualities we mention are not qualities we class as virtues. The virtues are now only a small part of the possible goodness of man, though to the ancient Greeks they were sometimes the whole of it, divided into his physical, his moral, and his intellectual, kinds of goodness.

The virtues now tend to be confined to what Aristotle called moral virtues; and these are, as he said, praiseworthy habits of choice. Man as he lives acquires habits of exercising his various powers of choice in particular ways, and if we praise such a habit we call it a virtue. (In ascribing this to Aristotle I am combining two assertions that he makes separately in his *Nicomachean Ethics*: 1103ᵃ9 and 1106ᵇ 36.)

It may be that our present use of the word 'virtue' is still narrower than this. It may be that not even all praiseworthy habits of choice are called virtues. For example, the habit of choosing happiness seems praiseworthy, and the habit of choosing unhappiness seems blameable; yet we do not call them a virtue and a vice. If so, we must ask what marks off those praiseworthy habits of choice that we do call virtues from those that we do not. Moore has plausibly suggested that 'virtues are distinguished from other useful dispositions . . . by the fact that they are dispositions which it is particularly useful to praise and to sanction, because there are strong and common temptations to neglect the actions to which they lead' (*Principia Ethica*, p. 172).

Virtues are good by definition. The mere calling anything a virtue is an implication that it is good. There is no proper place for an argument that virtue is good, except just this argument that virtue is good by the meaning of the word 'virtue'. The place for argument and exhortation is elsewhere, namely where the question arises which habits of choice should be praised as virtues and which should not. Plato in his *Republic* gave a list of four which has become famous: wisdom, courage, temperance, justice. It is often said that he took this tetrad from common Greek opinion; but I know no evidence for that, and I think it more probable that he was the first to pick out and set up just these four. Aristotle in his *Nicomachean Ethics* added about eight more, somewhat unconvincingly. He gave the impression of analysing very accidental opinions or usages, rather than of setting up an ideal of behaviour that a reflective person might adopt. Aquinas produced another famous list by combining Plato's four with the 'faith, hope, and love' celebrated by Paul. But this is a typical effort of Aquinas the Tinker, as I think he should be called, soldering together the Greek and the Christian as badly as postwar smiths solder silver. Paul's faith is incompatible with Plato's wisdom; and Paul's hope is too vague and slight a thing to be made a great virtue.

None of these thinkers supposed himself to be giving the complete list of human virtues. They knew well enough that there is no definite end to the dispositions we may want men to have or praise them for having. They were only setting up what they thought the most important virtues, those most often to be striven for and most worth remembering in a slogan, or those most in need of recommendation at the moment. They were not professing to abrogate all accepted evaluations of human character and start again, but only to alter slightly the emphasis accepted when they wrote, raising a little the importance of this and lowering a little the importance of that, rarely adding a wholly new ideal or completely rejecting an old one. I shall do the same. Starting with the current evaluations of human character, and retaining the greater number of them, I shall seek to raise your estimate of two of them and lower your estimate of two others. The two virtues which I wish to celebrate and support are reason and love, the first more Greek than Christian, the second more Christian than Greek. I suppose that Matthew Arnold had them in mind when he recommended 'sweet reasonableness'. Conversely I wish to reject as vices their opposites, which Plato called misology and misanthropy, the hatred of reason and the hatred of man (*Phaedo* 89 D).

2.502. *The word 'reason'*

There are at least three importantly different senses of the word 'reason'.

First there is the sense we are using when we say that the reason for having a long chimney is to make a better draught, or that someone offered no reason for his view, or that the reason for an act is not the same as the cause of the act. In these sentences the word 'reason', whatever it means, does not mean a virtue. Therefore it is not this sense that I am using when I say that reason is a great virtue.

Second there is a sense in which reason is the ability to think, or the exercise of that ability. 'Man is the rational animal' means 'Man is the animal that can think'. The word has this sense in Descartes' title *A Discourse of the Method of rightly conducting the Reason*; Descartes means that he is going to tell us how to think rightly. Ralph Linton was using this sense of the word when he wrote that 'reason is the ability to solve problems without going through a physical process of trial and error' (*The Study of Man*, p. 66). Reason in this sense of the word is, as Linton says, an ability, a power, a faculty.

The most striking part of thinking is reasoning. When we wish to call to mind an example of thinking, we tend to call up an example of reasoning. Yet on reflection we all agree that reasoning is not the only form of thinking. There are also wondering, imagining, composing, remembering, trying to remember, searching for ideas, getting ideas, calculating, reciting, and indefinitely many more. All these are indubitably thought. And reason in the sense of a human faculty is the faculty to do any or most of these, not just the faculty of reasoning. Hume, for instance, is too narrow in defining it as judgement from demonstration or probability, or later as 'the discovery of truth and falsehood' (*Treatise*, 2. 3. 3, 3. 1. 1).

Since a faculty is not a virtue, it is not this second sense of the word either that I am using when I say that reason is a great virtue.

But man can use his faculties badly or well, and to have the habit of using a given faculty well is to have a virtue. There is a virtue of exercising our power to think in good ways. There is a vice of habitually thinking badly, and a virtue of habitually thinking well. This virtue of habitually thinking well is what is meant, or obliquely referred to, by the word 'reason' when used in an honorific sense. The phrase 'it stands to reason that' means that, if you think *well*, you will certainly adopt the proposition in question. The phrase 'reason forbids' means that, if you think *well*, you will *not* adopt the proposal in question. If someone says that 'man is an *ir*rational animal', he is not contradicting the statement that 'man is a rational animal', but condemning the way in which man habitually conducts his reason. Man is a rational animal, that is, he thinks; and man is also an irrational animal, that is, he thinks badly.

To give an account of reason in the second sense is to write psychology, to describe human thinking as it occurs; and this is done in, for example, Professor Humphrey's book called *Thinking*. To give an account of reason in the third sense, however, is to write ethics, for it is to adopt or recommend particular habits of thought as being the *good* ways to think, to answer the question not how we do think but how we ought to think, to construct an ideal of thinking, a conception of intellectual virtue.

It is this third sense of 'reason' that I am using when I say that reason is a great virtue; and the following discussion of reason is my construction and recommendation of the ideal habits of thought.

2.503. *The love of truth*

In the ideal of reason I include the following eleven elements: love of truth, respect for reasons, consistency, deductiveness, preference for probability, tentativeness, respect for evidence, submission to criticism, selfcompatibility, impartiality, and the lessening of misery.

The first and foremost element in a good habit of thought is the love of truth, philalethy. The good man is philalethic, as Plato said. As Sir David Ross has said, 'intellectual integrity, the love of truth for its own sake, is among the most salient elements in a good moral character' (*The Right and the Good*, p. 153). The good thinker seeks always to arrive at true statements and opinions and to avoid adopting any false ones. Although it is too narrow to define reason as nothing but the judgement of the true and the false, yet the judgement of the true and the false is the basic interest and duty of reason. And, as one great champion of reason has written, 'he that would seriously set upon the search of truth, ought in the first place to prepare his mind with a love of it. For he that loves it not, will not take much pains to get it; nor be much concerned when he misses it' (Locke, *Essay*, 4. 19. 1).

2.504. *Respect for reasons*

If a man wishes to acquire truths, what principles and doctrines should he adopt for his work?

In the first place, he should learn what is wrong with the New Testament's distinction between belief and unbelief, and replace it with the three-part distinction between belief, doubt, and disbelief.

It is a very important part of good thinking to realize that there are three distinct possible attitudes towards every statement. You can believe it, or you can disbelieve it, or you can remain in doubt whether to believe or disbelieve it. In other words, you can assent or dissent or suspend judgement. The New Testament distinction conceals the difference between dissent and suspense of judgement. The 'unbelief' which it opposes to belief is either disbelief or doubt. It is correct to distinguish between believing a proposition and not believing it, and it may be useful sometimes to have the name 'unbelief' for not believing the proposition. But this name 'unbelief' is dangerous because it covers the two different attitudes, disbelieving the proposition and suspending judgement about it; and failure to distinguish these two leads to many errors. We are unlikely to adopt the right attitude towards a proposition if we assume that only two are possible. Pascal, for example, argued that we are immortal by assuming that we must either believe this statement or doubt it, and ignoring the possibility of firmly disbelieving it (*Pensées*, ix. 1, Havet).

There is another evil in the New Testament distinction between belief and unbelief, much greater than the first; and that is the implication that it is morally obligatory to believe and morally wrong not to believe. The New Testament habitually implies that it is wicked not to believe. This is to poison reason at its source. Reason commands a moral principle contrary to that of the New Testament, namely this: search for and weigh the reasons for and against each statement, and judge in the light of them whether you should assent to the statement or dissent from it or suspend judgement. Reason says that there is nothing wicked in disbelieving or doubting as such; what is wicked is to adopt your attitude in disregard of the available reasons.

You have here two fundamental and contrary principles for the conduct of your intellect, and you must choose between them. There is the principle implied by the New Testament, that it is right to believe and wrong not to believe. And there is the principle of reason, that it is right to believe or disbelieve or doubt in accordance with the balance of the reasons available, and wrong to doubt or disbelieve or believe in disregard of the reasons available. I have chosen the principle of reason, and I beg you to do so too.

This, then, is the first and greatest principle of reason: believe, or disbelieve, or suspend judgement about, each statement that comes to your notice, in accordance with the balance of the reasons for and against it available to you. More shortly, reason demands respect for reasons. In contrast to this, the New Testament principle may be summed as: avoid unbelief.

People sometimes come to prefer the New Testament principle through taking unbelief as equivalent to doubt and judging it better to believe something than to doubt everything. In this state of mind it seems to them reasonable to say that it is impossible to doubt everything, and therefore it is reasonable to believe. But unbelief is not equivalent to doubt; it is equivalent to either doubt or disbelief, and he who disbelieves something believes something.

I will develop this point, that he who disbelieves something believes something. To assert any statement is necessarily to reject its contradictory, and to reject any statement is necessarily to assert its contradictory. This follows from the nature of contradiction and the fact that every statement has a contradictory.

Every statement has a contradictory, because you can construct the contradictory of any statement by prefixing to it the words 'it is false that'. For example, the following are a pair of contradictories: 'there is a god' and 'it is false that there is a god'. (Langford in *Mind* for 1927 argued that singular propositions have no proper contradictories; but I will not go into this in an elementary lecture. Nelson discussed Langford's point in *Mind* for 1946.)

No statement has more than one contradictory. Its contradictory can, indeed, be expressed in different ways; for example, we can say 'there is no god' instead of 'it is false that there is a god'. But these different ways are equivalent and come to the same thing. Every statement has one and only one contradictory.

The definition of contradiction implied in this may be brought out as follows. The contradictory of any statement S is not-S. The contradictory of any statement not-S is S. Any two statements S and T are contradictories if and only if S is equivalent to not-T. Any two statements are contradictories if and only if the truth of either entails the falsity of the other and also the falsity of either entails the truth of the other.

Hence all statements fall into pairs of which one is true and the other is false. Hence, also, exactly half of all the statements that could be made are true, and exactly half are false. Hence, thirdly, and this is the important point for the lover of truth, to assert any proposition is to deny its contradictory, and to deny any proposition is to assert its contradictory; and everybody asserts exactly the same number of propositions as he denies.

The question about any statement is therefore not exactly whether to believe it or not; it is whether to believe it or its contradictory, for one of them must be true. This little shift of emphasis makes a big improvement in our mental attitude. It saves us from the common assumption that, other things being equal, it is good to believe as many things as possible and disbelieve as few things as possible. We see that this desired state is impossible, because every belief is necessarily also a disbelief, and conversely. It relieves us also from the feeling that, if we reject all the propositions presented to us, we are making no progress. On the contrary, since to reject a proposition is to adopt its contradictory, we are gaining just as many opinions as we are rejecting. It relieves us, thirdly, from the feeling that we are sceptics who ought to be believers. We see now that the difference between the sceptic and the believer cannot be that the believer believes much and disbelieves little, while the sceptic disbelieves much and believes little. Everybody, sceptic and believer alike, inevitably believes exactly the same number of statements as he disbelieves.

We must look elsewhere for a tenable distinction between the believer and the sceptic. We might say that the believer believes more affirmative statements, and disbelieves more negative ones, than the sceptic does. Or we might say that the believer more often picks the more consequential of the two contradictories; he more often picks the consequential statement that 'all Russians are suspicious', whereas the sceptic is the man who more often picks the inconsequential contradictory: 'at least one Russian is not suspicious.' Or we might define the believer as him who suspends judgement less often than the sceptic does. Many people, of course, tend to mean by 'the believer' simply the man who believes one particular statement, namely the statement that there is a god.

He who disbelieves something believes something. Therefore unbelief includes belief, since it includes disbelief. Therefore unbelief is not opposed to belief as doubt is. And the principle of reason is not a demand that we shall doubt every proposition. It is a demand that we shall decide in accordance with the available reasons whether to doubt the proposition or to believe it or to believe its contradictory.

2.505. *The love of consistency*

The next element in the ideal of reason is the love of consistency. This arises from the fact that certain statements follow necessarily from other statements. If a statement S follows necessarily from a statement R, I shall say that R entails S, employing the word 'entails' in a sense invented by G. E. Moore. Whenever S follows from R, R entails S. Conversely, whenever R entails S, S follows from R.

Whenever a statement entails a second statement, it is inconsistent with the contradictory of that second statement. If R entails S, R is inconsistent with not-S, and to assert both R and not-S is to be inconsistent. Hence whenever a man believes more than one statement, as we all do, there is a possibility that he may be inconsistent with himself. Reason demands that this possibility be avoided. We are to watch for inconsistencies among our beliefs; and, when an inconsistency appears, we are to drop one of the inconsistent statements and believe its contradictory instead. (The question which we are to drop, of the two inconsistent statements, has to be answered on further grounds. The mere demand for consistency will be satisfied by dropping either of them.)

A horrible example of acquiescing in inconsistency is provided by a certain common way of taking the doctrine that 'the exception proves the rule'. Many people take this to mean that, for example, you can prove that it is a rule that women are inferior to men by producing an exceptional woman who is not inferior. They imply that a universal generalization is proved to be true by the production of a case in which it is false! This is selfcontradictory and absurd. An exceptional woman who was superior to men would not prove a universal rule that all men are superior to all women. On the contrary, she would disprove it completely for all time. And as to a statement about averages, for example that the average man is superior to the average woman, it is neither proved nor disproved by any individual case of anything at all.

What then is the value of this common doctrine that 'the exception proves the rule'? Is it just a piece of insanity? Yes, as commonly used today it is just a piece of insanity. But it has arisen out of a sane procedure in the lawcourts. Wherever men make and enforce rules of action, it is possible for them to allow some exceptions to their rules. If a governor is known to have said 'I make an exception in your favour', this is good evidence that the governor generally follows a certain rule, which he is breaking in this special case. The fact that the governor says he is making an exception shows that he has a rule. The exception proves that there is a rule. This is sane inference. But when it is transferred from the sphere of human rules of action to the sphere of laws of nature, insanity results.

The phrase can also make sense if taken as a reference to the fact that apparent exceptions sometimes turn out on closer examination not to be exceptions at all, and thus strengthen our belief in the general statement. Thus punishing people for ignorance appears to be an exception to the rule that they should be punished only for their voluntary acts; but it may turn out that they are punished for ignorance only when that ignorance is due to a voluntary act of theirs.

The love of consistency is not the same as obstinacy. Some people obstinately refuse to change their opinion because they think to do so would make them inconsistent. A change of view does, of course, involve that my opinion today is inconsistent with my opinion yesterday. But there is no harm in that. What is objectionable is that one of my views today should be inconsistent with another of my views today. The reasonable man pursues consistency of his present opinions with each other. He does not pursue consistency of his present opinions with his past opinions. On the contrary, he changes his opinions whenever present considerations indicate that he should.

Just as the love of consistency does not involve the obstinacy of refusing to change an opinion, so it does not involve the vice of sneering at others for having changed their opinion, or pouncing on them for believing contrary to what they believed five years ago. The reasonable man objects to any inconsistency of your present opinions with each other, but not to any inconsistency they may have with your past opinions.

People sometimes confuse consistency with order and orderliness, and think that reason demands orderliness because it demands consistency. This confusion is often embodied in the word 'logical' used as a term for judging actions. People say it would be 'more logical' to do so and so when they mean it would embody a tighter order to do so. In this way they come to think that 'reason is that in us which demands sequence, regularity, and order in things; it resents mere accident and chance occurrence' (Bishop Gore, *Belief in God*, p. 53). This sometimes encourages tyranny in politics, by way of the view that it is unreasonable of people to be disorderly.

But consistency is not the same as tight and simple order, or as order of any kind. A disorderly arrangement of flowers in a bed is more reasonable than an orderly one, if it is more pleasing to the eye. There is nothing inherently more reasonable about order than about disorder. Reason forbids us to hold two propositions that are inconsistent with each other; but it does not forbid us to hold two propositions that fail to belong together in some neat and orderly arrangement. And the ideal of reason includes the love of consistency but not the love of order.

There are occasions when it is very hard to be consistent. That is, there are occasions when we feel very strongly impelled to believe both that R is true, and that R entails S, and that S is false. Such a difficulty is usually largely emotional, but sometimes it is purely intellectual. If Berkeley's arguments 'admit of no answer but produce no conviction', as Hume said, they provide a purely intellectual case of the difficulty. On such occasions we should not turn away our thoughts but keep on facing the difficulty and considering what we are to abandon, convinced that it is essential to abandon one of the three, either our belief that R is true, or our belief that R entails S, or our belief that S is false.

2.506. *Deductiveness*

The love of consistency is important because some propositions exclude others because they entail their contradictories. In that way the fact of entailment between propositions greatly determines the ideal of reason. I wish now to bring out another and more positive way in which entailment determines the ideal of reason. If it is reasonable to believe a given statement, it must also be reasonable to believe all the other statements which the given statement entails. Hence, given one reasonable belief, we can add to our store of reasonable beliefs by finding what it entails. To do this is to be deductive, and deductiveness is part of the ideal of reason. The reasonable man keeps looking for entailments, for 'therefores' and 'follows froms'. By the discovery of entailments he increases his stock of reasonable beliefs, he uncovers inconsistencies which he can then remove, and he brings to bear on each proposition a much greater amount of reasonable consideration and argument, thus making his decision about it much safer.

Deductiveness is the most striking of all the elements in the ideal of reason, and the most widely known. It is often falsely assumed to be the whole of reason. It is already fairly clearly expressed in the dialogues of Plato, both in the actual procedure of argument depicted there, and in phrases like 'wherever reason may carry us like a wind, there we must go' (*Rp.* 394 D). The magnificent passage on misology in the *Phaedo* is largely an endorsement of deductiveness: 'A man can suffer no greater evil than to have become a hater of deductions' (λόγους μισήσας, *Pho.* 89 D).

We must, however, make one correction in Plato's statement of the ideal here. Propositions cannot themselves blow us in any particular direction as a wind does. The statement R cannot take us by the hand and show us the statement S which it entails. Our creative effort is required in order to think of any of the other statements which a given statement entails and see that it entails them. The discovery of them is a slow process, though when one is discovered it is often hard to believe that our ancestors failed to realize it.

Thus Plato slightly misplaced the passivity which he assigns to the reasonable man in these passages. The reasonable man is passive in acknowledging and submitting himself to all the entailments which he perceives. But he is not passive in perceiving them, for there is no one to show them to him if he were just to sit expectantly waiting for them to appear. He is active in searching for these entailments. He is active in choosing in which direction to search, and which of the discovered entailments to follow up.

Plato's slight misconception here is reminiscent, and perhaps an ancestor, of the common view that it is bad to think of your conclusion first and then look for arguments for it afterwards. That is perfectly false. There is no harm and much good in thinking of your conclusion first. There is no harm, because the value of your argument is independent of the order in which you invented its parts. When you urge that 'S must be true because of R', the strength or weakness of that argument is nothing to do with the historical question whether you thought of S before you thought of R. There is much good in thinking of your conclusion first, because, if you do not think of it first, you will probably never think of it at all. Good arguments are mostly produced by people who want to prove some particular conclusion, not by people who want to use some particular premiss to prove—anything it will prove! If you hear a chemist say 'I believe so and so, and I am going to try to prove it', you should not suspect that he is a bad scientist. It is much more likely that he is a good one.

2.507. *The pursuit of certainty*

In seeking to decide which of a pair of contradictories is the true one, the reasonable man asks first whether they are analytic or synthetic statements. I explain and justify this rule as follows.

We want to avoid doubt or suspense of judgement if we reasonably can; for the task of reason or good thinking is to adopt the true one of each pair of contradictory statements and reject the false one. Provided that we include disbelief in belief, it is true to say that our aim is to believe as much as we reasonably can. We desire that, for as many statements as possible, we may reasonably abandon suspense and come down on the side of either adoption or rejection.

When, then, is it reasonable to abandon suspense about a proposition and either accept it or reject it? Once we have adopted a statement, reason bids us to adopt whatever other statements it entails, and to reject whatever other statements it is inconsistent with. But how are we to adopt the original statement reasonably? How are we to get started? This question is the search for the criterion of truth; for it is equivalent to the question what are the criteria for deciding which of a pair of contradictories is the true one. The first part of the answer to it is that the criterion of truth is different for different kinds of statement, so that we must make the relevant distinctions among statements, and assign its proper criterion to each kind that we distinguish.

Some statements are selfcontradictory, for examples 'no horse is a horse', 'a horse is an insect', 'a triangle does not have three sides', 'if two people are brothers one of them is a woman', 'x is a motor-car and x is not a vehicle'. We need no plainer criterion of a statement's being false than that it is selfcontradictory.

If a statement is false, its contradictory must be true. Hence the contradictory of a selfcontradictory statement is a true statement, for examples 'a horse is a horse', 'a horse is not an insect', 'a triangle has three sides', 'it is false that if two people are brothers one of them is a woman', 'either x is not a motor-car or x is a vehicle'.

These examples show that there is a class of statements for which the criterion of truth and falsehood is selfcontradiction. They are false if they are selfcontradictory, and true if their contradictories are selfcontradictory. I shall call them 'analytic' statements, 'analytic' falsehoods if they are selfcontradictions, and 'analytic' truths if they are the contradictories of selfcontradictions. Every statement that falls outside this class I call 'synthetic'.

If a statement is analytic, its contradictory is analytic too; and if it is synthetic, its contradictory is synthetic too. You do not change this character of a statement by prefixing to it the words 'it is false that'.

Analytic statements are analytic in virtue of their meaning alone. It is simply and solely what the words mean that makes it false that 'a horse is an insect'. It follows that we have to decide whether a statement is analytic solely by considering its meaning, and that when a statement is analytic we can tell whether it is true or false solely by considering its meaning, and cannot tell it in any other way. It follows also that, in seeking to decide which of a pair of contradictories is the true one, the reasonable man asks first whether they are analytic or synthetic statements.

This rule at first appears to be petty and unimportant on the ground that analytic statements are trivial. Who wants to be told that it is false that a horse is an insect, or true that a triangle must have three sides? But, on the contrary, the rule is of very great importance for two reasons. The first reason is that people who are not well aware of the distinction often spend hours of study and labour and come out with results to which they attach great importance, but which are in fact analytic truisms that could have been obtained without any labour at all. It has been my painful task to point out to a friend, who had taken to writing and composed after four years' research a very learned and obscure book, that the thesis he was seeking to recommend was true by its meaning alone, and all his erudition was irrelevant to its support. This misfortune is frequent. It may well be called 'the first distemper of learning', to borrow a phrase from Francis Bacon; and it may be said to consist in mistaking words for matter, in that it mistakes a statement true by its mere meaning for one that gives important information about the world.

We do not by the mere light of nature see in every case whether a statement is analytic or synthetic. Even when we set ourselves to decide a given case we sometimes have difficulty. And when we are not thinking of the distinction at all, and have our heads full of some concrete matter that we have studied, we often produce a statement which we assume to be an important description of the matter but which is in fact an analytic truth.

Here is the second reason why it is important to realize and apply the distinction between analytic and synthetic statements. Analytic truths are not all truisms, and analytic falsehoods are not all obviously false. Take any three large numbers. That the first when added to the second equals the third is either an analytic truth or an analytic falsehood; but you often cannot tell which without doing some calculation. That there is an infinity of prime numbers is an analytic truth; but it may take you a month to see it if you try to prove it for yourself; and even following Euclid's proof of it takes a number of seconds. Analytic truths, far from being all trivial, include the domain of mathematics, vast, difficult, rich, and important. Mathematical proofs are the means by which we realize the analytical truth of complicated or surprising analytical truths; for they are demonstrations of entailment, and entailment is an analytic relation. Whether one statement entails another depends solely on the meanings of the two statements, and has nothing to do with the contents of the world.

Mathematics has two extraordinary values. In the first place it is independent of all observation. It needs no looking or listening or touching or smelling or tasting. It needs no laboratories or field trips. It is all done in the head. It is purely intellectual. In the second place mathematics, or let us say more generally analytical science, is the realm of absolute conviction and, we believe, absolute knowledge and proof. In it we never need to content ourselves with mere evidence or likelihood. I do not mean that we have never been mistaken in this sphere or never shall be again. That would be false. I mean that we need not and should not acquiesce in mere probability in the realm of analytical science, but may and do set ourselves the goal of absolute certainty and proof, and believe that we usually achieve it, and I have no doubt are right so to believe. The reasonable man pursues certainty and eschews mere probability about all analytic statements.

2.508. *The pursuit of probability*

There was a time when the possibilities of analytic statements had been greatly developed, while the distinction between analytic and synthetic statements was still only faintly grasped. That time included the ancient Greeks, with their development of mathematics; and it also included the seventeenth century, with the further development of mathematics by Descartes and others. During this time there implicitly existed the hope that all statements whatever would turn out to be analytic, in other words that mere thinking without the aid of the senses would ultimately tell us the truth-value of every statement, in other words that the whole of science would become like mathematics, and specifically like what they regarded as the perfect form of mathematics, namely Euclid's *Elements*. This hope became clearest and strongest in the seventeenth century, when Spinoza composed an *Ethics* in Euclidean form, and Newton composed a kinetics in Euclidean form, and Steno composed a description of muscle in Euclidean form.

A consequence of this belief that all knowledge could become mathematical or analytical was that they expected and demanded to achieve in all spheres the wonderful certainty that we achieve in mathematics. All science whatever was to be absolutely certain and absolutely proved. Everything less than absolute certainty was useless and to be rejected. Descartes thought that he should reject, as absolutely false, everything about which he could imagine the slightest doubt. Accordingly, he had no use in his account of scientific method for the notion of hypothesis, or even for the notion of probability. It is a waste of time to be setting up hypotheses and estimating probabilities if we can obtain certainty. Every reasoning was either certain or no use at all. Pascal expressed the general attitude when he wrote: 'I am not content with the probable; I seek the sure.'

This hope was vain. Now that the distinction between analytic and synthetic statements has become much clearer, we see that it is false that all statements are analytic and ideally decidable by intellectual considerations alone. The question whether this lobster has recently shed his shell can never be reasonably decided without the aid of the senses; nor can the general question whether lobsters shed their shells from time to time. The laws of nature, if they exist, are not entailments, and cannot be discovered by mere logic and mathematics. The laws of nature hold between things; but entailments hold between propositions. Statements asserting laws of nature or facts of history are one and all synthetic, so that to decide on their truth-value without any appeal to experience would be folly. Even a great deal of what is commonly called mathematics is in fact synthetic and uncertain. For example, the geometrical theorems of Euclid are synthetic. What is analytic in Euclid's geometry is at most his proofs, that is, his statements that his theorems are entailed by his postulates. By far the greater number of the statements that seriously concern us are synthetic.

When people begin to realize that the Cartesian hope is vain, and that the absolute proof of mathematics never will be achieved for propositions describing the real world, they sometimes react with a despairing scepticism. They think that, if human thought cannot achieve mathematical certainty about existence, it is no good at all; and they resign themselves to the view that 'men cannot discover philosophical truths by the sole use of their natural faculties', or the more sweeping view that 'truth is impossible to attain'. 'I look on all sides', wrote Pascal (*Pensées*, xiv. 2, Havet), 'and everywhere I see nothing but darkness.' That was because to him darkness and certainty were the only alternatives. Hume was a sceptic for the same reason; he abandoned the Cartesian conviction that our knowledge could be mathematically certain, but retained the Cartesian conviction that it ought to be.

From this despairing scepticism it is an easy and common step to unreason. Pascal took it when he recommended us to decide whether there is a god by means of a wager (op. cit. x. 1, Havet). Many take it in the form of saying to themselves: 'Since certainty is unattainable, I can only believe whatever my intuition tells me.' Thus Newman (*Grammar of Assent*, p. 343), after deciding rightly that there cannot be a science of reasoning sufficient to compel certitude in concrete conclusions, infers wrongly that we should 'confess that there is no ultimate test of truth besides the testimony borne to truth by the mind itself'. Thus reason is brought into disrepute by being identified with the certainty and proof that are obtainable only concerning analytic statements, as it becomes clear that most statements are not analytic and cannot be settled by mere deduction.

The right reaction, to the discovery that mathematical certainty is impossible about most statements, is not to abandon reason, but to include in it the pursuit of *probability* as well as the pursuit of certainty. Then we can say, contrary to Hume, that it is by reason that we believe in the existence of bodies as well as in the truths of mathematics. The reasonable man does not say 'Give me certainty or I despair'. He looks for certainty about analytic statements only. About synthetic statements he is content with probability. On the considerations available to him at the time concerning a given statement, either the statement is more probable than its contradictory, or it is less probable, or it is equally probable. In the last case he suspends judgement; otherwise he adopts for the present the more probable of the two contradictories. In each pair of contradictories he habitually tries to estimate which is the more probable, and he habitually adopts that.

'All is uncertain', said Hume. But it is extremely unlikely that the probability of every proposition is exactly equal to the probability of its contradictory, so that we ought to suspend judgement about all propositions. It is still more unlikely that a pair of contradictories could both be improbable rather than probable. It is perfectly obvious, when you come to think of it, that some propositions are far more probable than their contradictories, and therefore ought to be adopted. If we were to follow Descartes's advice, and reject as false everything that is not mathematically proved, we should be rejecting both of two contradictories, which is absurd since one of them must be true. If we were to reject as 'invalid' every consideration that did not amount to a strict deductive proof, we should be perversely depriving ourselves of many reasonable aids to picking the true contradictory. The division of arguments into valid and invalid is a remnant of the exclusively deductive and mathematical way of looking at knowledge in general; it should be confined to mathematics. In questions of history and nature, we should give up bothering whether the proposition is certain or not. We should ask ourselves instead whether we will adopt the proposition or reject it, and in deciding we should remember the significant fact that to reject a proposition is to adopt its contradictory. It is not a 'burden of proof' that reason lays on us in existential and practical questions. It is a burden of judgement, of *judging* which is the more probable of the two contradictories in view of the available considerations.

Some people think that this is impossible because probability entails certainty, so that where nothing is certain nothing can be probable either. I myself argued this view at some length in my first book, *The Province of Logic*, London, 1931. I withdraw it now. I overlooked the fact that every statement has its contradictory, and that if the one is improbable the other must be probable.

To wild despairs such as 'truth is impossible to attain' the reasonable man opposes the following antiseptic reflection. Of any pair of contradictories, say 'there is a god' and 'there is no god', one is true and the other is false. Now each of these statements has been believed. Therefore somebody has believed a true statement. Therefore truth *is* possible to attain. If the sceptic replies that he meant that we cannot know for certain which is true, the reasonable man answers that we can often make a reasonable judgement as to which is more *probably* true, and then it is wise to be content with that. It is unwise to insist on all or nothing, for the result of doing that is to get nothing.

The probable must not be opposed to the true. Plato pointed out that it is wrong to say 'let us seek what is probable, not what is true' (*Phaedrus* 272 DE). That amounts to the immoral advice: 'seek to convince, and do not mind whether what you say is true.' The right maxim is: let us seek what is probably true rather than what is certainly true, since certainty is unobtainable outside mathematics. The probable is not opposed to the true or the false, but to the certain and the improbable.

2.509. *Respect for evidence*

Where synthetic statements are concerned, the pursuit of probability is the right middle way between two wrong extremes. One of these wrong extremes is the pursuit of certainty, which I have described. The other is the acquiescence in mere possibility. Some people speak as if they thought that, since certainty is unattainable, they might accept any proposition that is not known to be impossible. 'May it not be that . . . ?', they ask; and the implication is that if it is possible it is actual. You can be sure that anyone who recommends a proposition by prefixing to it the words 'May it not be that . . . ?' is less than a firstclass reasoner. For of course it may be. Every synthetic proposition is logically possible. But so is its contradictory. That too *may* be so. Hence the right question is not which of them *may* be so (for each of them may be so), but which of them has the better evidence. Similarly, the right question is not which of them has *some* evidence in its favour (for usually each of them has some evidence in its favour), but which of them has the weightier evidence in its favour.

I draw your attention to one specially bad and very common form of acquiescing in mere possibility. People sometimes adopt a proposition for true merely on the ground that they do not know it to be false. 'You cannot prove that it is false', they say; and they regard this as justifying them in holding it true. They speak as if our not knowing a certain statement to be false were good evidence that it is true. I call this the argument from ignorance, though I think it is not what everybody has meant by the phrase 'argument from ignorance'. It is fallacious, because ignorance is not a good ground for asserting anything except that we are ignorant. The question in matters of fact is not what we can or cannot prove, but which of the two contradictories has the better evidence. That we cannot prove that there is no god is irrelevant. The right question is which of the two contradictories, 'there is a god' and 'there is no god', has the better evidence. Even the enlightened Joseph Butler endorsed a case of this fallacy, when he wrote that 'due sense of the general ignorance of man would . . . beget in us a disposition to take up and rest satisfied with any evidence whatever, which is real' (*Sermon* XV, § 10). No amount of ignorance can make it right to consider only one side of a question. However ignorant we may be, we should consider the evidence for both of the two contradictories, and decide which is the heavier.

The argument from ignorance is often concealed in the form of a question. When a man has no argument whatever in favour of his thesis that pigs have wings, he can still impose it on many of the unwary by putting it in the form of a question: Who can say whether after all pigs may not have wings? The implication is that, in view of the general ignorance of man, you would be a rash fool to assert that pigs have no wings.

The worst form of the argument from ignorance masquerading as a question is the 'how can' or 'how could' form. For example, 'the problem still remains *how can* anyone understand the difference between good and evil unless he has been given at birth a natural feeling for it'. The writer of this sentence implies that your ignorance how this can be done is good evidence that it cannot be done. But, of course, it is no such thing. If it were, we could prove that the moon is made of green cheese, thus: 'Unless the moon were made of green cheese, *how could* it have that patchy and crumbly appearance?'

The 'how can' form of argument is dishonest. By using this form the speaker conceals the fact that it is he who is making an assertion and thus incurring a responsibility. He insinuates falsely that the responsibility is all on you for not admitting the assertion. Instead of openly making his assertion and taking the responsibility for it, he insinuates that you ought to believe it unless you can answer some 'how' question. The honest thing would be to say: 'The moon has a patchy and crumbly appearance, and most things of that appearance are made of cheese, therefore the moon is probably made of cheese.' And then the weakness of the thought would be apparent. The advantage of the dishonest 'how could' form is that, while it must mean just this, it declines to confess it and take the responsibility for it.

Often the best way to meet one of these bogus questions is to reply: 'A question is not an argument; only statements can be arguments. Your question is an argument only if it is a way of stating that. . . .' For thus you bring his assertion into the open and force him either to acknowledge it or to drop it. I recommend to you the idea that a question is not an argument. It invalidates a surprisingly large number of letters to *The Times*.

So much for the mistake of acquiescing in mere possibility. Concerning synthetic statements the reasonable man neither acquiesces in mere possibility nor demands mathematically certain proof, but estimates probabilities and adopts the more probable of the two contradictories.

The truth-value of a synthetic statement cannot be found by merely considering its meaning and entailments. It can be found only by both considering its meaning and doing something more. What more? What further criterion comes in? A great many synthetic statements profess to describe the world that is, or the world that has been or will be. This is done by all particular reports, such as 'the cat mewed when it saw her', and 'the sun will be eclipsed tomorrow', and 'Caesar crossed the Rubicon'. It is done by general reports, such as 'cats make a mewing sound but dogs do not', and 'eclipses of the sun are less frequent than those of the moon', and 'all bodies attract each other with a force inversely proportional to the square of their distance'. There is a class of synthetic statements which are all what we may call in a very general sense descriptions. This class includes all or most of the statements of history and natural science. It excludes statements of value, of goodness and badness.

The criterion of the truth-value of descriptive statements may be labelled 'correspondence'. These statements are false if they fail to correspond to the world, if what they assert to be so is not so. For example, if someone tells you that your waistcoat is on fire, you look down to see if it is. You look to see if what he asserts to be so is so, if his assertion corresponds to the facts.

How do we tell whether the statement corresponds to the world? It is impossible to answer this both generally and completely. It is a matter of gradually accumulating more and more knowledge, both about the meanings of statements and about the world they profess to describe. In the case of 'your waistcoat is on fire', it is a matter of knowing the rules for the use of 'your', the rules for the use of 'waistcoat', and the rest of the meaning, and then using your senses on the world to discover whether what you experience corresponds to what the statement asserts. The evidence for or against 'your waistcoat is on fire' is very simple. It is just what you can observe now in the region of your waistcoat. But evidence becomes a far more complicated and doubtful matter for statements describing absent parts of the world, and for general descriptions of the world, and for conditional descriptions of the world. Questions of judgement and choice soon enter in. Do you judge Tacitus to be a truthful and cautious historian? Was Fisher, or whoever it was, judicious in choosing the standard statistical deviation as he has?' These matters will never be completely decided. The process of improving and adding to our decisions is the study of evidence.

We have seen two great domains of statement in which the criteria of truth are different. For analytic statements the criterion is self-contradiction. For descriptive synthetic statements the criterion is the real world. There appears to be at least one more domain with its own criterion, and that is the domain of ethical and practical synthetic statements, such as 'we ought to tell the truth', 'Beethoven's music is better than Bach's', 'political equality is a good thing', 'disorder is undesirable'. In choosing between such a practical statement and its contradictory, we cannot use the criterion of self-contradiction because they are synthetic statements. Nor can we use the criterion of correspondence with the real world; for these statements do not profess to describe the world, and therefore nothing the world can do will make them either correspond to it or fail to correspond.

In the first and second domains men are very largely agreed as to what the right criterion is and how to use it. At least, they tend very largely to use the same criteria in the same way and come out with the same results, though they disagree in their theoretical account of the nature of these criteria. But in the third domain, that of practical statements, men neither give the same theory of the criterion nor use the same criterion nor come out with the same results. In one sense there is no criterion for this domain; that is, there is no universally agreed and reliable criterion. But people have their own criteria. I have told you earlier some of my own principles of judgement.

Does this mean that we cannot properly speak of evidence for and against practical propositions, and that the notion of reason as including respect for evidence has no application here? No, it only means that in this sphere evidence is more doubtful and shifting than in the other two. There still is evidence of a kind. Plenty of arguments are produced on practical matters, arguments about the factual situation on which practice has to be based, about the consequences of proposed actions, about the criteria to be employed, about their relative strengths, about the way to apply them. Here as elsewhere it is possible to distinguish between the reasonable man who finds and respects the evidence, and the unreasonable man who does not. It is common and correct to distinguish between those who adopt policies after careful consideration and those who do not.

Reason, then, includes respect for evidence. The decision which of two contradictories is the more probable is to be made by examining the evidence for and against each. And this apparently applies to all classes of statements, though the evidence is of very different kinds in the different classes.

Let us observe some of the forms of disrespect for evidence.

One common form of disrespect for evidence is the habit of believing a proposition not because it has the better evidence but because its contradictory is painful. Somebody has said that 'I could not rest in a truth were I compelled to regard it as hateful'. Christians often recommend their doctrines on the ground that they are comforting, whereas their contradictories are depressing. You can find a striking example of this in Newman's *Grammar of Assent*, p. 305, which shows how powerful it can be.

Whether to believe the contradictory that has the better evidence, or to believe the one that gives more comfort, is one of our profoundest and most important decisions. Each alternative is often chosen. I am strongly in favour of choosing to believe the contradictory that has the better evidence, because that makes us more likely to believe truly. That one of a pair of contradictories frightens me is no evidence as to which of them is true. Believing truly is in the long run likely to comfort us more than believing falsely; and anyhow it is beneath our dignity as human beings not to seek a correct view of things.

Another form of disrespect for evidence is to reject it in favour of intuitions or hunches. Intuitions are necessary sometimes, namely when we have to make a decision but cannot in the time available find any evidence on which to base it. For instance, if you must decide this instant whether an attacker will shoot at your head or your heart. Furthermore, intuitions are sometimes good evidence in themselves. If there is a person whose intuitions in a certain field have turned out right more often than not in the past, then the fact that he now intuits a certain statement in the field to be true is good evidence that it is true. But an intuition is at best only one piece of evidence among other possible pieces. It is always capable of being overthrown by further considerations. It never justifies us in neglecting to look for other pieces of evidence, or in neglecting to put them also on the scales when they appear. And Bishop Gore's view that we are justified in believing an intuition if it gives us strength is very bad indeed.

Another form of disrespect for evidence, which may overlap with the foregoing, is the fanatic's deliberate hostility to evidence and rejection of it, what Professor Campbell called 'the blind uncritical devotion to an idea or cause which is so utterly sure of its own rectitude that "examination of the evidence" seems mere meaningless waste of labour' (*Philosophy*, 1950, p. 119). 'I believe it because it is absurd.' The fanatic, if he has to defend his view, does so by force or fury or intimidation or sarcasm or authority or mollification, all means which, while they often convince, never contribute to the determination of a truth-value.

The commonest form of disrespect for evidence is mere carelessness or thoughtlessness or failure to realize what is required. We assume that our meagre experience of some foreign nation is good enough evidence for generalizations about it, not out of any contempt for evidence, but out of mere ignorance of what sort of data such generalizations demand. We write home that 'the hotels here are' so-and-so, after having stayed in one and looked into two others. Respect for evidence involves knowing that evidence usually does not come without work, and hence involves searching for the good evidence.

A subtler form of disrespect for evidence is pretending that we have evidence when we have not. We may do this to others or to ourselves. 'Evidence is accumulating', we say. But how much has actually accumulated? For only that counts. To assume that in the future there will be more is to disrespect evidence.

Respect for evidence, or at least respect for the evidence of the senses, is the main element missing from the ideal of reason in Plato's dialogues. We may roughly say that he found reason merely in deductiveness, but we find it in deductiveness plus inductiveness. Mere deductiveness by itself constituted reasonable thinking according to Plato. But, since the distinction between analytic and synthetic propositions has become plain, we have to say that mere deductiveness is reasonable only in mathematics. Everywhere else it must be joined with inductiveness.

The theory of deduction and induction is logic, and logic is thus an important part of the development of the ideal of reason. It is a normative science; that is to say, it lays down norms of how we ought to think; it states an ideal. But do not take me as implying that every respected textbook of logic does this adequately, or even tries to. Among those that make a good shot at it are Pascal's *Spirit of*

Geometry, the *Port-Royal Logic*, the third and fourth books of Locke's *Essay on Human Understanding*, John Stuart Mill's *System of Logic*, W. K. Clifford's *Ethics of Belief*, and Cohen and Nagel's *Introduction to Logic and Scientific Method*. Many other logic books are not normative at all, but parts of mathematics exploring the nature of entailment. In them you will find no practical help towards becoming reasonable. It is a pity that the same word 'logic' has to cover both a purely theoretical and a very practical inquiry.

2.510. *Tentativeness*

The reasonable man holds his views tentatively rather than dogmatically. He bears in mind the possibility that at some future time the weight of evidence may point the other way. He refrains from thinking that 'there cannot possibly ever be a good reason for changing this view, and so I will never listen to any argument against it'. His views are hypotheses rather than dogmas, laid down to be tested by their consequences and other connexions, and to be exchanged for their contradictories if the network thus revealed ever indicates so. Plato, to whom the tentativeness of reason was clear, made his 'Socrates' say that 'we must submit to the argument until somebody persuades us with a better one' (*Rp*. 388 E).

Tentativeness is not the same thing as hesitation or indecision. Holding one's opinions always tentatively neither is nor involves being always hesitating and indecisive. Descartes in a well known passage records his decision to act firmly on practical principles although they were provisional, and that was reasonable.

Tentativeness is not the same thing as the pursuit of probability; for we should be tentative about our mathematical opinions as well as about our physical and historical and practical ones. We may be wrong in thinking a certain proposition to be an analytic truth, as well as in thinking it to be synthetic truth. Euclid's postulate about parallels was for long mistakenly thought to be a mathematical certainty. The contrast between mathematics and chemistry is not that we are never mistaken in the one, whereas we are sometimes mistaken in the other. We are sometimes mistaken in each of them. The contrast is that the truth of true mathematical propositions depends only on their meaning, whereas the truth of true chemical propositions depends also on the nature of the world. Descartes should have extended to all his opinions the tentativeness which he rightly chose in practical matters.

Tentativeness does not involve always listening to every argument. If you were hurrying to a vital appointment, and a queer-looking stranger stopped you in the street and asked you to listen there and then to an argument that the earth is flat, reason would not require you to comply. Nor need you read all the volumes of the Society for Psychical Research before deciding that there are no ghosts. We could spend our whole lives listening to arguments and still not have heard all the persons who wish to persuade us. Hence we are obliged to choose what we will hear and when we will hear it; and we are not necessarily unreasonable because we have declined to listen to Mr. A's argument or read Mr. B's book. The ideal of tentativeness does, however, involve never deciding that 'under no circumstances will I ever consider any further argument against this proposition, or reconsider an old argument, with a view to possibly changing my opinion'.

The tentativeness of reason sets many people against reason, because they cannot bear to be uncertain. 'Man cannot live by merely tentative beliefs', they say; 'he demands security of mind, an assured faith.' (This statement of the objection is taken from Campbell, *Philosophy*, 1950, p. 130.) This is a common and natural feeling; but it is childish and ought to be overcome, like the fear of being alone in a house at night. It amounts to taking the absurd position that 'I am going to have certainty at all costs, even if I have to stifle reason to get it'. The desire for security, like other desires, is to be gratified when it can be gratified without grave loss to other interests; but it is not to be gratified at all costs. We know the havoc that a nation causes when its unbridled desire for security drives it to be always acquiring a little more buffer territory at the expense of a neighbour. An individual's private desire for intellectual security can cause as great a proportion of havoc in the intellectual life of himself and his associates. We all can and should learn temperance in the indulgence of our desire for security as in the indulgence of all our desires.

And what is this metaphor, taken from the Bible, that 'man cannot live'? Of course it does not mean that those who are undogmatic in their beliefs die of being so. I suppose it means that they become less happy for being so. But they become more happy for knowing that they are doing the reasonable thing.

Those who think that human reason suffices, and those who think that only a god and faith in him suffice, have in common that they all think that something suffices. And in this they are all mistaken, for nothing suffices. We are always, in any case, going to have mistakes and sufferings, and finally we are going to cease existing. The question we must ask is not what will give us *all* the help we want, for nothing can do that; but what will give us the *most* help possible. And the answer is reason. Reason is more likely to avoid mistake and suffering than is faith or any other way.

Yeats once complained that 'the best lack all conviction'. He may have been right in the way he meant it; but—a certain lack of conviction is the very thing that constitutes the best people.

2.511. *The submission of reason*

The essential part of bearing in mind the possibility that one is mistaken is not to begin each statement with the words 'I may be wrong but it seems to me that'. That would be very tiresome and quite useless. It is to allow free speech to others and weigh their ideas. Reasonableness includes listening to the other side, and giving the other side full liberty to argue. It includes submission to criticism.

The reasonable man behaves as a fallible being among fallible beings. The unreasonable man, on the contrary, sometimes talks as if you were fallible but he were a god. 'Don't trust man', he sometimes says, 'trust God.' This remark would be selfdefeating if he regarded himself as a man, for in that case he would be telling you not to trust himself and therefore not to trust this advice of his. So the implication is that when *he* speaks it is the voice of a god. Newman clearly makes this claim in the following sentence: 'Theological reasoning professes to be sustained by a more than human power, and to be guaranteed by a more than human authority' (*Grammar of Assent*, p. 377). Similarly, Rousseau at the beginning of his *Discourse on Inequality*, para. 7, quite clearly implies that, whereas other men's books are merely human and contain lies, this book of Rousseau's is the voice of nature herself and therefore must be true, though he says he may have added something of his own without intending to. The idea that 'when you talk it is merely your subjective opinion, but when I talk it is the objective truth', is thoroughly bad-mannered and unreasonable. We are all in the same boat, the predicament of subjectivity. Whenever any of us talks it is his subjective opinion; but it may also be true.

Submission to criticism excludes keeping one's opinion secret.

It involves making one's views known rather than concealing them. Reason is essentially public. The reasonable man submits to criticism, and he submits to the new evidence and new probabilities that criticism sometimes brings.

A very different kind of submission is sometimes demanded of reason, namely submission to authority. It is pointed out that no man can investigate all things for himself, and that we do in fact rely upon all sorts of authorities, and should be unreasonable not to do so. It is often suggested that a man has no right to have an opinion of his own on a subject about which he is ill informed. Even being in doubt about a proposition is disapproved by some people. Jeremy Bentham, and some others who shared his doubts about the thirty-nine articles of the Church of England, were induced, nevertheless, to sign them by a person who reproved their hesitation as 'presumption' (Jeremy Bentham, *Works*, ed. Bowring, x, 37).

It is true that no man can investigate for himself all the matters on which he needs to have an opinion, and that it would be foolish never to trust the authority of, say, a physician or an accountant. Yet the demand for submission to authority, as commonly made, is not a right conclusion from this, but on the contrary highly improper. For it is usually a demand that we should submit to a certain authority without having criticized his credentials, without having judged for ourselves whether he is justified in claiming to be an authority. It overlooks or suppresses the vitally important fact that each one of us has to decide who are the authorities.

The Medical Association is not the only set of persons claiming authority in medicine. There are the others, whom the Medical Association calls quacks. The patient has to decide between them; and sometimes he leaves one in disgust and goes to another. The Roman Church is not the only body claiming to be an authority about the gods. There are also the atheists, and the Moslems, whom the Roman Church calls infidels. There is no escape for any of us from choosing between these rival authorities. In adopting any one authority we are judging his rivals, in effect if not explicitly. Therefore we are all of us always inevitably judging the authorities, that is, criticizing them.

The only choices we have in this matter are whether to do this judging consciously or unconsciously, and whether to do it reasonably or unreasonably. Evidently it is better to do it consciously and reasonably. The person who submits to a priest because she found herself doing so when she woke up, and has never considered not doing so, is in a less reasonable and less safe position than the person who submits because she has criticized this authority and decided that it is better to submit. And it is better to review such decisions from time to time than to make them once for life. We should submit to no man in the sense of abandoning our own judgement for ever. Complete submission to an authority, far from being commendable, is a grave irresponsibility. We are responsible for all our opinions, however ignorant we may be in the field, because we are responsible for our choice of any authorities on whom we rely. All submission to an authority should be based on, and revocable by, our own judgement whether he is an authority; and this judgement should be revised from time to time in the light of the best considerations then available.

As to the doctrine that a man may have no right to an opinion on some matter, I suspect it of being held owing to ignorance of the fact that to adopt someone else's opinion is to have an opinion oneself. It is clearly wrong if it includes suspense of judgement in having an opinion. If a man is aware of a proposition he cannot help doing one of three, either adopting it or rejecting it or suspending judgement about it. If, however, we exclude the case of suspending judgement, as not properly falling under the expression 'having an opinion about', and say that having an opinion about a proposition is either accepting it or rejecting it, then it is true that sometimes a man may have no right to an opinion. But when? Precisely when he ought to suspend judgement about the opinion. And he ought to suspend judgement about it when he cannot find any good evidence for or against it; and this includes not being able to find an authority who has an opinion on the matter. If he can find an authority whom it is reasonable to follow on the matter, he ought to have an opinion because he ought to adopt the authority's opinion.

2.512. *Practical reason*

If a person confined his ideal of reason to what I have so far said, he would not call any *action* reasonable or unreasonable, except acts of thinking and of arriving at opinions and getting evidence for opinions. But we call actions of many sorts reasonable or unreasonable. Thereby we imply that there is such a thing as practical reason. We are right to do this. For we cannot help evaluating actions, and human actions are essentially thoughtful. Hence in evaluating actions we are evaluating something that involves thought. Hence our ideals for thought come into our ideals for action. Hence in evaluating actions we sometimes use the word that refers to our ideal for thought, and call them reasonable or unreasonable. Thinking includes choosing actions and principles of action, and this can be done well or badly.

Some great men have doubted whether there is such a thing as practical reason, or whether reason has anything to say about practice. That was because they confined reason to deductiveness and consistency. If we understand by 'reason' ideal thinking, as it is very common to do, and if we believe that thinking enters essentially into human action and largely helps to make it good or bad, then it is inconsistent for us to deny the possibility of practical reason. Practical reason is possible and to some extent actual. It is the same as wisdom.

Reason in action includes, first, all that reason in reflection includes. Reasonable action is based on opinions about the world reached by reasonable thinking.

As the reasonable thinker collects impartially all the considerations bearing on a question of fact, so the reasonable agent takes impartial account of all the interests affected and examines all the advantages and disadvantages of each course. There is, however, this difference of degree, that the urgency of time enters into action more than into theory, and makes it sometimes reasonable to act earlier without a full consideration instead of acting later with a full consideration.

Further, we all call it unreasonable to keep on doing two sorts of action such that the one sort defeats the aim of the other sort. Selfdefeatingness in practice is to be added to selfinconsistency in theory as part of unreasonableness. It is unreasonable, for example, to desire people's love and at the same time keep on hurting them. Such selfdefeatingness is often called inconsistency. But it is not a belief in two inconsistent propositions. The statement that 'I want people to love me' is consistent with the statement that 'I want to hurt people'. Selfdefeatingness is due to laws of nature, not laws of logic. It consists in pursuing two aims which nature has made incompatible; and only by knowing some laws of nature can we know what aims are incompatible.

We also call it reasonable to adapt one's means properly to one's ends, and unreasonable to try to achieve an end by a means which is probably ineffective, or which is effective but far too costly in relation to what the end is worth. To insist on achieving some end at all costs would be eminently unreasonable if we really meant 'at all costs'; but usually the context shows that we are referring only to a small part of all the possible costs.

We also call it reasonable to respect the aims and interests of all persons equally. Reason in this sense is referred to in some uses of the words 'impartiality', 'justice', and 'equality'.

So far I think I have mentioned only matters that most people include under reason in action. I myself include in it a further item which, I fear, is not so often included that I can claim that it is generally agreed. I mean the principle that the lessening of misery is the most important aim, and other aims should give way to it. If a man says he would rather all Englishmen were made miserable than that England should play second fiddle to the United States, I call him unreasonable precisely because he holds something else more important than the fight against misery. If a man says that a certain moral law is to be obeyed no matter how much misery it causes, because it is the command of a god or just because it is the moral law, I call him unreasonable for the same reason: he puts something else above the lessening of misery. In other words, pity is part of practical reason.

What is the relation of practical reason to the moral laws? I doubt whether Henry Sidgwick was right in believing that there is a 'common conviction that the fundamental precepts of morality are essentially reasonable' (*Methods of Ethics*, 5th ed., p. 383). I think that too many people dissociate morality from reason for this to be true. But the precepts of morality *ought* to be reasonable, and we ought to reject all moral laws that do not tend to diminish misery on the whole. The reasonable man desires to obey general principles that are impartial between men and men and could be obeyed by all to the common advantage. He submits himself to such rules of action as both are actually acknowledged and also impartially diminish misery.

2.513. *Depreciations of reason*

It is very common to depreciate reason or compare it unfavourably with something else. People say that reason tends to atrophy feeling, that it tends to make action feeble, that it is incompetent in certain spheres, that it cannot help to make us happy, that we should trust God not human reason, that to trust reason is pride, that reason cannot prescribe ends, that reason must be subordinated to faith or intuition, and that we should think not with reason but with the blood.

Yet it is absurd to talk against reason if the word means what I have suggested. Reason, I have suggested, is either the power to think or the good use of that power. As to reason as the power to think, nobody seriously holds the view that we had better not think, at least when it is thus expressed. And as to reason as the good use of the power to think, it is evident that to deny the goodness of that would be to say that something good was not good, a selfcontradiction.

How then do people come to talk against reason? They do so through fear of thought combined with the misconception that reason is a special faculty. Fear of thought is, of course, a common and natural occurrence, because thinking sometimes undermines a cherished belief or reveals an alarming situation. It is usually held in check by the fact that thinking is inevitable and sometimes supports a cherished belief or reveals a delightful situation.

The other element which leads people to talk against reason is the misconception that reason is a special faculty, not the general faculty of thinking but a special department of it. It is easy to regard reason as a faculty because in one correct sense the word does mean a faculty, namely the general faculty of thinking. It is also easy to regard reason as not being the general faculty of thinking but some specific or different faculty, owing to the other sense of the word, in which it means something different from the faculty of thinking. The sense in which reason is the power to think makes us regard reason as a power. But the sense in which reason is the ideal use of something makes us regard it as not the power of thinking. So we slide into regarding reason as some mental power other than the power of thinking. Reason now appears as one mental power among others, the others including probably intuition, faith, belief, memory, imagination, emotion, sight, hearing, and touch. The human mind, or the power of thinking, comes to seem like a toolbox; and these various faculties—reason, intuition, faith, and the rest—are the tools in the box. Kant called reason a *Werkzeug* (*Grundlegung*, pp. 395-6). Now the good use of a toolbox involves the good choice of which tool to use for each purpose. There are things that you can do well with a chisel but not with a hammer, and conversely.

Hence we come to think that there are things you can do with faith but not with reason, and so on.

Once we have come to regard reason as a special faculty, and as only one among many tools available to the mind, we can safely depreciate it, which we should not dare to do if we regarded it as the power of thinking in general. This gives opportunity to that fear of thought which is latent in most of us. Whenever thought leads to results that distress us, we can now say it was because we used reason when we should have used some other faculty, like prentice carpenters trying to make a screwdriver do the work of a chisel. Now we can talk about 'the bounds of reason', and about 'areas where reason is incompetent', thus taking the liberty to reject the results of our thinking when they distress us. Now we can retort, against those who appeal to reason, that they are concentrating on one particular faculty and neglecting all the other ways of knowing. Thus we shut people off from using their reason on our favourite doctrines.

All this is a mistaken thing to do. We should not let the distressing results of some thinking seduce us into inventing the myth of reason as a special faculty alongside intuition and faith and the rest. There are no such special faculties. Reason, in the sense of a mental power other than the general power to think, is a fiction, a dummy set up to be knocked down by those who favour not thinking about certain matters. The human mind is not a box of tools from which you can select. It has only the one tool, thought. And our only choice is whether to use it badly or well, and whether to inquire and learn how to use it well. The English word 'reason' is sometimes the name of this tool, thought, and sometimes the name of the ideal use of this tool, which we dimly perceive and try to perceive more clearly. To be against reason is therefore either to be against thinking as well as possible, or to be against thinking at all.

The bounds of reason are as wide as the bounds of statement and belief. Anything whatever that can be stated or believed should be stated or believed as a result of thought, which is one sense of the word 'reason'; and the thought should be as good as possible, which is the other sense. There is no 'area where reason is incompetent', in the sense of a set of propositions which are to be adopted or rejected without thought. To say that reason is incompetent about a given proposition is to say that it is not good to search for the considerations for and against this proposition, or to weigh them against each other, or to adopt a view accordingly, or to revise this view from time to time, or to listen to criticism of it. On all choices between adopting a proposition and adopting its contradictory either reason is competent or nothing is. The Pope in September 1952 said to astronomers that, when the human intellect has done all it can, faith must carry on. The implied contrast is false, for the human intellect will not have done all it can until the human race is extinct.

This confusion leads also to the idea that those who praise reason are neglecting nonrational methods of knowing, or denying their value. If reason is thought of as one peculiar mental faculty, and we recognize other rival mental faculties alongside it, it seems that those who praise reason are neglecting these other instruments. But when we see that reason is not a special faculty, but the good or ideal use of the general faculty of forming statements and beliefs, this opposition falls to the ground. Every special way of producing beliefs that there may be, either intuition or sight or hearing or telepathy or what you will, is to be examined and given whatever weight seems reasonable after examination; but none of them is to be set up as autonomous and immune from criticism. None of them is even to be assigned a special sphere in which it is uncriticizable. For example, sight is not supreme in the sphere of the visible. We check and sometimes reject its deliverances by the rational use of other faculties, especially touch and memory. Reason is supreme because it is not a special faculty, but the best use of the whole faculty of forming beliefs for the sake of forming them truly. The only alternatives to thinking with reason are thinking unreasonably and not thinking.

The misconception of reason as a special faculty is also responsible for the idea that 'it is beyond the power of reason to prescribe ends' (Harrod in *Mind* for 1936). Reason is the good employment of thought, and thought both can and should adopt ends.

The idea that to trust reason is pride is, we now see, the idea that it is pride to try to use one of our powers as well as possible, namely the power of thinking. They might as well say that it is pride to try to run as fast as possible, or to preach a sermon as well as possible. Or perhaps they mean that we should use our power of thinking as well as possible to arrive at a conclusion, but then out of humility reject our result and believe instead what is told us by some authority. On the contrary, the doctrines of authorities should be considered *before* we reach our conclusion and weighed along with the other considerations before us. They are not opposed to reason but part of the evidence which reason weighs.

Any virtue may become an occasion of pride, for the peculiarity of the vice of pride is that it finds its opportunity precisely in the presence of a virtue. But the virtue called reason is not a necessary nor even a specially likely occasion of pride. On the contrary, the submission of our thought to criticism and argument and evidence is a great and good humility; for an important part of 'the worth of men consists in their liability to persuasion', as Whitehead has written (*Adventures of Ideas*, p. 105). This sort of humility is often conspicuously absent from those who depreciate reason.

It would be a very sad thing if the good employment of our power of thinking tended to atrophy feeling, but fortunately it does not. Brutality and schizophrenia tend to atrophy feeling; but reasonableness does not. It is true that the unreasonable man is often emotional in a way that the reasonable man is not; he tends to anger when contradicted. It is true also that reason tends to atrophy painful and harmful feelings; for good thinking includes reflecting upon the emotions, and deciding which are to be preferred, and training oneself accordingly. But the result of such reflection is not that we are to discourage all emotion. It is that we are to discourage anger and hate and gloom and envy and jealousy, but encourage love and pity and respect and joy and what may well be called the emotion of reasonableness, the sentiment of desiring to listen to both sides, and of enjoying taking one's decisions in the light of all available considerations. We tend wrongly to call it the work of reason only when we decide to discourage the emotion or repress the desire. It can also be the work of reason when we decide to encourage or gratify. Perhaps Plato is partly responsible for this misconception; his works have a tendency to suggest that the business of reason with the emotions is to suppress them all.

As to thinking 'with the blood', all thinking has to be done with the blood in any case. No one can think unless there is plenty of good blood in his brain. If this crass literalism exasperates some disciple of D. H. Lawrence into exclaiming that 'you know what I mean', the answer is that we know that he means that he demands the right to be dogmatic and listen to no argument, and he demands that we follow him blindly.

If you dislike my account of reason, do not because of that reject reason, but give a better account of it. I have recommended the pursuit of reasons and consistency, deductiveness and inductiveness, respect for evidence, tentativeness, and submission to criticism, because I think they are our most likely means of coming to hold true rather than false beliefs. And I have recommended self-compatibility and impartiality and the rejection of misery because I think they are our most likely means of coming to good decisions. If you disagree, you should make your own account of what constitutes good thinking. You should not reject reason as such, because the word 'reason' is our name for the ideal of thinking, and our dignity as men demands that we conduct our power of thinking in the best possible way. Misology, the hatred of reason, is a great evil.

2.6. LOVE

Love the virtue is the right habitual conduct of love the emotion.

I think we know well enough what we mean by 'the emotion of love'. It is an emotion arousable only towards persons or living things, though there is no definite limit to what somebody may regard as a living thing. The love that one may feel for wine is a different sense of the word.

Love the emotion is not sexual desire or excitement; but it is often produced by sexual desire. There is in the erotic impulse a tendency towards the furthering of all life that is characteristic of love; and Eros is the most philanthropic of the gods, as Plato made his 'Aristophanes' say. The tenderness that can ennoble desire is a form of love.

The elevation of the right conduct of this emotion into a great virtue is the work of the New Testament, and the greatest novelty in the history of morals. But in what does the right conduct of it consist?

The right conduct of love is, in the first place, the withering of hate. 'Love your enemies.' Hate is an undesirable emotion and is to be discouraged.

The right conduct of love is, in the second place, the creation of pleasant converse. To converse with other living things in amiable and pleasant association—that is the end and essence of right love. The converse may be conversation, or silent being together, or stroking the dog, or working or playing together, or writing letters, or other. Love is primarily conversation. The loving man teaches himself to converse. That is not necessarily to talk and display himself, though some do this too little, and some wrongly despise it; but it is to be with others in understood and amiable communion.

The determined selfsacrificer will say with contempt that I have mistaken petty amiability for love. He is wrong, and he is a hindrance to the good life. The gospels emphasize selfsacrifice too much. 'Greater love hath no man than this, that a man lay down his life for his friends' (John xv. 13). If so, to show the greatest love one must have a friend. And that is my point. You do not get a friend by merely sacrificing yourself. People do not usually become friends with those they rescue from drowning at the risk of their own lives. You get a friend by creating loving converse. Selfsacrifice comes into our ideal of love, but its place is restricted. A person who is always sacrificing himself is destructive of everyone's happiness, except perhaps his own; and he creates no love.

Nor is love almsgiving, or 'charity' as that is sometimes wrongly called. 'The real love knows her neighbour face to face, and laughs with him and weeps with him, and eats and drinks with him, so that at last, when his black day dawns, she may share with him, not what she can spare, but all that she has.' Those fine words were written by Stella Benson (*Living Alone*, p. 92).

Nor is love even service. No doubt service, too, must come into our ideal of love. No doubt the loving person serves and helps. But the mere servant is colourless at best, and often a tyrant. He is the missionary, aiming at reforming you, a smug tyrant whom you cannot repulse in the ordinary way because he is shielded by his armour of religion. He is equally offensive whether he pities or reproves you. The duty of aiding persons in distress is not the same as the ideal of love.

If love is regarded merely as service, the problem how far to extend this service becomes pressing and unanswerable. Nearly all the world is worse off than you are; and everybody has his miseries and could do with some more help. Must you therefore devote all your energy to the service of other men? Yes, if love were primarily service. But no, because love is primarily conversation; and the point of service is to make happy conversation more frequent. The first task, therefore, which love lays on us is to be at least inoffensive, and if possible pleasing, to the other living things with whom we come in contact. Reasonable love demands pleasing converse with our neighbours rather than unpleasing service in Africa. No one should go to serve in slums unless he has good reason to think that he will be personally pleasing rather than repellent to those he is trying to serve. Daughters should not stay at home to look after parents unless they like it. We should seek to please rather than to serve.

The Christian story of Mary and Martha teaches the right ideal. Love lies in the conversation of Mary rather than in the service of Martha. It lies in the enjoyment of the being of other living things, and in friendly communication with them. It lies in amiability and in conversation, in personal relations. Service and selfsacrifice are secondary to this. They are that this may occur. It is for this that love does all those things Paul says it does (1 Cor. xiii), and also some others which he does not mention, including sympathizing, pitying, and imagining. It is for this that love is humble as Paul says it is, and not for the snobbish ends suggested by Luke (ix. 48 and xiv. 7-11). Love receives little children for the sake of converse with them, not in the hope of meeting a god. Love does not take a low seat at table in order to be put into a high one. It takes whatever seat seems most likely to contribute to loving converse at the meal.

A proper appreciation of the personal and conversational character of love sometimes leads people to repudiate the idea of loving the whole human race. They think that 'the human race is so big, so various, so little known, that no one can really love it' (James Fitzjames Stephen, *Liberty*, *Equality*, *Fraternity*, 1st ed., p. 289). But this may be going too far. Love is not to be confined to those whom we know and whose responses we can apprehend. It is good to say 'I wish you well' not merely to the unknown redcoat who turns his head as he marches by, but to the never seen, to the dead, to the unborn, and to the plant that never responds. What is true is that this love of the unknown and unknowable should always be an imagined extension of our communications with our intimates, rather than a service.

What mostly makes it hard to love living things is not their absence but the hatefulness of their presence. The ways of men and animals often strike us as too hateful to let us love them. As we grow older, men and women come to seem to us nastier and pettier, and full of pervasive and destructive defects. Hence the frequency of the complaint that 'I don't know what has come over people nowadays'. We must keep on fighting against the bitterness and disappointment that experience brings. It is necessary to bear in mind the maxim attributed to Helvetius, that if we are to love men we must expect little of them. Another helpful thought is that we seem as hateful to others as they do to us. Misanthropy, how inevitable soever, is still a great evil.

The only completely improper extension of love is its extension to the love of a god; and the New Testament's putting this first is a great defect in its formulation of the ideal. If there is a god, we should be on man's side against him; and in any case one cannot converse with a god. The doctrine that 'God is love' conflicts violently with other things that are said about him.

Though love is not service, it often commands service; and it is an unfortunate consequence of the New Testament's demand for love of a god that appeals for service are largely made in the name of a god, and that atheists are largely excluded from enterprises of service, or invited to join them under false auspices. Thus the great good of service under love is smeared with the dishonesty that widely infects theism; and the many people who reject theism are not properly mobilized for service. We need to remove the tendency to think that if you disbelieve in theism you reject service, and if you want to serve you must believe that there is a god. We need to put all service on a purely mortal ground, as do the societies against cruelty to children and animals.

So much for the great virtue of love.

2.7. CONSCIENTIOUSNESS

Besides reason and love, there are many more habits of choice which we include in our ideal of man. There is, for example, the great sphere of selfdiscipline, which includes selfformation and selfcontrol. The habit of selfformation tends to be repudiated today in contrast to our Victorian ancestors who insisted on it rather pedantically. Their lists of moral exercises to be done daily, their diaries for recording and discussing moral progress, strike us as only comic now. But a middle way is required; for certainly it is desirable to take oneself consciously in hand, and make of oneself, by training and maxims and routine, the best character one can. There is a good brief suggestion of how to do this in the beginning of the fifth book of Spinoza's *Ethics*.

PERSONAL GOODS 109

The other part of selfdiscipline is selfcontrol, and this we are still very conscious of. Selfcontrol divides into controlling ourselves against desire and pleasure, on the one hand, and against fear and pain, on the other. That is, it divides into temperance and courage. Both of them are always necessary, and both of them are goods.

Then there are indefinitely many other virtues, including generosity, industry, and taste or the pursuit of beauty. But there is only one of these further virtues that I wish to discuss, and that merely so far as to disagree with a certain estimate of its value. I mean the virtue of conscientiousness or morality. A conscientious man is 'one who when he deliberates always has ⟨the idea of rightness⟩ in his mind, and does not act until he believes that his action is right' (G. E. Moore, *Principia Ethica*, p. 179).

Conscientiousness is often considered the greatest of the virtues. Kant so represents it when, in the beginning of his *Foundations of the Metaphysics of Ethics*, he writes that 'there is nothing that can be held to be good without qualification except only a good will'; for by a good will he means one that always acts out of respect for the moral law. All other candidates for unconditional goodness can, he says, sometimes be 'evil and harmful' (*böse und schädlich*). The same estimate has been expressed by Sir David Ross, who writes: 'The infinite superiority of moral goodness to anything else is clearest in the case of the highest form of moral goodness, the desire to do one's duty' (*The Right and the Good*, p. 153).

Such an estimate of the value of conscientiousness often causes a man to take great interest in assigning moral praise and blame, and to busy himself in 'fixing the moral worth' of people and actions, as he is likely to put it, and in detecting as many outrages to conscience as possible. Thus Thomas Arnold prayed: 'May the sense of moral evil be as strong in me as my delight in external beauty, for in a deep sense of moral evil, more perhaps than in anything else, abides a saving knowledge of God' (according to Lytton Strachey, *Eminent Victorians*, p. 199).

Along with this estimate of the value of conscientiousness there usually goes an unbounded respect for conscience, which is regarded as sacredly uncriticizable. There also goes a terror of any future change in men's moral judgements, although it is recognized that they have changed in the past.

I dissent from this estimate of conscientiousness, and place it decidedly below reason and love in value. Kant's argument for it is a mistake. All other things, he says, can be evil and harmful, but the good will cannot. This is false. All the good wills that have ever existed or ever will exist have been harmful to some extent; for harmfulness, that is having some bad effects, belongs to everything whatever. The English nonconformists' tyrannous and harmful interference with the way other Englishmen spend their Sundays is done from conscientious motives. The massacre on Saint Bartholomew's Day was probably executed, on the part of many of those responsible, from conscientious motives. 'It is as certain as anything can be that very harmful actions may be done from conscientious motives' (G. E. Moore, op. cit., p. 180).

It is natural that conscience should be harmful sometimes, because conscience recks nothing of harm. It is an autonomous commander reckless of the consequences of its orders. It is by nature unreasoning and tyrannous. It gives orders without reasons, and rejects all requests for reasons.

The original conscience of any given individual in any given society is an historical accident, the result of the influences to which he has been subject. It is a set of taboos and compulsions, acquired from his associates in the same unreflecting way as all his other taboos and compulsions. It has only this much of reason in it, that rules of conscience which are very harmful tend by natural selection to be eliminated from a society in course of time, or else the whole society itself tends to be eliminated from the world because it has such bad rules of conscience. Hence there is some natural tendency for more beneficial and less harmful rules of conscience to reign in the world as history goes on; but it is a tendency that may easily be overcome at any time by other influences.

Autonomous morality can be a very low thing indeed. 'Most moralists are fools', said a frivolous writer with much excuse; I mean James Laver in *Nymph Errant*. A very serious writer, Alfred North Whitehead, has said that 'mankind has been afflicted with low-toned moralists' (*Adventures of Ideas*, p. 346). Sometimes a person writes to *The Times* to let us know with fatuous selfsatisfaction that her mother taught her, and she has always obeyed, some perfectly pointless moral rule. The moralizer far too easily becomes intolerant and even a bully. He may acquire the nasty habit of wanting to make people feel guilty. He does not realize that he is a tyrant, and has a perfectly good conscience about his behaviour.

We in England had and have far too much moralizing. As it has been put by one of the wisest members of my College, Matthew Arnold, the English middle class 'in the beginning of the seventeenth century entered ... the prison of Puritanism, and had the key turned upon its spirit there for two hundred years. ... They created a type of life and manners ... which is fatally condemned by its hideousness, its immense ennui, and against which the instinct of self-preservation in humanity rebels.' He goes on to refer to the Puritan Parliament disposing of the National Gallery, and to Milton's abusiveness (*Mixed Essays*, p. 78).

Some persons would be inclined to accept this estimate of conscientiousness if they believed that Jesus also estimated it low. I suggest that he did. Morality to him was embodied in the rules of the Pharisees, which he often spoke against. 'The sabbath was made for man, not man for the sabbath', he said as he broke one of their sabbatarian rules. The righteousness praised in Matthew's Beatitudes is probably not conscientiousness but piety. And his 'judge not, that ye be not judged' is a command not to take the moralizing point of view. The modern Christian's coupling of Christianity with the moralistic point of view is therefore a perversion of the founder's teaching. However, what Jesus subordinated conscientiousness to, namely the love of god and man, is not identical with what I subordinate it to, namely reason and the love of man.

Augustine subordinated conscientiousness to love in his famous *Dilige et quod vis fac*.

Conscience deserves no pious acceptance, and ought not to be worshipped as sacredly uncriticizable. 'It is as certain as anything can be ... that conscience does not always tell us the truth about what actions are right' (G. E. Moore, op. cit., p. 180). Conscience ought to be reflectively criticized and critically adopted or rejected. One of the great merits of utilitarianism was its emphatic suggestion that perhaps ordinary moral consciousness is *wrong* in some respects (cf. J. S. Mill, *On Liberty*, introduction, para. 6). This merit comes out by contrast if you read F. H. Bradley's essay on 'Pleasure for Pleasure's Sake' (in his *Ethical Studies*), and see how hopelessly imbued he is with the sacred uncriticizability of actual conscience.

The terror of future change in men's moral judgements, as found in Plato (*Laws* 798) and in many twentieth-century writers, would be justified only if most changes in men's moral judgements were for the worse. Plato thought they were, and the task was to restore the past golden age of decency. But our contemporary conservatives have not this justification; for they share the present belief in progress to the extent of holding that in the past men's moral judgements have on the whole improved, and that in particular they took a big step forward with the teaching of Jesus.

Some persons, when invited to criticize conscience, reply that there is nothing to criticize it with. There is no rule by which to overrule the rules of conscience. But there is. The criterion of moral rules is their tendency to decrease misery. As Aristotle put it, 'the right (in one sense) is that which produces and maintains happiness and the parts of happiness for society' ($N.E.$ 1129 ^{b}18). All moral rules should be submitted to the criticism of reason to determine whether their reign in a given society tends to lessen misery there or not. If it does not lessen misery, it is bad and to be abolished. A moral rule is an interference with freedom, and all interferences with freedom are to be abolished unless they produce a more than compensating advantage. The man who puts morality above everything else is to be faced with the following question: If you became convinced that your moral rules, when they reign in a society, definitely make that society more miserable upon the whole, would you still demand obedience to them? If he says yes, then this moralist is immoral; for the highest morality is that the diminution of misery is the supreme law. Obey those moral rules, and only those, whose reign in society would, reasonable examination concludes, lessen misery. Rise from the plane of morality to that of reason. Contrary to Thomas Arnold, I hope that the sense of moral evil will decrease, and pity for life's unhappiness increase.

Conscientiousness must be subordinated to reason and love. When so subordinated, it is a great virtue, though inferior to them. The lessening of misery urgently demands rules, rules of good faith and sincerity and respect for others' lives and persons and troubles and so on; and the man of good will therefore seeks and obeys the rules whose reign lessens misery. Respect and awe towards the moral law, when the moral law is regarded as the rules whose general observance would most contribute to the happiness of society, is one of the sentiments that reason encourages.

Morality, then, is not to be autonomous but prescribed by reason. But, if we accept this doctrine, we need to remind ourselves that reason has to work, not with an ideal society, but with the actual society we have here now, including its actual set of moral laws, acknowledged to a certain degree, and obeyed to a certain other degree. It can happen that a rule, which would not exist in an ideal society, nevertheless ought to be obeyed by us in this society. Conversely, it can be irrational to follow here a rule that would be universally followed in an ideal society. For that which most lessens misery in view of the taboos we actually have, may be different from that which would most lessen misery if we had no taboos or better taboos. We usually can do little to change even our own taboos, and still less to change those of other people. Hence we must work with the taboos there are, and make the best rules in view of them. In this way many difficulties and doubts and complications arise, and it becomes important to know to what extent such and such a taboo could if we tried be removed from our society; and the question what is the right action comes to depend sometimes in a very awkward way on the question to what extent some existing moral rule is dying out, or whether deliberate defiance of it by you would or would not do anything towards making it die out. This is where the conservative moralist argues that your rebellion will never change a rule, but only make people disobey all moral rules more often, while the reformer calls for deliberate and shocking disobedience in the name of a better society. To take an actual and therefore dangerous example, the present horror of male homosexuality is possibly an irrational taboo, but in spite of that every young male ought to be protected and discouraged from homosexuality, simply because the existence of this powerful taboo means that the male homosexual is exposed to terrible and crippling disapproval, and driven to furtiveness.

So much for the doctrine that conscientiousness is not the greatest virtue, and that conscience should be criticized by reason and love. And so much for virtue in general.

2.8. RELIGION

2.81. *Religion and reason*

I come now to something commonly accepted as a great good which I reject, namely religion.

Religion has held a big place in the thoughts and feelings of most of the human beings who have yet lived; and, though some have found it an inescapable evil, most have found it a great good. The founder of the Gifford lectures said that 'religion is of all things the most excellent and precious' (according to Sherrington, *Man on his Nature*, p. 360).

The religious man feels that his god is the supreme good, and the worship of him is the supreme good for man; and he obtains an immense satisfaction in worship and obedience. His creed gives him the feeling that the universe is important and that he has his own humble but important part in it. 'God is working his purpose out, as year succeeds to year'; and in this august enterprise the believer has an assured place. When he says that 'man cannot be at ease in the world unless he has a faith to sustain him', the faith he is thinking of is in part that there is something extremely important to do. Thus his religion lays that spectre of futility and meaninglessness, which man's selfconsciousness and thoughtfulness are always liable to raise. The convert says to himself, in the words at the end of Tolstoy's *Anna Karenina*: 'My whole life, every moment of my life, will be, not meaningless as before, but full of deep meaning, which I shall have power to impress on every action.' The great comfort of such a belief is obvious.

But this is still less than half of the comfort religion can give. For it is not yet an answer to man's greatest horror, the death of his loved ones and himself. If his religion also makes him believe that death is not the end of life, that on the contrary he and his loved ones will live for ever in perfect justice and happiness, this more than doubles his feeling of comfort and security. This doctrine of the happy survival of death is the chief attraction of the Christian religion to most of its adherents; and their first profound religious belief comes to them as a reassurance after their first realization that they are going to die. It is an easy defensive reaction against this terrible discovery. (This point is well put by Bergson in *Les Deux Sources*, &c., e.g. p. 137.)

Such is the enormous comfort that religion can give. Because of it a man who deprives the people of the comfort of believing 'in the final proportions of eternal justice' is often regarded as a 'cruel oppressor, the merciless enemy of the poor and wretched' (Edmund Burke, 'Reflections on the French Revolution', *Works*, v. 432.)

But is it a cruel oppression to preach atheism? There is a sinister suggestion in this idea, namely the suggestion that we ought to preach religion whether or not it is true, and that we ought not to estimate rationally whether it is true, which implies that truth is below comfort in value.

It seems to me that religion buys its benefits at too high a price, namely at the price of abandoning the ideal of truth and shackling and perverting man's reason. The religious man refuses to be guided by reason and evidence in a certain field, the theory of the gods, theology. He does not say: 'I believe that there is a god, but I am willing to listen to argument that I am mistaken, and I shall be glad to learn better.' He does not seek to find and adopt the more probable of the two contradictories, 'there is a god' and 'there is no god'. On the contrary, he makes his choice between those two propositions once for all. He is determined never to revise his choice, but to believe that there is a god no matter what the evidence. The secretary of the Christian Evidence Society wrote to *The Times* (19 March 1953) and said: 'When demand is made upon devout Christians to produce evidence in justification of their intense faith in God they are apt to feel surprised, pained, and even disgusted that any such evidence should be considered necessary.' That is true. Christians do not take the attitude of reasonable inquiry towards the proposition that there is a god. If they engage in discussion on the matter at all, they seek more often to intimidate their opponent by expressing shock or disgust at his opinion, or disapproval of his character. They take the view that to hold the negative one of these two contradictories is a moral crime. They make certain beliefs wicked as such, without reference to the question whether the man has reached them sincerely and responsibly. This view, that certain beliefs are as such wicked, is implied in these two sentences in John's gospel (xvi. 8-9 and xx. 29): 'He will reprove the world of sin . . . because they believe not on me', and 'Blessed are they that have not seen, and yet have believed'. There is an extensive example of this attitude in Newman's fifteenth sermon.

Along with the view that certain beliefs are as such wicked there often goes, naturally, the view that it is wicked to try to persuade a person to hold certain beliefs. The believer's complaint, 'you are undermining my faith', implies that it is wrong as such to try to convince a man that there is no god. It implies that whether one believes the proposition or not, and whether one has a good reason to believe it or not, are irrelevant, because it is just wrong in itself to recommend this proposition. This view is contrary to the search for truth and the reasonable attitude of listening to argument and guiding oneself thereby.

If theology were a part of reasonable inquiry, there would be no objection to an atheist's being a professor of theology. That a man's being an atheist is an absolute bar to his occupying a chair of theology proves that theology is not an open-minded and reasonable inquiry. Someone may object that a professor should be interested in his subject and an atheist cannot be interested in theology. But a man who maintains that there is no god must think it a sensible and interesting question to ask whether there is a god; and in fact we find that many atheists are interested in theology. Professor H. D. Lewis tells (*Philosophy*, 1952, p. 347) that an old lady asked him what philosophy is, and, when he had given an answer, she said: 'O I see, theology.' She was nearly right, for theology and philosophy have the same subject-matter. The difference is that in philosophy you are allowed to come out with whichever answer seems to you the more likely.

In most universities the title of theology includes a lot of perfectly good science which is not theory of god, and which I do not reject, I mean the scientific study of the history of the Jews and their languages and their religious books. All that can be reasonable study, and usually is so. But it is a hindrance to the progress of knowledge that we are largely organized for research in such a way that a man cannot be officially paid to engage in these branches of research unless he officially maintains that there is a god. It is as if a man could not be a professor of Greek unless he believed in Zeus and Apollo.

Religious persons often consider gambling to be a bad thing. It certainly causes a great deal of misery. But much of the badness of gambling consists in its refusal to face the probabilities and be guided by them; and in the matter of refusing to face the probabilities religion is a worse offender than gambling, and does more harm to the habits of reason. Religious belief is, in fact, a form of gambling, as Pascal saw. It does more harm to reason than ordinary gambling does, however, because it is more in earnest.

It has been said that the physicist has just as closed a mind about cause as the Christian has about god. The physicist assumes through thick and thin that everything happens according to causal laws. He presupposes cause, just as the Christian presupposes god.

But the physicist does not *assume* that there is a reign of law; he *hopes* that there is. He looks for laws; but, whenever a possible law occurs to him, he conscientiously tries to disprove it by all reasonable tests. He asserts at any time only such laws as seem at that time to have passed all reasonable tests, and he remains always prepared to hear of new evidence throwing doubt on those laws. This is far from the Christian attitude about god. The Christian does not merely hope that there is a god and maintain only such gods as the best tests have shown to be more probable than improbable.

The main irrationality of religion is preferring comfort to truth; and it is this that makes religion a very harmful thing on balance, a sort of endemic disease that has so far prevented human life from reaching its full stature. For the sake of comfort and security religion is prepared to sophisticate thought and language to any degree. For the sake of comfort and security there pours out daily, from pulpit and press, a sort of propaganda which, if it were put out for a non-religious purpose, would be seen by everyone to be cynical and immoral. We are perpetually being urged to adopt the Christian creed not because it is true but because it is beneficial, or to hold that it must be true just because belief in it is beneficial. 'The Christian faith', we are assured, 'is a necessity for a fully adjusted personality' (a psychiatrist in the *Radio Times* for 20 March 1953, p. 33). Hardly a week passes without someone recommending theism on the ground that if it were believed there would be much less crime; and this is a grossly immoral argument. Hardly a week passes without someone recommending theism on the ground that unless it is believed the free nations will succumb to the Communists; and that is the same grossly immoral argument. It is always wicked to recommend anybody to believe anything on the ground that he or anybody else will feel better or be more moral or successful for doing so, or on any ground whatever except that the available considerations indicate that it is probably true. The pragmatic suggestion, that we had better teach the Christian religion whether it is true or not, because people will be much less criminal if they believe it, is disgusting and degrading; but it is being made to us all the time, and it is a natural consequence of the fundamental religious attitude that comfort and security must always prevail over rational inquiry.

This pragmatic fallacy is not the only fallacy into which religion is frequently led by preferring comfortingness to truth, though it is the main one. The religious impulse encourages all the fallacies. It encourages the argument *ad hominem*, that is the argument that my adversary's view must be false because he is a wicked man: the atheist is impious, therefore he is wicked, therefore his view is false.

Religion encourages also the argument from ignorance: instead of rejecting a proposition if it is probably false, the religious man thinks himself entitled to accept it because it is not certainly false. Biased selection of the instances is also very common in religious language. Any case of a man getting his wish after praying for it, or being struck by lightning after doing something mean, is taken as good evidence that there is a god who gives and punishes. Contrary cases are not looked for; and if they obtrude themselves they are dealt with by the further hypothesis that 'God's ways are inscrutable'. Religious arguments even exhibit, very often, what seems the most fallacious possible fallacy, namely inferring a theory from something that contradicts the theory. Thus we often find: 'since no explanation is final, God is the final explanation'; and 'since everybody believes in God, you are wrong not to believe in God'.

I have been saying that religion is gravely infected with intellectual dishonesty. You may find this very unlikely for a general reason. You may think it very unlikely that such widespread dishonesty would go unnoticed. I do not think so. I think, on the contrary, that it is quite common for a moral defect to pervade a certain sphere and yet escape notice in that sphere, although the people concerned are wide awake to its presence in other places. I think there are plenty of other cases of this. One of them is that the English, who are great haters of the bully and the might-is-right man, nevertheless bully and intimidate each other when driving a motor-car. They know that power does not confer any right, but they assume that horse-power does. Life is full of such inconsistencies, because we can never see all the implications and applications of our principles. In religion it is particularly easy for intellectual dishonesty to escape notice, because of the common assumption that all honesty flows from religion and religion is necessarily honest whatever it does.

2.82. *Faith*

According to Christianity one of the great virtues is faith. Paul gave faith a commanding position in the Christian scheme of values, along with hope and love, in the famous thirteenth chapter of his first letter to the Corinthians. Thomas Aquinas held that infidelity is a very great sin, that infidels should be compelled to believe, that heretics should not be tolerated, and that heretics who revert to the true doctrine and then relapse again should be received into penitence, but killed (*Summa Theologica*, 2-2, 11, 4).

According to me this is a terrible mistake, and faith is not a virtue but a positive vice. More precisely, there is, indeed, a virtue often called faith, but that is not the faith which the Christians make much of. The true virtue of faith is faith as opposed to faithlessness, that is, keeping faith and promises and being loyal. Christian faith, however, is not opposed to faithlessness but to unbelief. It is faith as some opposite of unbelief that I declare to be a vice.

When we investigate what Christians mean by their peculiar use of the word 'faith', I think we come to the remarkable conclusion that all their accounts of it are either unintelligible or false. Their most famous account is that in Heb. xi. 1: 'Faith is the substance of things hoped for, the evidence of things not seen.' This is obviously unintelligible. In any case, it does not make faith a virtue, since neither a substance nor an evidence can be a virtue. A virtue is a praiseworthy habit of choice, and neither a substance nor an evidence can be a habit of choice. When a Christian gives an intelligible account of faith, I think you will find that it is false. I mean that it is not a true dictionary report of how he and other Christians actually use the word. For example, Augustine asked: 'What is faith but believing what you do not see?' (*Joannis Evang. Tract.*, c. 40, § 8). But Christians do not use the word 'faith' in the sense of believing what you do not see. You do not see thunder; but you cannot say in the Christian sense 'have faith that it is thundering', or 'I have faith that it has thundered in the past and will again in the future'. You do not see mathematical truths; but you cannot say in the Christian sense 'have faith that there is no greatest number'. If we take Augustine's 'see' to stand here for 'know', still it is false that Christians use the word 'faith' to mean believing what you do not know, for they would never call it faith if anyone believed that the sun converts hydrogen into helium, although he did not know it.

A good hint of what Christians really mean by their word 'faith' can be got by considering the proposition: 'Tom Paine had faith that there is no god.' Is this a possible remark, in the Christian sense of the word 'faith'? No, it is an impossible remark, because it is self-contradictory, because part of what Christians mean by 'faith' is belief that there *is* a god.

There is more to it than this. Christian faith is not merely believing that there is a god. It is believing that there is a god no matter what the evidence on the question may be. 'Have faith', in the Christian sense, means 'make yourself believe that there is a god without regard to evidence.' Christian faith is a habit of flouting reason in forming and maintaining one's answer to the question whether there is a god. Its essence is the determination to believe that there is a god no matter what the evidence may be.

No wonder that there is no true and intelligible account of faith in Christian literature. What they mean is too shocking to survive exposure. Faith is a great vice, an example of obstinately refusing to listen to reason, something irrational and undesirable, a form of self-hypnotism. Newman wrote that 'if we but obey God strictly, in time (through His blessing) faith will become like sight' (*Sermon* XV). This is no better than if he had said: 'Keep on telling yourself that there is a god until you believe it. Hypnotize yourself into this belief.'

It follows that, far from its being wicked to undermine faith, it is a duty to do so. We ought to do what we can towards eradicating the evil habit of believing without regard to evidence.

The usual way of recommending faith is to point out that belief and trust are often rational or necessary attitudes. Here is an example of this from Newman: 'To hear some men speak, (I mean men who scoff at religion), it might be thought we never acted on Faith or Trust, except in religious matters; whereas we are acting on trust every hour of our lives. . . . We trust our *memory* . . . the general soundness of our reasoning powers. . . . Faith in ⟨the⟩ sense of *reliance on the words of another* as opposed to trust in oneself . . . is the common meaning of the word' (*Sermon* XV).

The value of this sort of argument is as follows. It is certainly true that belief and trust are often rational. But it is also certainly true that belief and trust are often irrational. We have to decide in each case by rational considerations whether to believe and trust or not. Sometimes we correctly decide *not* to trust our memory on some point, but to look the matter up in a book. Sometimes even we correctly decide not to trust our own reason, like poor Castlereagh deciding he was mad because the Duke of Wellington told him he was. But Christian faith is essentially a case of irrational belief and trust and decision, because it consists in deciding to believe and trust the proposition that there is a god no matter what the evidence may be.

Another common way to defend Christian faith is to point out that we are often obliged to act on something less than knowledge and proof. For example, Newman writes: 'Life is not long enough for a religion of inferences; we shall never have done beginning if we determine to begin with proof. Life is for action. If we insist on proof for everything, we shall never come to action; to act you must assume, and that assumption is faith' (*Assent*, p. 92).

The value of this argument is as follows. It is true that we are often unable to obtain knowledge and proof. But it does not follow that we must act on faith, for faith is belief reckless of evidence and probability. It follows only that we must act on some belief that does not amount to knowledge. This being so, we ought to assume, as our basis for action, those beliefs which are more probable than their contradictories in the light of the available evidence. We ought not to act on faith, for faith is assuming a certain belief without reference to its probability.

There is an ambiguity in the phrase 'have faith in' that helps to make faith look respectable. When a man says that he has faith in the president he is assuming that it is obvious and known to everybody that there is a president, that the president exists, and he is asserting his confidence that the president will do good work on the whole. But, if a man says he has faith in telepathy, he does not mean that he is confident that telepathy will do good work on the whole, but that he believes that telepathy really occurs sometimes, that telepathy exists. Thus the phrase 'to have faith in x' sometimes means to be confident that good work will be done by x, who is assumed or known to exist, but at other times means to believe that x exists. Which does it mean in the phrase 'have faith in God'? It means ambiguously both; and the selfevidence of what it means in the one sense recommends what it means in the other sense. If there is a perfectly powerful and good god it is selfevidently reasonable to believe that he will do good. In this sense 'have faith in God' is a reasonable exhortation. But it insinuates the other sense, namely 'believe that there is a perfectly powerful and good god, no matter what the evidence'. Thus the reasonableness of trusting God if he exists is used to make it seem also reasonable to believe that he exists.

It is well to remark here that a god who wished us to decide certain questions without regard to the evidence would definitely *not* be a perfectly good god.

Even when a person is aware that faith is belief without regard to evidence, he may be led to hold faith respectable by the consideration that we sometimes think it good for a man to believe in his friend's honesty in spite of strong evidence to the contrary, or for a woman to believe in her son's innocence in spite of strong evidence to the contrary. But, while we admire and love the love that leads the friend or parent to this view, we do not adopt or admire his conclusion unless we believe that he has private evidence of his own, gained by his long and intimate association, to outweigh the public evidence on the other side. Usually we suppose that his love has led him into an error of judgement, which both love and hate are prone to do.

This does not imply that we should never act on a man's word if we think he is deceiving us. Sometimes we ought to act on a man's word although we privately think he is probably lying. For the act required may be unimportant, whereas accusing a man of lying is always important. But there is no argument from this to faith. We cannot say that sometimes we ought to believe a proposition although we think it is false!

So I conclude that faith is a vice and to be condemned. As Plato said, 'It is unholy to abandon the probably true' (*Rp*. 607 C). Out of Paul's 'faith, hope, and love' I emphatically accept love and reject faith. As to hope, it is more respectable than faith. While we ought not to believe against the probabilities, we are permitted to hope against them. But still the Christian overtones of hope are otherworldly and unrealistic. It is better to take a virtue that avoids that. Instead of faith, hope, and love, let us hymn reason, love, and joy.

What is the application of this to the common phrase 'a faith to live by'? A faith to live by is not necessarily a set of beliefs or valuations maintained without regard to evidence in an irrational way. The phrase can well cover also a criticized and rational choice of values. To decide, for example, that the pursuit of love is better than the pursuit of power, in view of the probable effects of each on human happiness and misery, and to guide one's actions accordingly, is a rational procedure, and is sometimes called and may well be called 'a faith to live by'. In this case a faith to live by is a choice of values, a decision as to great goods and evils, and is what I am doing in these lectures. On the other hand, many 'faiths to live by' are irrational and bad. Some people will not count anything as a faith to live by unless it deliberately ignores rational considerations; so that what they will consent to call a faith to live by must always be something that is bad according to me. Other people refuse to count anything as a faith to live by unless it includes a belief that the big battalions are on their side, so that according to them a man who rationally concludes that he is not the darling of any god by definition has no faith to live by.

2.83. *There is no god or afterlife*

Good evaluation has to be made in the light of good judgement as to what the facts are, what our situation is. Among the questions of fact on which it is important to have a right judgement are the questions whether there is a god and whether there is a life after death. My answer to each of these questions is 'No'. Ought I to give you the considerations on which I base these answers? That is a hard choice, because, on the one hand, it seems wrong to offer no reasons on these immensely important questions, but, on the other hand, all imaginable reasons have already been exhaustively discussed by both sides for centuries, and we are perfectly sick of them. I have concluded that I had better give something on this topic, but make it merely a brief indication.

Whether there is a god, and whether there is a life after death, are questions of existence, of what there is or what happens. They are not questions of mathematics, nor questions of law or necessary connexion. They are like the questions whether there is a tribe of people on the Amazon who eat their parents, and whether there are flying saucers. They cannot be answered by mathematical proofs, but only by travellers' reports, or at any rate by something far more like a traveller's report than a mathematical proof.

Mathematical proofs can show non-existence but they cannot show existence. (They can show that there 'exists' a prime number greater than the millionth power of ten. But that is another sense of 'exists'. It is not the natural existence in time or place that I am speaking of.) For mathematics can only show that certain conceptions are selfcontradictory and others are not. If a conception is selfcontradictory, as is the round square, that shows that nothing of the sort exists. But if a conception is selfconsistent, as is the round area, that does not show whether anything of the sort exists. Thus mathematics may be able to show that certain conceptions of god or immortality are selfcontradictory and therefore nothing of the kind exists. But, if there is any selfconsistent conception of god or immortality, mathematics will not show in the least whether anything fulfilling this conception exists.

In the Christian religion, though perhaps not in any other, we frequently find a conception of god that is selfcontradictory and therefore corresponds to nothing. That is the conception formed by the following three propositions taken together:

1. God is all-powerful.
2. God is all-benevolent.
3. There is much misery in the world.

A god who was all-powerful but left much misery in the world would not be all-benevolent. An all-benevolent god in a world containing much misery would not be an all-powerful god. A world containing a god who was both all-powerful and all-benevolent would contain no misery.

Here, then, we have a mathematical proof bearing on a common religious doctrine. Anyone who is confident that he frequently comes across misery in the world may conclude with equal confidence that there is no such thing as an all-powerful and all-benevolent god. And this mathematically disposes of official Christianity, as has long been known (though people have fought endlessly against it by means of the doctrine of free will).

That, however, is as far as mathematics takes us. (And even there we are relying also on our judgement and experience to get the conclusion that misery does occur.) When we turn to consider all the selfconsistent conceptions of gods and devils and angels that have been invented or might be invented, mathematics gives us no help, and we are confronted with the truth that anything whatever *might* exist so long as it is selfconsistent.

In order to decide what *does* exist, among all the things that *might* exist because they are selfconsistent, we have to use our judgement on the reports and experiences available to us. It is a question of using the *judgement*, of deciding *judiciously* between the two contradictories; and more than half the battle consists in getting oneself into a sincerely judicious frame of mind and out of the injudicious determination to believe the affirmative answer if one possibly can. The rest of it consists in learning by experience what kinds of inference are reliable in questions of existence. For, whereas in mathematics we learn by logic what kinds of inference are valid, in questions of fact we learn only by experience what kinds of inference are judicious. Only experience has taught us that, for example, when a person looks at a police line-up and says confidently that 'this is the man who attacked me', she is sometimes wrong.

What is good evidence for the presence or existence of a person, and have we such evidence for the existence of a superhuman person?

Suppose you wish to decide what kinds of mammal exist. You collect your memories of mammals you have seen. You collect zoologists' descriptions of mammals they have seen. You collect travellers' accounts. And so on. You try to judge which of these you should accept and which you should reject. 'I am sure I remember seeing a panther, but do I really remember seeing something called an "ocelot", or was that a dream? I am sure the reports of okapis in the Congo are true, but can I trust the reports of abominable snowmen in the Himalayas? Among travellers I judge that X is nearly always both honest and correct, Y is always honest but often incorrect, and Z is plain dishonest.' All this is clearly fallible, however copious our information and however much we compare and counter-check. But nothing better can possibly be found. And there are plenty of cases where the judicious man properly comes to a confident judgement as to whether a given thing exists.

Suppose now that instead of mammals I wish to make a list of all the gods there are. Here again I can only rely on my own memories, the reports of travellers, the accounts of scientists, and so on. The scientists in this case will not be zoologists but theologians, prophets, mediums, psychical researchers. Again I have to judge which of their reports to accept, which of them are both honest and aware of the dangers of error, and so on.

Many of their reports have the remarkable feature that they tell us that the god they have experienced is the only god who exists. There is nothing like this in the case of mammals. No one comes back from the Congo and tells us that the kind of mammal he saw there is the only kind of mammal there is. These reports must be unjustified because experience cannot tell us that there is only one of a certain sort in the whole universe. If you carefully examine the whole of this room you will perhaps be justified in declaring that there is one and only one Scotsman in this room. But, since you cannot examine the whole of the universe, you cannot justifiably tell us that there is one and only one god in the universe.

Many of these reports tell us of a god who is infinite or perfect. They must be unjustified, because one cannot experience infinity or perfection. However long a time I may have experienced, I have not experienced infinite time. However much goodness I have experienced from a person, I have not experienced infinite goodness or perfection at his hands. It is only a finite god that we could have evidence for. Have we good evidence for such?

All of these reports have the remarkable feature that they tell us that the gods are experienced and yet not perceived. One may, it is said, sometimes perceive manifestations of the gods, visions, miracles, and, of course, images. One may also perceive a man and infer from the miracles he does that he is also a god. But one cannot perceive the god directly with eyes or ears. And yet one experiences him. Experience without perception is, of course, usually a mark of the subjective; what I experience without the aid of perception is primarily my own inner life, my thoughts and imaginations and moods and so on. But we are told that there is also experience without perception of at least one kind of objective reality, namely god or the gods.

This universal feature of the reports makes them all incredible. That is not because a claim to have experience of other persons without perception of them is always to be declared false. It is because such claims require confirmation by subsequent perception, and there is no evidential value in such a claim if it is never confirmed by perception. Even if experience without perception were good evidence, there would be nothing to show that the various believers were all experiencing the same god. A hundred people all having religious experience at the same time in the same church might each be in communication with a different god, since no god ever presents himself to their bodily perception for them to see whether they are talking about the same person.

What about inferring the existence of a god, as opposed to experiencing him? Sometimes we properly and correctly infer the existence of a person in a house, although we do not perceive anyone there. Can we similarly infer the existence of a god in the universe, although we do not perceive one? No, we cannot. The fundamental defect of all such inferences is that they require perceptual confirmation and they never get it. Inferences that there is someone in the house are sometimes confirmed by subsequently seeing him. If they never were confirmed by subsequent perception they would never be proper. But inferences from something or other to the conclusion that there is a god in the universe are never confirmed by subsequently seeing him here.

In the early days of Christianity the favourite phenomenon from

PERSONAL GOODS 127

which to infer the existence of a god was miracles. But the inference is worthless. It is worthless to monotheists, because all religions have their miracles, so that if miracles were good evidence for one god they would be good evidence for all the gods. It is worthless to every judicious reasoner. For a miracle is an event which astounds us by seeming to contradict the laws of nature. But our being astounded proves nothing but our ignorance. And if an event really contradicts what we thought was a law of nature, that just shows that we were wrong about the laws of nature. We very often *are* wrong about the laws of nature. They are not to be known by instinct, but only by the endless labours of science.

Another phenomenon from which people infer the existence of an unperceived god is the multitude of convinced and sincere testifiers. 'How could all those intelligent and honest men be mistaken?' This inference is also worthless. If we took the existence of a multitude of convinced and sincere testifiers as good evidence for a belief, we should have to believe not in one religion but in all the conflicting religions that have obtained; we should have to believe both that the sun goes round the earth and that the earth goes round the sun; we should have to believe both that the world ended at several different dates in the past and also that it is still going on; for it is a characteristic of Christianity that from its beginning down to at earliest 1900 it has produced groups of earnest persons who were convinced that the world was going to end within ten years. In 1846, for example, the Irvingites were convinced that the world was going to end in 1847. They were sober and intelligent persons living in London. They included the solicitor to Rugby School, and the banker who founded the chair of political economy in Oxford University. No one is a good reasoner about matters of fact until he has realized that it is very common for a gross falsehood to be firmly and sincerely believed by a great number of superior persons, and that therefore there is nothing in the argument from the consensus of mankind.

Another phenomenon from which many have inferred that there is an unperceived god is the designedness of the world. Since the world is designed, they have thought, it must have a designer. Here it is not the inference that is injudicious but the premiss. The world does not appear to be designed. Little bits of it appear to be designed from time to time, but as a whole it strongly appears not to be designed. When lightning kills a mean bully and leaves his victim unharmed beside him, that looks like somebody's design; but the complete picture of all the lightning-damage in a given country in a given century looks very undesigned.

Recently it has become common to infer that there is a god from the phenomenon of conscience. Human beings have consciences, uninferred convictions that certain kinds of action are wrong, and they feel guilty if they do an action belonging to one of these kinds. This phenomenon, it is thought, could only be caused by a god. But to lay it down that a certain phenomenon can only be caused by a certain something is to claim to know the laws of cause and effect by instinct and without inquiry. No one knows by instinct what the laws of nature are; they have to be laboriously hunted and proved by experiment. Since experiment is largely forbidden on human beings, the laws of human nature are particularly difficult to find; but the phenomenon of 'wolf children', that is human children brought up by wolves without contact with human beings, suggests, so far as I have read the reports, that conscience is caused by association with other human beings.

All the evidence and argument offered for the existence of a god, is, I judge, injudicious, in so far as we mean by a 'god' a superhuman person, and do not use the word as a mere question-mark to indicate an unknown something or other. I have shown briefly what seems to me the badness of some of the common reasons given for believing that there is a god. The eternal persistence with which people bring forward these bad arguments is probably caused by our need for the comfort and security of having a perfectly reliable father. This need often seduces us into very bad methods of argument. For example, some people will be tempted to sneer at the brevity and simplicity of these remarks of mine, saying loftily that the question of religion is not to be settled in five minutes. The question of religion will, indeed, probably never be settled. That is, there will probably never be universal agreement about it. But arguments about it are better when they are short than when they are long. Long arguments should always be suspected of being designed to intimidate or hypnotize rather than to explain. And we should reject the common assumption that no one has a right to assert atheism unless he asserts it at great length with great learning. If, however, anyone wishes for a longer statement of my position, there are plenty in existence. I will mention only David Hume's essay on miracles and his *Dialogue concerning Natural Religion*.

And now as to life after death. Endless life after death would be a form of infinity, and for actual infinities there can be no good evidence. But is there good evidence for any life after death?

A great deal of the evidence offered for life after death depends on the doctrine that there is a god, and is valueless because that doctrine is false. However, some people have believed that there is no god and yet is an afterlife; and spiritualists and mediums offer us evidence of survival independent of the question whether there is a god. I have never attended a spiritualist performance, but I have read some of their reports. I think I can safely say that no afterlife of any difference in quality from this life has been reported, and no afterlife of any interest. The stuff they offer us is deadly dull. However, it might be true for all that. Homer believed that there is an afterlife and it *is* deadly dull.

I judge that it is false, and that all these reports of messages from the dead are false. (By which I do not mean that they are all frauds or lies. No doubt many of them are sincere. It is desirable to repeat from time to time that a falsehood is not the same as a lie. A falsehood can be sincerely uttered, and a lie can be true.) These reports have the pattern of inventions, the vagueness, the poverty, the similarity to each other, the comfortingness, and the insistence on circumstances that make criticism difficult, such as darkness and reverence.

My main reason for thinking there is no afterlife is that it seems immensely probable that everything we know as life depends on there being a living body. All that part of life which consists in the activity of a living body selfevidently depends on there being a living body, for example, eating, tasting, running, laughing, kissing. The life that does not selfevidently depend on there being a living body is the interior life of the mind, including reasoning, imagining, dreaming, and other activities and experiences. But it seems quite clear that we have overwhelming physiological evidence that this mental life, too, depends on the activity of a living body, and ceases when there is no longer a good brain with good blood flowing through it in the right quantity.

For this reason I am confident that there is no life after death. However, no one who believes that there is a life after death will be disappointed, because, if there is no life after death, he will not be alive to be disappointed. Only those who believe that there is no life after death can possibly find that experience disproves their answer to this question.

So much for the questions whether there is an afterlife and whether there is a god, on our answers to which a great deal of our evaluations and actions should depend. One thing, however, which should not depend on these answers is our evaluation of religion as we know it now and have known it in the past. Religion as it has so far appeared is upon the whole a bad thing whether or not there is a god or an afterlife, because it is a fundamental rejection of the ideals of truth and reason.

2.84. *Religion and reasons for morality*

It is often held that religion is the only basis for ethics, that only religion can show a good reason why we should obey any moral laws, and only religion can make us in fact obey them. People holding this view tend to regard the assertion of atheism as an attempt to undermine the morality of the nation; hence they try to prevent atheism from being recommended on the B.B.C., in which they are almost completely successful.

It is false that religion is the only basis for ethics. If we had to choose between the two sweeping assertions 'religion is the only basis for ethics' and 'religion is not a basis for ethics at all', the latter would be preferable. Religion is in fact not a proper basis for ethics at all.

What is a basis for ethics? The phrase refers either to reasons for the moral law, or to causes which make people keep the moral law. It means either that the only good reasons to justify the moral law are religious reasons, or that the only stimulus which effectively causes people to obey the moral law is religion, or both. Let us consider each of these in turn, beginning with reasons. Does religion provide good reasons for the moral law, and does it provide the only good reasons for it?

Let us divide reasons into entailing and non-entailing reasons. An entailing reason for a moral law is one that entails it. A non-entailing reason for a moral law is one that does not entail it but nevertheless seems to somebody to be a good reason for it.

It has been made perfectly clear that there can be no entailing reason for a moral law except another moral law. Probably the first person to point this out unmistakably was H. A. Prichard in his article in *Mind* for 1911, 'Does Moral Philosophy rest on a Mistake?' (reprinted in his *Moral Obligation*). A sentence beginning 'thou shalt' or 'thou shalt not', or containing the words 'ought' or 'ought not' or 'right' or 'wrong', can be entailed only by a sentence also containing one of these expressions. For example, the sentence 'thou shalt not kill' is not entailed by any of the following: 'there is a god who hates killing', 'there is a god who punishes killing with eternal fire', and 'there is a god who is our father and commands us not to kill'. None of these is an entailing reason for the law that 'thou shalt not kill'. The following, however, *is* an entailing reason for this law: 'God commands us not to kill, and thou shalt do whatever God commands.' This is an entailing reason because it contains a 'thou shalt', and therefore is itself a moral law. A moral law can be entailed by a sentence about a god only if that sentence is itself a moral law. It cannot be entailed by a sentence which merely informs us that there *is* a god, and what his commands are. The moral laws as a whole are not and never will be entailed by anything. In other words, there is a good sense in which ethics has no basis and cannot have a basis. There is a good sense in which there is no such thing as 'the foundations of morality'. Mr. Hare stated this point very clearly, with special reference to Christian thought, in *Philosophy* for 1950, p. 376.

There could be a man who said: 'There is one and only one moral law, and it is that we ought to do whatever God commands.' If this man believed it possible to discover what his god did command, he could then go on to discover it and do it; and he would then be acting morally because he would be acting under a moral law, a sentence with an 'ought' in it. There could be another man who said: 'I am determined to devote myself utterly to God, and to do whatever he commands.' If he also believed that it was possible to find out what his god commanded, he, like the former man, could go on to discover it and do it. But unlike the former man he would not be acting morally, because he would be acting from a principle which contained no 'ought' and no 'thou shalt', but merely said 'I will'. His procedure would be like that of a man who gives up trying to do right and tries instead to please his mistress. He would simply have taken a god for his mistress. To devote oneself utterly to a divine being, and decide to do everything he ordered, would not be to base ethics, but to abandon it and substitute another way of living. We get an entailing religious basis for ethics only if we adopt the moral law that we ought to do whatever our god commands.

Now let us turn to non-entailing reasons for moral laws. There could be, and no doubt there is, a logically minded theist who agrees that religion can provide no entailing reason for the moral laws, but says that it can provide a good non-entailing reason for them, and nothing else can do that. The only good non-entailing reason for the moral laws, he may say, is that there is a god who commands us to obey them and will burn us eternally if we do not. Contrast this with my view that the only good reason for a moral law is that its reign in a society substantially decreases misery in that society.

If it really were probable that we should burn eternally, or not burn eternally, according as we disobeyed or obeyed a certain set of moral laws, that would, indeed, be an excellent reason for obeying them. But, while it would be an excellent reason for *obeying* them, it would be a poor reason for *respecting* them, or regarding them as worthy of reverence and awe. On the contrary they, and the god who imposed them on us in this unbelievably brutal way, could only be regarded as beneath contempt. And in fact it is very improbable that hell-fire exists, or that an afterlife at all exists. And we have only very poor evidence indeed that there is a god of any kind, and yet enormously poorer evidence as to what his commands and threats are if he does exist. And it is always possible that, if he exists and ordains certain laws, these laws are in conflict with those that would do most to lessen misery on earth. Because of these facts the religious reason for obeying the moral laws is a very poor reason. On the other hand, we can hope to get good evidence whether obeying a certain set of laws does or does not substantially decrease misery in a given society; and hence, if we take the decrease of misery as the criterion of a right moral law, we are likely to be able to form a reasonably probable opinion as to what the right moral laws are.

People talk disapprovingly of 'moral anarchy'. This phrase 'moral anarchy' is always a muddle, and should be given up. If it refers to the fact that people often disobey the moral laws, it is a bad way of referring to it. Correct phrases for the purpose are 'immorality', 'wickedness', 'disobedience to the moral law', and many others. If it refers to the fact that people disagree to some extent as to what moral rules should be obeyed, that is not something for disapproval; two people can disagree without either of them being reprehensible. If it refers to the fact that no government on earth is trying to enforce legally all the recognized moral rules, it refers to something that is to be approved, not disapproved. If it refers to the fact that many people have given up deducing moral laws from statements about gods, it refers to something good, since moral laws are not in truth entailed by anything but moral laws. If it refers to the fact that a great many people today, in deciding what moral laws to adopt, do not accept the authority of any church or priest or god, but freely criticize them all, it refers to something highly approvable, to that coming of age of man's reason which is an encouraging feature of our time. The truly moral world is essentially anarchical, in that to be a really moral agent a man must judge and choose for himself. A world in which people follow authority and obey an 'arch.y' for their moral opinions and choices is an imperfectly moral world. The disapprovable thing is moral 'archy', not moral anarchy. Great harm is done to morality by its authoritarian connexions, by the notion that the parson is the depository of it, by the habit of turning to the parson when the question is what is morally right. The average parson is a worse judge of right and wrong than the average layman, and that is simply because he takes his moral laws on authority. Never go to church to learn how to behave unless the sermon is preached by a layman.

So much for religion as a reason for obeying moral laws.

2.85. *Religion and causes of morality*

Now let us turn from reasons to causes and consider the proposition that 'the only *cause* which in fact makes people obey moral laws is their believing some religious proposition'.

The first and most important point to make about this proposition is that, whether it is true or false, to use it as an argument in favour of religious belief is a disgraceful thing to do. To do that is to commit the pragmatic dishonesty of arguing that a creed is true because it is useful that people should believe it. I know that this argument *is* used extremely frequently, and in the most respected quarters. Nevertheless, it is selfevidently null both in logical effectiveness and in common decency. That it would be very convenient if people believed the Christian creed is nothing whatever to do with the question whether that creed is true. And to recommend a proposition on the ground of the convenience of having it believed is just as dishonest as telling a lie. The improper appeal to expediency, which religious people are fond of imputing to their opponents, is in truth made by the religious themselves enormously more often than by the irreligious. To say in a solemn and intimidating tone of voice that, in so far as atheism comes to be believed, murder and theft and rape increase in the world, is part of an immense number of Christian arguments; and it is thoroughly immoral.

If it were true that a general belief in atheism caused a high frequency of murder and theft and rape, while a general belief in theism caused a low frequency of them, and at the same time atheism were true and theism were false, we should be compelled to make a painful choice. There would be nothing for it but either to preach the true doctrine and see murder and theft and rape increase in consequence, or to keep down the rate of crime by preaching the false doctrine. That would be a hateful dilemma indeed. Yet there is no doubt which course we ought to take if we ever were obliged to make this choice. We ought to preach the true doctrine and endure the consequent increase in crime. To preach a false doctrine, or to preach a doctrine without considering whether it is false or true, is base and beneath human dignity. It is an abandonment of the great good of truth, and a treachery towards our fellows worse than exposing them to a greater risk of crime.

That is the first and most important point about the proposition that 'the only cause which in fact makes people obey moral laws is their believing some religious proposition'. However true it may be, to use it as an argument in favour of religious belief is logically null and morally indecent.

The second aspect of this proposition which I wish to consider is how one would test it. To what branch of inquiry does it belong? Either to history or to anthropology or to sociology. It is a sociological sort of proposition, because it offers a general rule about a causal connexion between human beliefs and human behaviour. So we must ask: What is good method in sociology? How can one reach a justifiable judgement on a general proposition asserting that a certain kind of belief tends to be accompanied by a certain kind of behaviour?

To obtain a justifiable judgement on such a proposition is a matter of statistics and mass observation, and hence a very large undertaking. Sociologists and anthropologists have scarcely ever ventured, yet, to make any such sweeping statement about man in general. They have confined themselves almost wholly to saying things about particular groups of men. I think they have been wise to do so, and the apologists for theism are unwise when they offer us unrestricted generalizations about the effects of theological beliefs on human behaviour.

Even when we have abandoned talk about human behaviour in general, and confined ourselves to a particular society, the inquiry is still laborious in procedure and doubtful in result. Consider, for example, how you would test the proposition that 'from 1700 to 1900 moral and law-abiding behaviour declined in England because religious belief declined'. This involves three different questions: (1) First, did moral and law-abiding behaviour decline in England during this period? (2) Second, did religious belief decline in England during this period? (3) Third, if so, were the two causally connected? We can obtain a probable answer to only one of these three questions, the one about religious belief. The quantity of churchgoing affords a good rough measure of the quantity of religious belief; and we can find out something about that for the period in question.

We have no good way of answering the question whether moral and law-abiding behaviour declined in England during this period. Perhaps we know the population in 1700 well enough to compare with the population in 1900, which we do know. But police figures are not available to give any reliable comparison on the legal side; and on the moral side there is no record and no way of coming at the proportion of moral offences committed. If a centenarian tells us that people were much more moral in his young days, or much less so, that is very poor evidence indeed in view of the deceptiveness of memory, the bias of the old, and the fragmentariness of any one person's experience. Also the centenarian is most unlikely to be sociologically judicious and able to tell good evidence from bad in such matters.

Another difficulty in any such inquiry is as follows. When we speak of the morality or immorality of Englishmen in 1700, do we mean the extent to which they obeyed *their own* moral laws, or the extent to which they obeyed the moral laws *in which we believe now*? Our decision on this point may make a big difference, for the reigning body of moral laws may have changed somewhat between then and now. For example, perhaps there was a double standard of sexual morality then, and perhaps there is not now. If so, James Boswell, when he got an illegitimate child upon a girl and then rebuked her for her behaviour, was perhaps obeying his own moral laws though he was certainly disobeying ours. It is possible that by the code of 1700 Englishmen of 1700 were more moral than those of 1900, while at the same time by the code of 1900 Englishmen of

1700 were less moral than those of 1900. If we compare our fidelity to our code with the fidelity of an earlier society to our code, we are likely to come out nearly always with the conclusion that we are more moral than they were. But, if we try to compare our fidelity to our code with their fidelity to their code, the conclusion may be different; or there may be no conclusion because we cannot be sure what their code was.

For my part I think that we in England today both have a better code of morals, and obey the reigning code of morals better, than Englishmen did in the eighteenth century. But I also think that this is a precarious judgement, worth mentioning only as a counter-weight to the low estimates of present morals which we often hear from bishops and writers to the press. In any case I have no doubt that much of what is said from pulpits today about the immorality of the present generation may properly be described as irresponsible abuse. It is a bad habit that Christians have contracted from certain verses of the gospels.

But suppose we had reliable answers to both the first and the second question. That is, suppose we could say with confidence just how religious belief had changed in these two centuries and just how morality had changed. We should still have no reliable means of knowing whether they were causally connected. A single case of concomitant variation is no evidence of causal connexion in matters so delicate and complicated as religious belief and moral fidelity. Many other possible causes would require to be excluded; and this would require similar knowledge of the variations in moral fidelity and other possible causes at other times and places. I judge that no reliable conclusion is to be obtained here.

I judge also that, when people think they can reach a reliable conclusion here, this is often because they are improperly thinking of the obvious proposition, which needs no statistics for its support, that, 'if the only cause of a man's acting morally is his fear of hell-fire, he will cease to act morally when he ceases to believe in hell-fire'. That is true by the mere meaning of 'only cause'. But it has no application to our question, because fear of hell-fire is not the only cause of moral action. We know that, because we are acquainted with at least one man who acts morally but disbelieves in hell-fire.

There certainly are some people who obey moral laws only from fear of a god or that god's hell-fire; and it certainly does happen sometimes that a person of this sort ceases to believe that there is a god and thereupon ceases to obey moral laws. There is truth in the story of a Papist priest saying to a pair of well-behaved atheists: 'I can't understand you boys; if I didn't believe in God I should be having a high old time.' Nothing that I have said denies the possibility of this kind of human nature. My view is that *indefinitely many* kinds of human nature are possible, and hence we must not make sweeping statements to the effect that only one kind of human nature is possible and all others are impossible. The proposition that 'the only cause which in fact makes people obey moral laws is their believing some religious proposition' is in effect an assertion that it is impossible for there to be a kind of human nature which obeys moral laws from a non-religious cause. Such assertions of impossibility are injudicious. We do not know all that human nature may do, and we do know that it may do a great many different things, and react in a great many different ways.

The false assumption, that nothing but religious belief will ever make people obey the moral laws, is widespread in the occidental world, and it has harmful effects. It leads people into all kinds of intellectual dishonesties in their frantic efforts to save religious belief for the sake of saving morality. It leads many of those who reject religious belief into immorality, because their idea of obeying the moral laws was bound up with their idea of a god. It leads everyone who holds it to neglect the attempt to base morality on something not religious, and to neglect to teach their children a morality independent of religious opinion, that will remain in being however often they may change from theism to atheism or back again.

In other words, what may well be called the capture of morality by religion, which was an achievement of the Jewish religion in particular, has turned out harmful for the world now that religion is declining; and it is an urgent task to set morality free again and give it an independent position, dependent only on its serving the earthly good of man, which is his only good. We are not doing all we could in that matter. For example, atheistic parents usually do not try to find atheistic schools for their children. That is a wrong attitude. At theistic schools children are taught that the reason for morality is hell-fire or God's command. This false reason is likely to collapse in later life; and if it does so it leaves the person with no reason for morality unless he thinks one out for himself. Parents ought to demand a school which teaches that the reason for morality is the alleviation of suffering. If you are rich, you could do a great service by helping to maintain a school where morality was taught in this honest way. You would be doing a great deal to make our lives more sincere and our morality more enlightened.

Christianity in a sense captured common decency and made itself the guardian thereof. Nevertheless, it did not itself act in a decent way. According to the Christian historian Professor Herbert Butterfield, 'the Christian church began a cruel policy of persecution from the earliest moment when it was in a position . . . to do so; while at the other end of the story both Catholic and Protestant churches fought to the last point of cruelty not merely to maintain their persecuting power—but fought a separate war for each separate weapon of persecution that was being taken from them' (*The Listener*, xli. 582-3). The Roman Church is still officially against freedom. A book published in 1948 with the imprimatur of a Roman archbishop says that a Roman State 'could not permit ⟨members of a dissenting religious group⟩ to carry on general propaganda' (*Catholic Principles of Politics*, by John A. Ryan and Francis J. Boland, New York, Macmillan, 1948, p. 320); and this immoral policy was being practised in Spain in the 1940's and 50's.

There may be another harmful aspect to the capture of morality by religion. It may be that the gods are inevitably immoral, that is, that any god that ever has been or will be conceived acts immorally in some ways. We can, of course, all easily see that other people's gods are immoral. Zeus behaved immorally; so did Moloch; and so on. I suggest that you will find that your own god is immoral too, if you can bring yourself to apply to him the moral standards that you apply to men. Surely it is immoral to condemn people to everlasting fire, or to blame them for the sins of their ancestors. Surely it is immoral to be omnipotent and yet allow the vast and continuing miseries of living things, or to demand that people believe without regard to evidence. All such conventional phrases as 'God's ways are inscrutable' are in use partly because they help to prevent us from seeing the immorality of the god we have conceived.

Now it seems likely that this immorality of all the gods so far invented is not an accident, but a necessary consequence of the religious impulse. It is probably connected with the element of worship in religion. One cannot abase oneself before a perfectly moral person, because a perfectly moral person treats one as an equal and as having a right to one's way of life.

If the gods are inevitably immoral, the idea that they are the guardians of morality is bound to do some harm. The rules of morality will be distorted from time to time by the bad behaviour of their guardians. This, then, seems to be a way in which the capture of morality by religion is always unfortunate.

It sometimes happens, however, that the captive eats the life out of his captor. The capture of morality by religion ends, sometimes, in religion's becoming nothing but a picturesque or mythical form of morality. This was the position of Matthew Arnold in *Literature and Dogma*, where he wrote that 'religion is . . . morality touched by emotion' (p. 47), that 'the object of religion is conduct' (p. 144), and that God is the eternal Power, not ourselves, that makes for righteousness (p. 303). In this stage people make no independent effort to communicate with their god or find out his nature; they infer his nature from their own moral views. Plato knows that 'God likes a joke' (*Cra.* 406 C) simply by knowing that it is good to joke sometimes. Benjamin Franklin knows that 'God helps them that helps themselves', although this contradicts the New Testament, because as a sturdy Yankee trader he knows that you ought to help yourself. His famous phrase is simply a mythical form of the moral law 'help yourself'. To many people nowadays god is merely the myth to which they attach their valuations. Religion, which often used to be entirely independent of morality, has become in these people nothing but morality itself in mythical guise.

If a man's religion just is his morality, then certainly he loses his morality if he loses his religion. But in maintaining that we know of no causal connexion between religion and morality, I have, of course, been speaking of religion as the worship of the gods, a combined creed and attitude which has no necessary connexion with morality at all.

The general conditions which tend to make a man behave morally are two. (1) First, his circumstances must not make it very difficult for him to obey the moral law even if he wants to. He must not be exposed to strong temptation to break it. For example, he must not be starving and penniless among people who have food but will not give him any. (2) Second, the moral law must be generally obeyed, respected, and recommended, by those among whom he lives. Departures from it must be generally met with disapproval or something more painful. Where these conditions obtain, the moral law is mostly obeyed. Where they do not obtain, it is largely disobeyed. To destroy or diminish these conditions in a community is easy, for it can be done by a devastating war. To introduce them where they do not obtain is very much harder. Each of us, however, has from time to time opportunities to do a tiny bit towards maintaining or improving the reign of the moral law.

2.86. *The ethics of the synoptic gospels*

What are Christian ethics? Many people talk as if we all knew perfectly well what they are, and the only trouble were that some of us wickedly refuse to obey them. But it seems to me that what Christian ethics are is obscure and confused and uncertain.

The cause, which makes people confident that they know what Christian ethics are, is often that they assume that they can tell them by intuition. They have only to use their intuition, which when it deals with moral questions is called conscience, and the rules of Christian morality are known to them.

All that a man can find out by intuition is what he himself considers to be the right moral laws. He cannot find out what anybody else thinks right without studying the utterances or other acts of that person. The question what Christian ethics are, however, is an historical question. It is the historical question what rules are or were recommended by the Christians. Any responsible answer to it must proceed by historical method, by ascertaining and studying the texts uttered by the Christians.

Who are the Christians? There have been Christians for nearly 2,000 years, and thousands of them have published statements claiming authority on Christian doctrine. One could hardly read them all; but it takes little reading to discover that they do not altogether agree with each other. When they disagree, which has the better right to the title 'Christian'?

The word 'Christian' is made from a title, 'Christ', given to Jesus of Nazareth. It therefore seems that the writings closest to Jesus have the best claim to be the authority on Christian doctrine. Therefore the New Testament has a better claim than any subsequent writing by fathers or bishops or doctors or theologians or popes. Within the New Testament itself we can distinguish changes or at least additions of doctrine. There is a great deal in the epistles that is not in the gospels. There is a great deal in John's gospel that is not in Matthew, Mark, or Luke. There is a great deal in Matthew that is not in Mark. On the whole, Matthew, Mark, and Luke, stand together against John, and are much closer to each other than any of them is to John. For this reason it is often convenient to refer to the three of them together as 'the synoptics'. The synoptic gospels, then, seem to have the best title of any book to give the Christian ethics.

If, then, we wish to answer the question What are Christian ethics?, the first thing to do is to read the synoptic gospels and try to interpret them correctly.

The interpretation of a book written far away and long ago is always very liable to error. The interpretation of the synoptic gospels suffers from two additional and unusual sources of error. The first of these is that an overwhelming host of other interpreters has gone before us, and their results are ringing in our ears, and many of their results are more familiar to us than the words of the gospels themselves. The second is that we have been given an immensely strong bias to believe that whatever is affirmed in these gospels is rightly affirmed, and hence we have a perverting tendency to read into them whatever we personally think to be the true values, and to read out of them any false values they may at first appear to us to preach.

Even the most learned and responsible interpreters make this second mistake, and misinterpret a passage through the conviction that it cannot really be intended to recommend something which the interpreter is sure is disapprovable. Thus Dr. Lonsdale Ragg says of the passage on the ravens which neither sow nor reap, &c. (Luke xii. 22 ff. *Commentary on Saint Luke*, London, 1922, p. 181), that it 'cannot really be intended as a counsel of improvidence. It is rather a warning against that over-reliance upon dividends, and that degeneration of thrift into grasping greed which are characteristic of our time.' Dr. Ragg gives no reason for his statement that this passage cannot be what it seems to be, a recommendation of improvidence and a rejection of thrift. But it is obvious what reason he had in mind: he was saying to himself: 'Improvidence is bad, and Jesus never recommended anything bad; therefore he never recommended improvidence; therefore this passage is not really a recommendation of improvidence though it seems to be.'

Yet, when you come to think of it, the principle that 'Jesus never recommended anything which we think bad' is one that would make it rather useless to read the gospels. In interpreting them so that they always agreed with our valuations, we should be teaching Jesus rather than learning from him. In any case, it is a principle that is most unlikely to be true, and therefore most unlikely to guide us aright in interpreting the gospels; for the fluidity of human affairs, and the huge difference between our society and heritage and those of Jesus, make it extremely unlikely that all our valuations would be the same as his. If we suspect that a passage in the gospels does not mean what it appears to mean, then the test to apply to it, or rather the background against which to examine it, is not the valuations of the twentieth century but the rest of the gospels. The best way of deciding the meaning of any passage in the synoptic gospels is to look at it against the background of those gospels as a whole.

To interpret the gospels correctly you must read them with what may be called interpreter's piety, that is, the will to receive into your mind the exact meaning the author intended, however strange or repellent or boring it may turn out to be. I urge you to do this, or at least not to use the phrase 'Christian values' until you have done it. I do not mean to say that it will never help to study Palestinian history, or that you need never ask a learned scholar the meaning of some peculiar phrase. I mean that the chief thing you need to do is to read the gospels for yourself, in the original Greek if you know Greek, with the open mind of the pious interpreter, and try to see for yourself what they say.

I will now describe the ethical teaching of the synoptic gospels as it appeared to me the last time I studied it. After that, I will ask to what extent this teaching should be accepted.

These writings are by no means wholly, or even primarily, concerned with ethical teaching, that is, with telling us what things are good and what acts should be done. As one learned and responsible exponent has put it, namely T. W. Manson in his book *The Teaching of Jesus*, pp. 285-6, 'the "ethics of Jesus", in the sense in which . . . many . . . think of them, do not exist, and never have existed'. He explains that this is because 'the moral teaching of Jesus is part and parcel of his religion and is not separable from it except by violence'. What the synoptics are mainly concerned to do is to tell a story, the story of the wonderful life, death, and resurrection, of Jesus of Nazareth. Each of them is in form a biography rather than a collection of commandments and valuations. In each of them, and especially in Mark, Jesus is primarily not a teacher or moralist but a mysterious and miraculous divine leader.

However, this divine leader occupies himself largely with ethical teaching, especially according to Matthew; and we can give some general account of the nature of this teaching.

In the first place, it is quite unsystematic. There is nothing like a treatise. There is hardly even a methodical list like the Ten Commandments of the Old Testament. The teaching appears to consist of many separate and independent sayings. Unities like Matthew's Sermon on the Mount appear to be conflations by the writer, not original and connected discourses by Jesus. In one saying Jesus says which is the greatest commandment and which is the second greatest (Matt. xxii. 37 ff.); there is no other mention of the question how all these precepts and valuations are to be co-ordinated.

In the second place, a great deal of the teaching is vague, puzzling, or obscure. Much of it consists of fascinating but mysterious stories whose point is doubtful, such as that of the wise and foolish virgins. One does not know what to make of sentences like: 'The foxes have holes, and the birds of the air have nests; but the Son of man hath not where to lay his head.' Many even of the direct exhortations are very uncertain in meaning. For example, 'blessed are the pure in heart'; what is purity in heart? Is it virtue in general or is it a special virtue? In many cases little can be done to elucidate an obscure saying by comparing other parts of the texts, owing to their fragmentary or atomic character. Sometimes, however, light can be brought by scholars who are familiar with other Jewish writings. In this way, for example, it can be made probable that 'give not that which is holy unto the dogs' means 'do not tell my gospel to anyone who is not a Jew'.

The teaching includes both very general precepts on which great emphasis is laid, and discussions of middling matters including divorce, and some small change of moral advice, such as 'if thy brother shall trespass against thee, go and tell him his fault between thee and him alone'.

The teaching is paradoxical and intended to be so. The writers represent Jesus as one who repeatedly uttered statements, valuations, and commands, that seemed to most people odd or shocking. He is given to sayings like 'the last shall be first, and the first last', and 'whosoever will be chief among you, let him be your servant'. Though in one saying he condemns making a scandal (Matt. xviii. 6 ff.), yet in another he implies that his own preaching makes scandal (Matt. xiii. 21); and Matthew often speaks of people being scandalized by him. Most people are in fact scandalized by the saying that 'whosoever hath, to him shall be given, and he shall have more abundance; but whosoever hath not, from him shall be taken away even that he hath'.

The teaching has a prominent strain of harshness in it. Jesus threatens weeping and gnashing of teeth. He threatens great misery to those who do not receive his missionaries (Mark vi. 11). He threatens damnation to those who do not believe in his gospel (Mark xvi. 16), and to those who blaspheme against the Holy Ghost (Mark iii. 29). He is remarkably abusive (cf. Matt. xi. 20), especially towards the Pharisees, with whom he at least once engages in cleversilly argument (Matt. xxii. 15-22). He harshly neglects his family relations for his gospel (Matt. xii. 46 ff.). He expects his gospel to result in parricide and in the betrayal of brothers and children to death (Matt. x, especially verse 21). He withers a fig-tree and destroys a herd of swine. Matthew Arnold seems to me far from the truth when he finds 'sweet reasonableness' in Jesus. There are a few 'sweet and comfortable sayings'; but the prevailing atmosphere is harsh. One of his most judicious twentieth-century followers, Professor T. W. Manson (*The Sayings of Jesus*, p. 75), acknowledges 'the seeming harshness of Jesus and His almost brutal thrusting into the background of natural feelings and obligations', but puts it down to 'the overwhelming urgency of His task'.

So much for the general character of the sayings; and now for the five main commandments which I find.

(1) According to Matthew the first words of the preaching both of John the Baptist and of Jesus were: 'Repent, for the kingdom of heaven is at hand.' Later Matthew says that Jesus said: 'Thou shalt love the Lord thy God with all thy heart, and with all thy soul, and with all thy mind. This is the first and great commandment.' Devotion to God, or piety, stands out as Jesus' main precept. It appears in two different forms, love and righteousness. On the one hand, we are to love God. On the other, we are to repent and be righteous.

This first precept appears to be absolute in Jesus' mind. No other precept or interest may in any circumstance override it. He demands its fulfilment no matter what the damage to all other interests, and he expects the damage to other interests to be very great. Among these consequent damages may be strife, the sword, and the denial of family claims. Devotion to God will involve the keen disapproval of others: 'blessed are ye, when men shall revile you, and persecute you, and shall say all manner of evil against you falsely, for my sake.' It will involve poverty: 'ye cannot serve God and mammon'; 'blessed be ye poor, for your's is the kingdom of God'. Jesus is against all prudent provision of material goods to avoid poverty and provide for the future. That would interfere with devotion to God, and is unnecessary because the kingdom of God is at hand. He frequently and consistently recommends improvidence and taking no thought for the morrow. 'Lay not up for yourselves treasures upon earth.' Imitate instead the fowls of the air, which neither sow nor reap nor gather into barns. Sell everything you have and follow me (Luke xviii. 22). Give to everyone who asks you (Luke vi. 30). He is against attempting to make ourselves materially secure; and he gives the impression of never having had the thought that, if we all followed his advice, everybody would soon be permanently poorer. His famous story of the Prodigal Son is the story of a waster who got on as well as or better than his careful and responsible brother; and he has several other stories to urge the same moral, that the laborious preserver of material goods neither gets nor deserves more reward than his opposite. As a complete substitute for thrift and prudence he recommends prayer and faith. 'Ask, and it shall be given to you.'

(2) Closely related to this first precept, but distinguishable therefrom, comes what appears to be Jesus' second command: 'Believe in me.' Jesus is represented by the evangelists as constantly demanding faith in himself and declaring it a sin not to believe in him.

The expression 'believe in me' seems obscure. Sometimes Jesus merely says 'believe' or 'have faith', expressions which are more obscure. The naïve reader today feels inclined to ask: 'Believe *what* precisely?' The answer is not 'believe that I can do miracles', for the evangelists assume that everybody who had heard of Jesus already believed that. The answer, if it is given at all, is given in a few obscure phrases such as 'that Jesus is the anointed' or that 'he is the son of man' or that 'he is the son of God'. But Jesus is represented as noticeably unwilling to utter such phrases himself. He tries to get others to utter them without uttering them himself.

The notion of faith, later to become a characteristic and prominent Christian virtue, appears in the gospels mainly in connexion with this precept, 'believe in me'.

This precept is probably much the most novel of Jesus' precepts.

Learned commentators show anticipations by other rabbis of most of Jesus' other rules; but naturally there are no anticipations of the rule that we should believe in Jesus.

(3) Jesus' third precept is the love of man. 'Thou shalt love thy neighbour as thyself.' He numbers it as second in importance; for he does not reckon his 'believe in me' when the question is what the commandments are. He regards the command to love the neighbour not as his own invention but as one of the established commandments. It does in fact occur in Lev. xix. 18. But he regards himself as extending it by adding: 'Love your enemies, do good to them that hate you, bless them that curse you, pray for them that despitefully use you.' He does not say explicitly that this applies even to Gentile enemies; but his story of the Good Samaritan, told in answer to the question 'Who is my neighbour?', probably means that we should love and help every human being.

He regards his extended law of love as entailing non-resistance to evil. 'To him that smiteth thee on the one cheek offer also the other; and from him that taketh away thy cloke withhold not thy coat also.' It entails also generosity: 'Give to everyone that asketh thee; and of him that taketh away thy goods ask them not again.' It entails the golden rule: 'As ye would that men should do to you, do ye also to them likewise.' It entails forgiveness, even for the seventy-times-seventh offence. No doubt it is the reason for the beatitudes: 'Blessed are the gentle. . . . Blessed are the merciful' (Matt. v. 5-7). No doubt it is the source of the few comfortable and kindly sayings ascribed to Jesus in these gospels, such as: 'Come unto me, all ye that labour and are heavy laden, and I will give you rest' (Matt. xi. 28).

It is difficult to see, however, what Jesus' law of love can amount to in practice in view of his overwhelming insistence on the priority of the law of piety. We cannot give material help to our neighbours because the law of piety demands improvidence and poverty. We cannot take family love very seriously because it may interfere with our devotions. Any two rules of conduct will conflict in some cases; and it seems quite clear that Jesus' first two rules must conflict very often. But, in accordance with the unsystematic character of Jesus' teaching, there is no recognition of this in the gospels. There is hardly a recognition of any possibility of conflict between any two rules; but perhaps Professor Manson is right in saying that the verse, 'There is none other commandment greater than these' (Mark xii.

31), implies that the first two commandments may clash with the rest, and declares how such a clash is to be decided (*The Sayings of Jesus*, p. 227).

(4) Jesus' first three precepts are, then, love God, believe in me, and love man. I know no obvious name for or summary expression of what appears to be his next most important precept. I will call it purity of heart, though this involves a mere guess as to how he himself actually used the word 'pure'. The precept is that we are to regulate our thoughts in the same ways as we are to regulate our actions, that the laws are to be maintained internally as well as externally. It is suggested at length in Matt. v. 21 ff.: 'Ye have heard that it was said by them of old time, Thou shalt not kill. . . . But I say unto you, That whosoever is angry with his brother without a cause shall be in danger of the judgment'; and so on. It is also probably the meaning of the doctrine that 'that which cometh out of the mouth, this defileth a man'. It is probably the cause of the critical and reserved attitude of Jesus towards the explicit rules of law and behaviour and ceremony reigning in his society and maintained by the priests. He repudiates the idea that ritual, and ritual laws, can exist for their own sake, appealing to the saying that 'I desire pity and not sacrifice'.

(5) The fifth and last of the major precepts I find in the synoptic gospels is the demand for humility. We are to ταπεινοῦν ourselves, to humiliate or lower ourselves. This will involve preventing ourselves from feeling contempt; we are not to despise one of these little ones, which probably implies that we are not to despise anyone. It will involve not judging people. 'Judge not, that ye be not judged.' It will involve avoiding displays of superiority; for example, we should do good in secret, not in public. It will involve not caring about one's prestige, and not demanding honours or recognition, though perhaps accepting them when offered. It will involve serving others, including serving them in low ways such as washing their feet. It will involve, or be, something more central than all these, something inward and mental, which Jesus does not define and I am not prepared to define, but which is suggested by this lovely story: 'Two men went up into the temple to pray; the one a Pharisee, and the other a publican. The Pharisee stood and prayed thus with himself, God, I thank thee, that I am not as other men are, extortioners, unjust, adulterers, or even as this publican. I fast twice in the week, I give tithes of all that I possess. And the publican,

standing afar off, would not lift up so much as his eyes unto heaven, but smote upon his breast, saying, God be merciful to me a sinner.' (Luke xviii. 10-13).

These, then, are the five major precepts I find in the synoptic gospels: love God, believe in me, love man, be pure in heart, be humble. We may infer that the greatest virtues are piety, faith, love, purity, and humility; and that the only great goods beyond these virtues are God and Jesus.

Does Jesus offer reasons why we should adopt these precepts? In keeping with the unsystematic and gnomic character of his sayings in general, he has no elaborate argumentation in favour of them. He has, however, two brief reasons for them, which he frequently utters. One is that the kingdom of heaven is at hand. The other is that those who obey these precepts will be rewarded in heaven, while those who disobey will have weeping and gnashing of teeth. 'Your reward shall be great in heaven.' It is a plain matter of promises and threats.

Certain ideals that are prominent elsewhere are rather conspicuously absent from the synoptic gospels. It is important to notice these because, if they have been strongly adopted since Jesus' day, they are liable to be wrongly labelled Christian and included in the Christian values.

The ideal of beauty is wholly absent from this teaching. Beauty is entirely ignored, unless in the reference to the lilies of the field it is used to enforce the lesson of improvidence.

The ideal of truth and knowledge is wholly absent from this teaching. On the contrary, Jesus poured contempt on the professors of knowledge, and declared that the kingdom of heaven is hidden from the wise and prudent and revealed unto babes. He frequently inclined to secrecy. At the same time as he was making public demonstrations of miraculous power, he kept trying to keep it a secret that he had this power, according to frequent statements by Mark and some statements by Matthew. He has some sayings according to which his teaching is a mystification rather than a spreading of truth: 'Unto you it is given to know the mystery of the kingdom of God: but unto them that are without, all these things are done in parables: That seeing they may see, and not perceive; and hearing they may hear, and not understand; lest at any time they should be converted, and their sins should be forgiven them' (Mark iv. 11-12).

As Jesus never recommends knowledge, so he never recommends the virtue that seeks and leads to knowledge, namely reason. On the contrary, he regards certain beliefs as in themselves sinful (such beliefs as that 'Jesus is not the son of God'), whereas it is an essential part of the ideal of reason to hold that no belief can be morally wrong if reached in the attempt to believe truly. Jesus again and again demands faith; and by faith he means believing certain very improbable things without considering evidence or estimating probabilities; and that is contrary to reason.

The virtue of conscientiousness, of respect for the moral law, has been placed very high by many subsequent Christians, especially among the Protestants; but it is not placed high by Jesus. The mere keeping of moral commandments appears to offend Jesus rather than to please him, and he condemns it as Phariseeism.

Jesus says nothing on any social question except divorce, and all ascriptions of any political doctrine to him are false. He does not pronounce about war, capital punishment, gambling, justice, the administration of law, the distribution of goods, socialism, equality of income, equality of sex, equality of colour, equality of opportunity, tyranny, freedom, slavery, selfdetermination, or contraception. There is nothing Christian about being for any of these things, nor about being against them, if we mean by 'Christian' what Jesus taught according to the synoptic gospels.

The Jesus of the synoptic gospels says little on the subject of sex. He is against divorce. He speaks of adultery as a vice, and perhaps includes in adultery all extramarital intercourse. The story of the woman taken in adultery, which is of a synoptic character though it appears in texts of John, preaches a humane and forgiving attitude towards sexual errors. Jesus shows no trace of that dreadful hatred of sex as such which has disfigured the subsequent history of the Christian churches, or of the disgusting idea that sexual intercourse is sinful in itself, and that, as the English prayer book has it, marriage 'was ordained for a remedy against sin, and to avoid fornication ⟨for⟩ such persons as have not the gift of continency'. The nearest he comes to that is saying that 'there be eunuchs, which have made themselves eunuchs for the kingdom of heaven's sake' (Matt. xix. 12). But he declares that 'he which made them at the beginning made them male and female, and said, For this cause shall a man leave father and mother, and shall cleave to his wife: and they twain shall be one flesh' (Matt. xix. 4–5); and this cannot mean sexless marriage.

2.87. *Criticism of the synoptic gospels*

Now I come to the attempt to judge these precepts and say which of them we should accept.

If one has been brought up in the Christian religion, it is easy to feel that there is something fundamentally wicked in judging whether to adopt these precepts. But this feeling we ought to repress. It is easy to fall into an attitude of superstitious and unquestioning awe towards the precepts in the gospels, and to adopt every one of them in automatic and thoughtless submission. But this we ought not to do. We ought to judge these precepts as we judge any other precepts or valuations, weighing their value in the light of reason and love, considering whether to adopt or reject them by asking whether they lessen human misery or do not lessen it.

As a corrective to the uncritical attitude, it is well to bear in mind that the synoptic gospels are very like folktales. Like good folktales, they are strange and beautiful and suggestive, and often embody principles that we wish to adopt. Also like good folktales, however, they often embody principles that we judge barbarous and wish to reject.

Evidently the precepts of Jesus do not provide all the values and rules we need. They do not preach the three great Greek inventions, truth, beauty, and justice, which we certainly must have. They do not recognize the inevitability of conflict between the commandments, and hence give little or no judicious guidance in cases of conflict. Evidently, also, their completely unsystematic character entitles us to pick and choose among them, accepting some and rejecting others if we so judge.

Newman said that when non-Christians read the Christian Bible 'they are much struck with the high tone of its precepts' (Sermon on John xiii. 17). That is contrary to my experience. I shall never forget the first time I read the Old Testament after I had acquired the habit of independent judgement. I was horrified at its barbarity, and bewildered that it had been widely held up as a store of ideals. It seemed to describe a savage people, fierce and brutal, no more admirable than the worse of the savage cultures that anthropologists describe to us today, and a great deal less admirable than the gentler cultures they report. The only major difference between the Old Testament, and an anthropologist's report of a rather brutal culture, seems to be that the Old Testament is written by members of the culture described, who adopt its superstitions and approve of its habits.

Nor will Newman's words fit the impression made by the synoptic gospels. They are a beautiful and fascinating piece of literature; and they preach the great precept 'love thy neighbour'. But this precept is overshadowed in them both by the harsh unloving behaviour of the preacher, and by its absolute subordination to the unreasonable commands to love God and believe in Jesus.

We should reject Jesus' first two precepts, love God and believe in me; and we should reject the values that he associates therewith, piety, faith, and improvidence. It is improbable that there is a god; but, even if it were probable, that would not justify Jesus' demand for piety, because he makes his demand without reference to probability, and because he is reckless of its effects on humanity. Whether the pious man is a benefit or a terror to his fellow men depends, of course, on what he believes his god tells him to do; but it is evident that many of man's most terrible actions have been done out of piety, and that piety is responsible for our shameful wars of religion, and that concern to obey a god is less likely to diminish human misery than is concern to diminish human misery.

It is most important to reject the view that it is a sin not to believe in Jesus; for the view that a belief can be sinful is very harmful and wrong. It destroys the whole ideal of knowledge and reason, and prevents man from achieving the knowledge in which much of his dignity and much of his safety lie. No belief is as such morally wrong; but it is morally wrong to form one's beliefs in view of something other than truth and probability; and Jesus demanded this moral wrong. It is a moral wrong whose harmful and degrading effects penetrate widely and are great. It is terrible to think how many million people have, as a result of those passages in the gospels about having faith, done what probably each one of us here did in his childhood, tried to hypnotize himself into some particular belief and to disregard whatever scraps of judgement he possessed. The fine things in Jesus' preaching have been and will be greatly harmed by this blasphemy against reason.

It is a typical nemesis on blasphemy against reason that through it Jesus came to exhibit in himself or ascribe to his god some of the bad qualities against which he warned humanity. While he preached humility, he weakened his effect by insisting with considerable asperity on his own divinity or semi-divinity, and demanding that everyone should believe in him. While he preached to men that they should forgive, he threatened unforgiving damnation to those who disbelieved himself or his missionaries, and represented his god as going to produce weeping and gnashing of teeth. While he preached love, he showed an unloving god. To demonstrate his miraculous power he destroyed useful living things.

We should reject also that praise of poverty and improvidence which he bases on these precepts. Human life depends on material resources, and they should not be neglected or thrown away. A proper concern for the misery of creatures involves the husbanding of our wealth.

At the same time we all know that some of Jesus' words on this matter hint at something acceptable and important, especially his 'how hardly shall a rich man enter into the kingdom of heaven'. That many rich people succumb to a frozen and hideous inhumanity, while the poor are sometimes gloriously lovingkind to each other, is clear to see among us. But what principles are there to guide us aright in this matter? It seems that we have not yet discovered them. The best that we have so far is Aristotle's doctrine that property should be private in ownership but public in use, if this is to be interpreted as saying that every owner of material goods is to act with the aim of making them as widely used and enjoyed as possible. He is to fence off his snakeflowers, for example, because otherwise they would all be eradicated in a few years; but he is to take all means he can of letting as many persons as possible enjoy them without destroying them.

We should accept the precept to love our neighbours, extended as Jesus perhaps extended it to love of all humanity, and still further to love of all life, as he certainly did not extend it. And if we reject his precepts to love god and believe in himself, this precept to love man will be able to amount to something and deeply affect our lives. We should accept most of the consequential attitudes that he indicates, generosity, gentleness, mercy, and the observance of the golden rule.

Forgiveness is also to be accepted. But there seems to be something injudicious in his 'seventy times seven', and something still more injudicious in his doctrine of non-resistance. Invariable non-resistance certainly does harm to the world that could be avoided by resistance on occasion. It is no contribution to human happiness always to yield to bullies, but very much the reverse. It is true, however, that many people resist too often.

As to the fourth precept, that we are to regulate our thoughts in the same ways as we are to regulate our actions, it seems to condemn imagination. In imagination, in painting and sculpture, and most of all in fiction, we enjoy the imaginative contemplation of acts that we ought not to do. There is a great and permanent and rather evenly balanced difference of valuation here, half the world approving and the other half disapproving of the contemplation of evil in imagination and art. I am among the approvers, because I find in this activity great interest and happiness, and because I believe that it discourages more than it encourages the performance of wrong acts. I believe that wrong acts are done much more by the unimaginative than by the imaginative, and much more by those who have not contemplated wrong acts in fiction than by those who have. I therefore do not much care to adopt and recommend this precept. However, some writing, and some thinking, are precisely a creation of the intention to do something wrong, and these must be wrong if the thing to be done is wrong. If we understand the precept as directed against this it seems trivial; while if we understand it as against imagination it seems bad.

There is a third way in which we might understand this precept, namely as an injunction not to encourage dangerous emotions or desires, such as anger with one's brother and sexual desire for a forbidden person. And this is the most favourable way to interpret it. It is certainly a distinct interpretation from the first, for imagination and emotion are not the same thing and need not go together.

The fifth and last precept was that of humility. The words 'humility', 'pride', and 'vanity', indicate a complicated and mysterious set of questions about human nature and the evaluation thereof. Though I have thought about this mysterious complex for years, I have not yet reached views on it in which I can rest. Only the following points seem clear to me.

First, it seems undesirable either to lie about one's own value or to be mistaken about it, and this seems to be so whether the false statement overestimates or underestimates one's value. The only good estimate of one's value to have, or to utter, is, surely, the true estimate. The value of humility cannot override the value of truth.

Secondly, it seems clear that we should act according to our actual superiorities and inferiorities. The superior man in a group should lead the group and not hang back. The less informed man in a group should hang back and not offer to inform the company.

Thirdly, it is clear that we often have a choice, between uttering and not uttering remarks about our own value and superiority or inferiority, and between calling attention to our value and not doing so. That being so, the right choice will usually be to refrain from drawing attention either to our superiorities or to our inferiorities. The main criterion of good conversation is what will please others; and the boaster and the selfdepreciator are both unpleasing. But where the conversation has an ulterior purpose, such as the appointment of an officer, these considerations are overridden.

Fourthly, to insist on the recognition of one's superiorities by others, as Aristotle's megalopsychic man so remarkably does, is rarely good, though occasionally it is required. It is not a common vice nowadays. The virtue of modesty is in fashion. Not that the vice of pride has disappeared. It is flourishing mightily in the place where it has hidden itself, namely in politics. Though most people are modest about themselves, nearly everybody insists far too much on the excellence and prestige and honour and glory of his own State, and almost nobody ever recommends his own State to behave humbly, or talks humbly about it.

Fifthly, we should know the true value of others as well as of ourselves; and in that sense we should reject Jesus' 'judge not'. It would be absurd to give up the lawcourts and the accusation and judgement of suspected persons. It would be absurd never to decide that an act was wrong, or an agent inclined to do wrong. 'Judge not' may serve, however, to suggest two desirable principles, first that it is easy to spend too much time in remarking other people's defects, and second that contempt is an emotion for which there is very little place in a good man's heart. Not contempt, but a certain kind of respect, is always required towards all persons, however petty their capacities and however loathsome their crimes. This respect is required towards all higher animals as well, and for the same reason, namely that they are all sufferers and have the rights which suffering gives. I would say they are all equal in this way, were it not that there are more obvious kinds of equality which are bad.

Finally, the reasons that Jesus gave for his precepts, namely his promises and threats, are quite unacceptable. They are false, since there is no heaven or hell; and anyhow they make his precepts precepts of prudence instead of precepts of morality. To obey rules because otherwise you will go to hell is prudence, not morality. The good and moral reason for a moral precept is that its reign in a society lessens misery in that society.

2.88. *The human situation*

The human situation is this.

Each one of us dies. He ceases to pulse or breathe or move or think. He decays and loses his identity. His mind or soul or spirit ends with the ending of his body, because it is entirely dependent on his body.

The human species too will die one day, like all species of life. One day there will be no more men. This is not quite so probable as that each individual man will die; but it is overwhelmingly probable all the same. It seems very unlikely that we could keep the race going for ever by hopping from planet to planet as each in turn cooled down. Only in times of extraordinary prosperity like the present could we ever travel to another planet at all.

We are permanently insecure. We are permanently in danger of loss, damage, misery, and death.

Our insecurity is due partly to our ignorance. There is a vast amount that we do not know, and some of it is very relevant to our survival and happiness. It is not just one important thing that we do not know. If it were, we might hope to discover that one important thing and live secure ever after. That one important thing would then deserve to be called 'the secret of the universe'. But there is no one secret of the universe. On the contrary, there are inexhaustibly many things about the universe that we need to know but do not know. There is no possibility of 'making sense of the universe', if that means discovering one truth about it which explains everything else about it and also explains itself. Our ignorance grows progressively less, at least during periods of enormous prosperity like the present time; but it cannot disappear, and must always leave us liable to unforeseen disasters.

The main cause of our insecurity is the limitedness of our power. What happens to us depends largely on forces we cannot always control. This will remain so throughout the life of our species, although our power will probably greatly increase.

There is no god to make up for the limitations of our power, to rescue us whenever the forces affecting us get beyond our control, or provide us hereafter with an incorruptible haven of absolute security. We have no superhuman father who is perfectly competent and benevolent as we perhaps once supposed our actual father to be.

What attitude ought we to take up, in view of this situation?

It would be senseless to be rebellious, since there is no god to rebel against. It would be wrong to let disappointment or terror or apathy or folly overcome us. It would be wrong to be sad or sarcastic or cynical or indignant. A. E. Housman has imagined some of the wrong attitudes very poetically for us.

> High heaven and earth ail from the prime foundation;
> All thoughts to rive the heart are here, and all are vain :
> Horror and scorn and hate and fear and indignation—
> Oh why did I awake? when shall I sleep again?

Or the words he gives to Terence Hearsay:

> Therefore, since the world has still
> Much good, but much less good than ill,
> And while the sun and moon endure
> Luck's a chance, but trouble's sure,
> I'd face it as a wise man would,
> And train for ill and not for good.
> 'Tis true, the stuff I bring for sale
> Is not so brisk a brew as ale:
> Out of a stem that scored the hand
> I wrung it in a weary land.
> But take it: if the smack is sour,
> The better for the embittered hour;
> It should do good to heart and head
> When your soul is in my soul's stead;
> And I will friend you, if I may,
> In the dark and cloudy day.

No; in a dark and cloudy day a book of humour is better than *The Shropshire Lad*; and one of the important parts of 'training for ill' is to acquire cheerfulness.

Cheerfulness is part of courage, and courage is an essential part of the right attitude. Let us not tell ourselves a comforting tale of a father in heaven because we are afraid to be alone, but bravely and cheerfully face whatever appears to be the truth.

The theist sometimes rebukes the pleasure-seeker by saying: 'We were not put here to enjoy ourselves; man has a sterner and nobler purpose than that.' The atheist's conception of man is, however, still sterner and nobler than that of the theist. According to the theist we were put here by an all-powerful and all-benevolent god who will give us eternal victory and happiness if we only obey him. According to the atheist our situation is far sterner than that. There is no one to look after us but ourselves, and we shall certainly be defeated.

As our situation is far sterner than the theist dares to think, so our possible attitude towards it is far nobler than he conceives. When we contemplate the friendless position of man in the universe, as it is right sometimes to do, our attitude should be the tragic poet's affirmation of man's ideals of behaviour. Our dignity, and our finest occupation, is to assert and maintain our own selfchosen goods as long as we can, those great goods of beauty and truth and virtue. And among the virtues it is proper to mention in this connexion above all the virtues of courage and love. There is no person in this universe to love us except ourselves; therefore let us love one another. The human race is alone; but individual men need not be alone, because we have each other. We are brothers without a father; let us all the more for that behave brotherly to each other. The finest achievement for humanity is to recognize our predicament, including our insecurity and our coming extinction, and to maintain our cheerfulness and love and decency in spite of it, to prosecute our ideals in spite of it. We have good things to contemplate and high things to do. Let us do them.

We need to create and spread symbols and procedures that will confirm our intentions without involving us in intellectual dishonesty. This need is urgent today. For we have as yet no strong ceremonies to confirm our resolves except religious ceremonies, and most of us cannot join in religious ceremonies with a good conscience. When the *Titanic* went down, people sang 'Nearer, my God, to thee'. When the Gloucesters were in prison in North Korea they strengthened themselves with religious ceremonies. At present we know no other way to strengthen ourselves in our most testing and tragic times. Yet this way has become dishonest. That is why it is urgent for us to create new ceremonies, through which to find strength without falsehood in these terrible situations. It is not enough to formulate honest and high ideals. We must also create the ceremonies and the atmosphere that will hold them before us at all times. I have no conception how to do this; but I believe it will be done if we try.

3

POLITICAL GOODS

3.1. The State	158
3.2. Equality	173
3.3. Freedom	187
3.4. Tolerance	198
3.5. Peace and Justice	219
3.6. Democracy	228

3.1. THE STATE

3.11. *Political goods*

POLITICAL goods are goods arising out of the existence of governments. Some of them are goods which governments are designed to obtain, as peace and security; but the phrase 'political goods' does not mean goods which governments are designed to obtain, for it covers also goods which governments lessen rather than increase, as freedom. Political goods are those goods which arise out of the existence of government, either as aims of government or as aims against government or in some other way. They include peace, security, freedom, equality, justice, democracy, tolerance, and the State.

There is a tendency to set up as one's great goods either personal goods or political goods but not both. Plato, though profoundly interested in politics, finds his ideal in philosophic contemplation of the eternal forms; his justice is more a personal virtue than a political good; and the only political goods which he strongly favours are order and peace. Aristotle, though he wrote a wise book on politics, also expresses his ideal in terms of contemplation and personal virtues. The New Testament recognizes no political good whatever, so that phrases like 'Christian justice' have no proper meaning. G. E. Moore in his *Principia Ethica* concluded that the only two great goods were personal affection and the enjoyment of beauty.

Those, on the other hand, who do proclaim political goods tend to proclaim only political goods. On the whole, the more leftwing a party is the more it seems to recognize no goods but the political. Conservatism, on the contrary, tends to recognize very few political goods, and to hold that the proper aim of politics is only to foster personal goods. Liberalism is a middle attitude which fairly explicitly recognizes both personal and political goods; this is my own position.

The assumption that all great goods are purely political appears to me to be part of the barbarism of Marx's followers, and to have nothing to recommend it. The opposite extreme, however, that no political good is in the first rank, has several plausible arguments.

In the first place, many people believe it because they believe that political goods are all means, not ends. Peace and justice and security, they think, are merely conditions necessary for us to pursue and enjoy the true ends of man. These ends themselves are all of another nature, such as contemplation and love.

Others omit the political goods because they judge them thoroughly empty or confused. Thus Croce, according to Professor Berlin, held 'that such concepts as liberty or equality, as they occur in the polemical writings of e.g. Marxists or anti-Marxists, are, as a rule, quite wooden and without application. Any attempt to hold up such uninterpreted notions as ideals, or to continue to speak of them in accordance with some dogmatic formula, necessarily springs from, and leads to, a distortion both of thought and of action' (*Mind*, 1952, p. 576).

A third reason for the view that no political good is in the first rank is the negative air of several of the political goods. Freedom appears to be merely the absence of compulsion, security merely the absence of disaster, peace merely the absence of violence, equality merely the absence of humiliation, and so on.

I do not find these considerations convincing. The distinction between means and end, when applied to the question what things are good, appears to me to lead to an absurd devaluation of nearly all values, as I have argued at length in an earlier lecture. The vagueness and negativity of most political goods, which I admit, appear to me powerless to disprove our conviction that these goods do very strongly engage our hearts and may rightly do so. Love is vague, and non-resistance is negative; but no one thinks that these are good reasons for excluding love and non-resistance from a list of great goods. I proceed to examine some things that are considered great goods in the political sphere, hoping that, where I adopt the common opinion that it is a great good, my discussion will show the reasonableness of doing so.

3.12. *Is the State a great good?*

In the sphere of politics one of the things that are greatly valued is the State. The State is often regarded as a kind of god on earth, demanding our worship and service, and worthy of them. It is thought to be the source of all that is noble and free and moral in human nature and society, the means of our control of ourselves in the interest of the good. According to Acton (Fasnacht, *Acton's Political Philosophy*, p. 139), the State was the ideal of Richelieu, of Peter the Great, of Frederick the Great, of Napoleon, and of Bismarck. Down to the 1950's or later, members of the British Labour Party could be heard talking of 'the State' in tones of emotional and moralistic approval. On this view we are called upon to worship the State, and to make the good of the State our ultimate good, that is, to sacrifice our own good to the good of the State when there is a conflict.

In what consists this good of the State for which we are called upon to sacrifice ourselves? Strange to say, many of the State's admirers, while they call upon us to sacrifice ourselves to its good, leave us rather in the dark as to what they conceive that good to be. This is notably true of Plato and Aristotle, both of them admirers or worshippers of the City-State, but neither of them very explicit about its good. Plato vaguely gives the impression of thinking that the good of the city lies in a beautiful condition of harmonious order, like a handsome statue or painting. Aristotle seems to find it rather in the citizens' being virtuous.

In modern times two other conceptions of the State's good have come forward. One of these is that the State's good lies in its reputation or prestige. Actions and omissions are frequently recommended or deplored today on account of their effect on the State's prestige. Every aspect of life is liable to be drawn into the service of the State's prestige. People demand more support for whatever they are doing on the ground that the present level of support is inadequate to the State's prestige, and liable to put the State behind in the race against other States for top prestige. There have recently been astounding manifestations of this spirit in games and physical sports, so that the Olympic festivals have come to look like mock wars, less dangerous but more ill-tempered than the real ones. The prestige idea has also invaded what used to be called the international realm of science; and not merely journalists, but often also the scientists themselves, report their progress as being 'a satisfactory indication of Britain's determination to keep in the forefront' (*Times Science Review*, 1952, Winter, article on the radio telescope at Jodrell Bank, Cheshire). Every history of science or invention tells us that nearly all the great advances have been made by fellow citizens of the author.

Lastly, the good of the State is nowadays often thought to lie in its power. 'The State strives after power, just as a man strives after food', and 'an elemental power-impulse must already be present in the statesman himself, because without it he would not do his job properly' (Meineke, *Machiavellism*, tr. by Douglas Scott, pp. 6-7, 403). As a popular British song has it, 'God who made thee mighty make thee mightier yet'. Power over what, and to do what? This is not said, but the implication must be: power over individual men, whether foreigners or its own citizens, and power over other States. Only one State at most can fully achieve its good on this view, for the good of States is competitive.

The setting up of some particular State as one's own particular god is known as nationalism, and has been common since the eighteenth century. Some one 'country', as a State is usually called in this connexion, is then regarded by the individual man as his god; and he looks on other States as devils rather than gods, or at best as gods that have no concern with him, though he unquestioningly recognizes their existence. He is then inclined to think that every other good in the world should be sacrificed to the good of his State when it conflicts therewith. Thus Hitler gave the impression of thinking that the God-State Germany had the right to pursue its own good at the expense of all foreigners and all other States, and even at the expense of all individual Germans.

3.13. *No State should be worshipped*

In opposition to this view I propose to argue that States are not gods, and no State should be worshipped, and the good of the citizens should not be sacrificed to the good of the State.

(1) No decent end for the State has been proposed. Those who worship the State always find its good in ends which, the more they

are faced, the less they can be adopted. How does prestige differ from reputation? Reputation is for decency or virtue or skill; but prestige is for power, and there is something pretentious about it. The word comes through French from the Latin *praestigium*, a juggler's trick. (It is not the only French word that takes on a nasty meaning when used in English politics.) The modern worshipper of a State conceives its good to lie in its power and prestige, and he devotes himself to the aggrandisement of these. His god is a juggernaut, whose glory lies in its cruel and crushing power.

(2) Many have been able to worship the State because they confused the good of the State with the good of its citizens, and were thus able to regard all those who were cool towards the State as being cool and selfish about their fellow citizens. But State-worship does not coincide with an altruistic attitude towards fellow citizens. On the contrary, it necessarily fails to coincide therewith, because the attitude of worship demands that the aim of the worshipped god shall be held to be something other and 'grander' than the good of his worshippers. State-worshippers usually conceive the aim of their god to be his own power and prestige; and the power and prestige of a State can perfectly well conflict with the good of its citizens. The surest way to try to secure the good of the individual citizens is to aim precisely at that, and not to aim at the good of the God-City on the assumption that this will always be identical with, or lead inevitably to, the good of the citizens. Dr. Popper has made this point in his discussion of Plato in *The Open Society*.

(3) States have acted more often like devils than like gods, to be execrated rather than worshipped. Do you know of a State of more than fifty years' standing that has not committed at least one crime? Is there a State to which historians give a clean record (excluding the historians who are citizens of that State)? If so, it must be a little State with little power to offend. All the great and powerful States have committed crimes, either by breaking a treaty, or by inventing an excuse for aggressive war, or by extorting unfair advantage with threats. Dr. Ewing has pointed out (*The Individual, The State, and World Government*, p. 224) that politicians never recommend a measure as good for the world though bad for this country. Such unselfish behaviour is as yet non-existent in States.

(4) Nationalism, the pursuit of power and prestige for a particular State, is a vicarious form taken by the sin of pride now that Christian teaching has largely suppressed its direct and original

manifestation. Public opinion today requires us to talk humbly about ourselves; but it does not yet require us to talk humbly about our State, and into the latter our thwarted pride therefore tends to find its way.

Pride is a peculiarly destructive vice. As in the *potlatch* once practised on the north-west coast of North America, pride easily tends to find its good in the destruction of more obvious and simple goods. Hence it is that a man may think that the good of Germany might demand the misery of all Germans. Hence the anger and abusiveness, the touchiness about sovereignty, the uprooting and oppression of thousands of simple people, that are characteristic of nationalism today. Pride is the chief motive of many States in their dealings with other States.

(5) Nationalism tends to involve myth. It usually involves the anthropological myth that the citizens of the State are all of the same race and culture and comprise everybody who is of that race and culture. It usually involves also some historical and half-religious myth about the past wrongs suffered by the State. George Orwell brought out this point.

(6) The worshippers of the State usually talk about it in the singular number, as if there were only one in the world. They thus get the advantage of monotheism. But they are not entitled to it because there are at present more than a hundred States. You will find that if, in their worshipping and solemn pronouncements, you replace their singular 'the State' with the correct plural 'States', the whole becomes much less plausible. Will you try this experiment on the following passage from Lord (*The Principles of Politics*, pp. 283-4)?

We must insist on the reality of the State and of its absolute right. It is impossible justly to understand human political experience if we reduce the State to a mere convention, an artificial device of individuals to secure their own rights or the objects of their desires, or if we fail to appreciate the sense in which the State is a necessary and natural being, and even prior to the individuals themselves. It does not merely follow from the good pleasure of its citizens; neither do its rights depend solely upon their permissive agreement.

If you mentally substituted the plural 'States' for each occurrence of 'the State' in this, you probably found that the atmosphere of worship evaporated and the sentences lost conviction. It is indeed hard to believe that those imperfect politicians at Versailles, carving the Austrian Empire into a plurality of States on Woodrow Wilson's principle of selfdetermination, were thereby procreating several 'necessary and natural beings, even prior to the individuals themselves'.

(7) The power and action of the State manifest themselves through governors, members of parliament, civil servants, city councillors, and city clerks. To worship the State is to worship what comes through these persons. To increase the power of the State is to increase the power of these men.

(8) The State gains worshippers and reputation through being confused with other things. We have already seen that the State's good is sometimes confused with the good of its individual citizens, so that to refuse to aim at the State's good looks like being selfish towards fellow citizens. Let us now see that the State itself often gets undeserved credit by being confused with other entities.

The State is often referred to as 'the country' or 'my country' or 'the fatherland'. It is not, however, a part of the earth's surface, but a political organization in control of a part of the earth's surface. It often loses or obtains or tries to obtain control over a particular piece of land. By the expression 'my country' one can refer to Epping Forest as well as to a State. The beauty of mountains is not the beauty of a State.

A State is not a people, for 'the people of the plains' and 'the people who like opera' are not States. A State is a certain political organization of certain people.

A State is not a government, but it has a government. Just so a man is not a heart, but he has a heart. A State is a set of human beings politically organized so that a government is distinguished among them. But the State and its government are often confused, for example when it is said that 'the State is a committee for the management of the affairs of the bourgeoisie'. The State is that corporate body which through its government claims sovereign power in the land, and if there is no such body in a land there is no State there.

The people who are organized into some one State are not necessarily all of the same race and culture. To see this we must see the difference between race and culture. Race is something you are born with and cannot do anything about, such as the colour of your skin and the type of your blood. It is those inherited features of your physical makeup in which you differ from many men and are identical with many other men. No man can change any man's race, except that he can choose whether or not to have a child and whom to have it by. Your race depends wholly on who your parents were, and which selection of their genes they transmitted to you in your conception.

Culture, on the other hand, is something you are not born with but receive after your birth from those you live with. You get it from your parents only if you live with your parents after your birth. You get it from all whom you live with and to the extent to which you live with them. It is a vast complex of habits and traditions of speech and thought and song and action and love and hate.

The concepts of race and culture are widely misunderstood at the present time, and often confused with each other. Here is a passage in which the author speaks of race but means culture. 'All of this Arctic country, from the tree-line north, is inhabited by a single race—the Eskimoes. They *are* a race, in spite of their dispersion and lack of social organization. They speak fundamentally the same language and their customs are basically the same' (p. 6 of *Inuk*, by Roger P. Buliard, London, Macmillan, 1956). Very likely the Eskimo are all of one race; but the reasons that Mr. Buliard gives here have nothing to do with race. They are reasons for believing the Eskimo to be all of one culture. Language and custom are matters of culture, not race. Dispersion and lack of social organization are liable to produce differences of culture, not of race.

Most States admit to their citizenship persons of various race and various culture. These 'naturalized' persons are then part of the whole people whose political organization under a particular government constitutes that State. This shows that a State is different both from a race and from a culture, and that the members of a given State need not be all of the same race or culture, and need not include all the members of some race or culture.

Is a State a nation? The question is too vague to answer because the idea of a nation is too vague. I think it is mostly used by people who have not yet distinguished race from culture, and are unconsciously assuming that race and culture always go together. By a 'nation' they mean, then, a set of people who constitute all the examples of a certain race and also all the examples of a certain culture, and they believe that there are such sets. In this sense of the word, however, there no longer are any nations. Every culture now has among its bearers people of more than one race, and every race has among its members people of more than one culture.

Is a State a society? I do not understand how people use the words 'society' and 'social' nowadays. For example, I do not understand what they mean by 'social justice', because I do not see how there could be a 'non-social justice' or a 'personal justice'. I am mystified by Tawney's talk of 'social emphasis' and 'social compunction' and social anything and everything. But in the plain dictionary sense of an 'aggregate of persons living together in a more or less ordered community' (*S.O.E.D.*), it is clear that all States are societies but most societies are not States. So much as clarification of the conception of a State, for I shall not go into the hard question of sovereignty and whether a federated State is really a State.

When the State is distinguished from all these other things, from land and people and government and race and culture and nation and society, and seen to be a political organization, which may or may not cherish certain people and preserve some valuable land or culture or race, the impulse to worship it evaporates. It is an organization like other human organizations, more powerful than most of them, hence more capable of evil, but capable also of helping things that may be much better than itself, namely human beings and their cultures.

Those are my reasons for the policy of not worshipping States, and of not putting the good of the State above everything else. They are not mathematical demonstrations, for no argument for an action or policy or evaluation can be a mathematical demonstration. They will not change a fanatic who cares for nothing but the power and prestige of his own country. But most men do care deeply for many other things, including the sorrows of individual men, and therefore can be influenced against nationalism by arguments which distinguish the good of the State from other goods and show that it may conflict therewith. I mention this point, the possibility of reasonable argument against taking the State as the supreme good, because it seems to be denied by T. D. Weldon in the gloomy last chapter of his book *States and Morals* (especially pp. 292-3).

These are not reasons for abolishing the State or declaring it useless. They are reasons for not worshipping the State or setting it up as a god whose will is paramount. They are reasons for holding that 'reason of State' or *raison d'état* ought not to be an ultimate reason, and that the appeal to national pride and prejudice ought not to be the easiest way for a politician to get followers.

They are reasons against nationalism rather than against

patriotism. 'Patriotism' is an approving name, and is usually applied to something that is indeed approvable, to wit, love and service towards the culture in which one shares, and towards those who share it with one. It is often described as love of one's country; but one's country here is more one's culture than one's State. One of the main uses of a State is to preserve a culture, and so one of the main good reasons for going to war in defence of a State is to preserve a culture which that State protects; and the patriot who does this deserves and receives honour. The culture is good in itself (if it is so; not all cultures that have existed have been good on the whole); but the State is not. Thus patriotism as I understand it may be good though nationalism is not. And if a Welshman says that he is in favour of cultural nationalism but not of political nationalism for Wales, he means by 'cultural nationalism' what I am here calling patriotism. I admit, however, that culture too can be made a fetish and often has been made one, especially in Germany. Some Germans have implied that German culture is the only good culture, and that, if German culture is being adulterated by degenerate influences from a foreign country, this justifies making war on that country.

The State, then, is to be treated with reserve and suspicion, as a necessary evil rather than as a great good. We should not listen to the politicians who magnify its power and prestige, but rather study the anthropologists who disclose to us the nature of culture, so grossly misunderstood by most of us, and so much worthier of our love. Let us never prefer the good of a State to the goods of human beings. Do not worship your State or even love it. Love instead your land, your fellow citizens, and the culture you share with your fellow citizens. Do not sing *Rule, Britannia* or *Land of Hope and Glory*. Sing instead something like this:

> This is Raroia,
> The land of the cool winds.
> The song of joy mingles
> With the noise of the breakers.
> Here is our country.
>
> (From *The Happy Island*, by Bengt Danielson, London, Allen & Unwin, 1952.)

On the other hand, States, like all erring moral beings, are to be treated on occasion with charity and forgiveness. We should avoid the common error of letting our attitude towards a State be fixed for ever by certain crimes it has committed in the past. States should confess their crimes, and those that genuinely repent should be forgiven. England should confess her past crimes towards Ireland, and the Irish should forgive them. Voters should vote for politicians who confess the country's crimes rather than for those who do not.

There is a fine statement of this point in Laurens van der Post's *Venture to the Interior*, pp. 16–17:

> The suffering which is most difficult, if not impossible, to forgive is unreal, imagined suffering. There is no power on earth like imagination, and the worst, most obstinate grievances are imagined ones. Let us recognize that there are people and nations who create, with a submerged deliberation, a sense of suffering and of grievance, which enable them to evade those aspects of reality that do not minister to their self-importance, personal pride or convenience. These imagined ills enable them to avoid the proper burden that life lays on all of us.
>
> Persons who have really suffered at the hands of others do not find it difficult to forgive, nor even to understand the people who caused their suffering. They do not find it difficult to forgive because out of suffering and sorrow truly endured comes an instinctive sense of privilege. Recognition of the creative truth comes in a flash: forgiveness for others, as for ourselves, for we too know not what we do.
>
> This perpetuation of so-called 'historic' and class grievances is an evil, dishonest and unreal thing. It is something which cannot be described adequately in the customary economic, political and historical clichés. The language that seems far more appropriate is the language of a pathologist describing cancer, the language of a psychologist describing a deep-seated complex and obsessional neurosis. For what is Nazism, or present-day Malanism in this Southern Africa of my youth, but the destruction of the whole by an unnatural proliferation of the cells of a part, or a wilful autonomous system that would twist the whole being to a partial need?

3.14. *States are moral agents*

You observe that I have not taken the positivist line that States do not exist. I have said that they do exist but are not worshipful. States exist, and they cannot be analysed away. That is, there are true propositions containing the word 'State' which are not equivalent to any proposition lacking that word and all its equivalents. For example, the true proposition that 'States ought to keep their treaties' is not equivalent to the proposition that 'Governments ought to keep treaties made by themselves or their predecessors'.

And the latter proposition cannot even seem equivalent to the former except by a tacit reference to the State at two points. For 'treaties' in it means agreements to which the government commits *the State*; it does not include agreements which the government may make with an hotel to buy a dinner. And 'predecessors' means predecessors as the governors of *the same State*; it does not include the men who preceded them as occupiers of a given room or as contractors with a given photographer. That 'States ought to keep their treaties', and that 'Governments ought to keep treaties made by themselves or their predecessors', are two distinct propositions. Both of them are true, and the latter follows from the former plus some other true propositions about governments and their relation to States. The latter would, however, be more accurately expressed by saying: 'Governments ought to see that their State keeps the treaties to which it is committed.'

I believe that all other reductions of a sentence about a State to one about a government also fail, except when the word 'State' was wrong in the first place because the sentence was really about a government. Analysts also try sometimes to reduce sentences about States to sentences about people; but this is still less plausible. Mr. Urmson in his *Philosophical Analysis*, pp. 151-2, shows the non-equivalence of 'England declared war' to any statement about English people.

'But surely', we are inclined to say at this point, 'England is not an entity over and above the English people.' I think that England *is* an entity over and above the English people; and our reluctance to believe so arises partly from reading too much into the word 'entity', or never having known what this technical term was invented to mean. An entity is a thing in the widest possible sense of 'a thing', that is, anything that can be referred to, anything except the non-entities. Since there is a word for referring to England, England is an entity. In calling England an entity, we do not decide what kind of entity it is. We do not decide whether it is a piece of matter or a colour or a relation or a group of people or none of these. We decide only that England is talkable about and referable to.

'But is this entity over and above the English people?' Well, it is not identical with the English people, since sentences about the one cannot be converted into sentences about the other. We should hardly care to say it is 'among' the English people, or 'beside' them, or 'round' them. If we want a spatial metaphor, the best one seems to be 'over and above'. Non-metaphorically, England and the English people are distinct and related. England presupposes but is not presupposed by the English people.

Reference can be definite or indefinite. 'Some enemy hath done this' is an indefinite reference. The word 'England', being a proper name, looks as if its use would be to make definite references only, and all of them to one and the same particular. But some thinkers have held that this appearance is deceptive. In reality, they believe, the word 'England' is used to make indefinite references. Just as 'one of the children has done this' means 'either John or Joan or Jane did this' if we have just those three children, so, it is thought, 'England declared war' means 'Either the Cabinet voted unanimously for war, or all of them but Mr. A voted for war, or all of them but Mr. B voted for war, or all of them but Mr. A and Mr. B voted for war, and so on'. 'The point of such a statement as "England declared war",' wrote Mr. Urmson, op. cit., p. 182, 'is precisely to let us know the sort of thing that Englishmen did without saying precisely how'. I do not think so. I think that 'England declared war' is a definite reference to a particular thing, the State of England.

But surely 'the history of States is not another branch of history with a different subject-matter alongside the history of individuals' (Urmson, op. cit., p. 181). Histories of States are distinct from histories of individuals, and the two can stand alongside on a shelf. Their subject-matters, the States and the individuals, are not exactly alongside, but rather above and below, like a history of birds and a history of the great auk. But they are much more different from each other than a history of birds would be different from a history of the great auk, because the race of birds is not a political organization. What J. R. Green gave us under the title of 'A History of the English People' was in fact mainly a history of the English State. Something like a real history of the English people was attempted by Trevelyan; but he called it 'English Social History', perhaps because Green had pre-empted his proper title. Historians mostly write about States, and about men only so far as men are officers of States or otherwise specially important to States. To put it another way, the word 'history' is never used now in its original wide sense of 'inquiry', and hardly ever used even so widely as to mean 'inquiry into the course of past events'. It is usually restricted to 'inquiry into the course of past events concerning States', so that an inquiry into how people fastened their boots in the Middle Ages is not history. Similarly, the 'prehistoric' period is the period before there were States rather than the period before there were writings.

We must go much farther than merely to say that England is an entity over and above the English people. We must say that England is a moral agent distinct from any or all of the English. That States are moral agents is implied by saying that they ought to keep their treaties; and it seems perfectly clear that States ought to keep their treaties, and that this is not equivalent to any proposition about governors. Since States ought to keep their treaties, the governor of a State ought to see that his State keeps its treaties; but this conclusion is not equivalent to the premiss from which it is deduced. States can do right and wrong. They can have virtues and vices. They are morally responsible. The 'perfidy of Albion' may or may not be a fact; but the phrase is significant, and it does not signify the same as any phrase about English people. 'My country right or wrong' is a wicked slogan but not an absurd one; it is not like saying 'My country odd or even'. We all use such language frequently, and it is not an abbreviation of something about individuals.

'You will be saying next that States are persons.' Well, what does the word 'person' mean? Do you use it as a synonym for 'human being'? A State, of course, is not a human being. A State is unlike a human being in that you cannot converse with it; it has no sex and no imagination; and we are entitled to bring it to an end on many more occasions than we are entitled to bring a human being to his end. Though it has a beginning and an end, and exists continuously from one to the other, it does not have the seven ages of a human being, but is equally likely to behave in a mature or an immature way at any period of its existence. The fact that the U.S.A. came into existence later than some other States is no ground for calling it an 'adolescent' country; for swelling breasts and sprouting beards cannot be observed in States.

Thus States are not persons if you use the word 'person' as a synonym for 'human being'. But that is not the only meaning of the word. Theologians use it otherwise when they say that God is three persons. Lawyers use it otherwise when they say that a corporation may be a legal person. One existing and important use of the word 'person' is precisely to indicate that the entity referred to is morally or legally responsible, a moral or legal agent. The word 'person' appears to be in fact the only single-word name that we have for a moral or legal agent, for what Maitland wellcalled 'a right-and-duty-bearing unit'. All States are moral persons, and in so far as they can sue or be sued in some court they are also legal persons.

Some thinkers have said that this is refuted by the consideration that a State has no existence apart from those who compose it. They might as well say that a man is not a moral person because he has no existence apart from the cells that compose him. They might as well say that all statements about a man can be analysed into statements about cells. The question whether X is a moral person has nothing to do with the question what X depends on for its existence. To say that a State did so and so is no more and no less analysable than to say that a man walked. You can analyse the contractions of his muscles and the impulses of his nerves; but that is not his walking. You can analyse the arguments and voting in the Cabinet; but that is not the State acting. To borrow an example from Dr. Ewing (op. cit., 176), you might as well try to reduce 'this house is comfortable and convenient for a small family' to a statement about its materials.

Some thinkers have believed that if a State were a moral person it could do no wrong or would be 'above morality'. This must be false because it is selfcontradictory. That X is a moral person entails that $\dot{X}$ *can* do wrong, for X's being capable of doing wrong is part of what is meant by saying that X is a moral person.

Some thinkers have believed that if States were moral persons they would be bound by the same moral principles as individuals are, whereas they cannot be. But neither of these premisses is probable. That States are moral persons entails only that they are bound by *some* moral principles, not also that they are bound by precisely those moral principles that govern individuals. On the other hand, States probably are bound by the same moral principles as bind individuals. This would not make their particular duties always the same as those of individuals, because one's particular duty depends not merely on one's general obligations but also on one's particular circumstances.

We should beware of making bad arguments to urge that a State is not a moral person, when all we really want is to get people to give up worshipping States. It is easy to confuse the two, because the phrase 'belief in the State' may mean either the belief that there are such things as States or the belief that they ought to be worshipped. We want people to abandon the belief that the State ought to be worshipped, but we do not want them to abandon the belief that the State exists and is something to be praised or blamed. States exist, and we shall not counteract their dangers by trying to persuade people that they do not exist. You cannot counteract the dangers of physical disease by trying to persuade people that it does not exist; and positivism about States is as misguided as 'Christian Science' about disease.

3.2 EQUALITY

3.21. *Equality in political power*

Equality is often put forward as a great political good. Of all the ideals offered us in politics it is probably the most puzzling both to understand and to evaluate. Equality is an abstraction, a generality. To put it forward as a political good is very different from putting forward a particular thing like France or some other State. There is only one France. There are only about a hundred States. But there are indefinitely many ways in which men can be equal or unequal. They can be unequally tall, heavy, healthy, wealthy, witty, strong, charming, clever, instructed, good, beloved, and so on for every adjective that involves the possibility of different degrees. These examples are not political; but within the sphere of politics there is also an indefinitely large number of ways in which men can be equal or unequal, even on the narrowest reasonable interpretation of the word 'politics'. They can be equal or unequal in voting power, and this for each sort of vote, as municipal or national, and on each matter of voting, as financial or not financial. They can be equal or unequal in office, in function, in right of bringing cases to a court, in right of being represented in a court. They can be equal or unequal in liability to tax, and this for each kind of tax, in liability to military service or any other compulsory public service. And so on indefinitely.

Do I wish all men to be exactly equal in all respects? Anybody who explicitly asks himself that question answers no. I do not wish everyone to have a headache when anybody has a headache. I do not wish all men to be produced by division of the same egg, so that they all have the same genes, appearance, character, and behaviour. I do not wish all girls to be equally black-haired, or all boys equally good at running a mile.

There are, however, many people who have never asked themselves this question, and are demanding whatever equalities have engaged their emotions, without considering how far equalization should go or what is the good of it. That is a great pity, and we ought to bring the question to people's attention as widely as we can. A reasonable ideal of equality must be, in fact, a demand for the creation of certain specific equalities. And, since equalities demanded by one person may be distinct from those demanded by another, the discussion of this ideal must divide into the discussion of various possible equalities; and must break off unfinished, because it is impossible to run through all conceivable equalities, and impossible to foresee which of them may be considered important in the future. I shall discuss the possibility or desirability of equality in political power, in legal rights and privileges, in wealth, and in respect.

Do I wish all men to be exactly equal in political power? To answer yes is to be an anarchist. The anarchists are the only complete egalitarians in politics; for as soon as you have political organization you have at least one governor or administrator, and he inevitably has more power than other people so long as he governs. There is a fundamental and inevitable inequality in politics, namely that what constitutes a political society is precisely a distinction between the governor and the rest. There is further the paradox that every time you pass a law to maintain a new kind of equality in the future you have to provide administrators to execute the law, and you thereby create some more persons with unequal power. Hence it is impossible for all persons to be equal in political power except in a mere crowd that has no organization and so no politics. Equal political power can only be zero political power.

This being the situation, it is better to abandon the ideal of equality in political power and retain or institute some government. I shall not argue for this here; but my discussion of the uses of government will provide reason for it.

On the other hand, the powers of officers can vary enormously in degree; and therefore equality in political power can be more or less approached although it can never be reached. And it ought to be approached to a considerable extent, because inequality of power is a dangerous state. In Acton's never-to-be-forgotten phrase, 'power tends to corrupt, and absolute power corrupts absolutely'. Men are not to be trusted with power over their fellows. Hence the power of the governors should be controlled by whatever suitable devices can be thought of. The greatest of these is no doubt democracy—the election and dismissal of the rulers by the whole people at frequent intervals. I shall discuss whether this device is desirable in a separate lecture on democracy. But it is important to note that the question of democracy is by no means the whole of the question about equality of political power. We have to ask also how many officers there are, and how much power they have while they are in office; for this is independent of whether the constitution is democratic or not. A dictatorship can have very few laws and consequently very few officers to administer those laws. A democracy can have a great many laws involving great control of the citizens' lives, and then it will require many officers to administer these laws, and these officers will have much power. Every socialist law that gives more power to administrators increases the inequalities of political power in the country. There is furthermore the very important question how many and which of the officers are removable by popular vote. In the United States some judges are removable by popular vote, but in the United Kingdom none are. In neither country are civil servants removable by popular vote, nor is there anything like the ancient Athenian public examination of officers at the expiration of a term of office. The American Congress does sometimes succeed in examining and controlling civil servants through its committees. But in the United Kingdom and its dependencies the power of civil servants is at present secret, irresponsible, and largely irresistible. According to Lord Hemingford in *The Times* (21 January 1954), a British governor or civil servant in the Gold Coast in 1948 promulgated a regulation under which he could intern anyone without the possibility of a writ of *habeas corpus* or any other appeal to the courts, and in Buganda shortly afterwards a British governor or civil servant promulgated a regulation under which he could deport anyone without the possibility of his action being questioned in court in any way. On 5 May 1953 the Chancellor of the Exchequer told Parliament that 'he had the greatest difficulty in controlling government departments'. In the next year a scandalous piece of administration by a civil servant resulted only in his transfer to another senior post, while his unfortunate minister resigned. There is certainly room in the United Kingdom now for a closer approach to equality in political power.

3.22. Equality before the law

I pass now to equality before the law. According to Article 7 of a 'Universal Declaration of Human Rights Approved by the General Assembly of the United Nations, Paris, 10th December, 1948 ... all are equal before the law and are entitled without any discrimination to equal protection of the law'. Equality before the law is often demanded; but its air of being selfevidently correct is deceptive. The phrase can mean two quite independent states of affairs. First, it can mean that the law makes no distinctions among human persons, but prescribes exactly the same voting rights for foreigners as for citizens, exactly the same penalty for child murderers as for adult murderers, exactly the same military service for women as for men, and so on. In this sense, equality before the law is a character of the kind of law that is on the statute book; and a student can tell in what respects a State has this kind of equality by reading its laws. But the phrase often carries another meaning, in which you cannot tell whether a State has equality before the laws by reading its statutes, but only by observing how its policemen and judges and jailers carry these statutes out. Do they carry them out impartially on all sorts and conditions of persons, or do they prosecute lawbreakers of class A while forgetting to prosecute lawbreakers of class B? Do they, for instance, prosecute poor young men who steal bread for food and omit to prosecute rich young men who steal street-signs for fun? Do they prosecute pedestrians who occupy a square yard of the road for an hour, and omit to prosecute parking motorists who occupy eight square yards of it for eight hours? And do they extend to all men equally such protection as the law indicates, or do they turn a blind eye to the injuries suffered by some while prosecuting the injuries suffered by others?

Each of these two kinds of equality before the law can exist without the other. Hence we need to ask of each separately whether it is desirable. Should the law, whatever it is, be equally applied to all sorts of persons by its executioners? That is to say, when the law does not itself direct its officers to make discriminations or use their discretion, should they nevertheless do so?

A certain amount of discrimination is inevitable. No law can save the public prosecutor from all need of deciding for himself whether to prosecute a particular person. There are bound to be doubtful cases. There will often be more cases than he has men and money to deal with. He must pick and choose. He may, therefore, do this choosing rightly or wrongly. Is it any use telling him that the principle of right choice is that all are equal before the law? I think it is sometimes of some use. It may remind him of certain specific inequalities which he is tempted to regard but ought to disregard, though he will have to know by some other means what these inequalities are. It may remind him that the inequalities he ought to regard, although they are not mentioned in the law, are only such as are consistent with impartiality and fairness, for example, the inequality between first offenders and habitual offenders, or between young and old offenders. On the whole, it is significant and right to demand equality in the administration of the law, although the administrator will always have to make choices and notice inequalities.

And what about equality in the intention of the law? Most of us are now certain that the law should refuse to notice certain inequalities which it formerly did notice, for example the inequality of freeman to slave, and of nobleman to commoner. Whether it should notice differences of colour is still largely in dispute. But it seems perfectly clear that we shall always want the law to notice some inequalities in some respects, for example the inequality between citizen and foreigner when it comes to electing officers, and that between rich man and poor man when it comes to paying tax. Hence in writing laws we cannot follow blindly the principle of equality before the law. Or, to speak more accurately, equality before the law cannot be our principle or starting point. It can only be a reminder of certain specific equalities which we have decided to adopt. Nor is it by any means the case that legislation tends constantly to notice fewer inequalities. Legislation in the twentieth century probably makes more difference than before between citizen and foreigner.

What I have salvaged in the ideals of equality in power and equality before the law is only a distorted version of a much greater political good, namely the rule of law. That law should rule, and that it should rule the governors as well as the subjects, is a far more important thing than that it should rule equally. Half the use of governors is to maintain laws. All of their use is likely to change to harm if they do not act in accordance with known laws, and cannot be summoned to give account of their acts in a court of law.

Every law is by its nature a kind of equality, however many

inequalities it institutes. Suppose a law to say that white subjects may vote and black subjects may not. Then, while it makes blacks unequal to whites, it leaves every black equal to every other black and every white equal to every other white, and it makes every black and every white equally subject to itself. This measure of equality is inherent in every law that really is a law and not a mere decree about some particular named person. But it is better to call it the rule of law than to call it any kind of equality. (I owe this point to Professor Berlin's excellent article on equality in *Proceedings of the Aristotelian Society*, 1955-6.)

3.23. *Equality in wealth*

In England today the equality most commonly demanded is that of wealth, that is, possession or consumption of material goods or power to possess or consume them. This seems to be what the British Labour Party has always chiefly meant by 'equality', for example in R. H. Tawney's book of that name. It half seems to be what Matthew Arnold meant by it in his essay of that name; for, although he says he means 'social equality ... this Frenchified sense of the term', his slogan is Menander's 'choose equality and flee greed', and his only particular proposal is to change the law of bequest and abolish primogeniture.

The demand for equality in wealth appears to be killed by the following question: If you could double everyone's consumption by making and maintaining a few millionaires, would you do so? This is a question which the demanders of equality in wealth do not face. They imply without realizing it that they would rather have everyone undernourished and equally undernourished, than have everyone well nourished but some very rich; or that they would rather have a society in which everyone was miserable but equally so, than one in which everyone was happy but unequally so. Stale fish for all is better than fresh fish for coastdwellers only.

I see no reply to this except one that nobody would care to make, as follows: 'The imagined society, in which everyone is happy but unequally so, is impossible because men are made unhappy by the mere fact of seeing that others are more happy than they are.' No one would care to make this reply because it reveals something that lurks in the demand for the equalization of incomes, namely the vice of envy.

The sinister side of the demand for equality is that much of it is a new and imposing version of the ancient vice of envy. Those who demand equality of incomes in this country always intend that the richer inhabitants of this country shall be brought down to the level of the poorer inhabitants of this country. They are never thinking of the fact that *all* the inhabitants of this country are richer than most of the inhabitants of Jamaica. They are never demanding that their own standard of living shall be lowered to raise that of the Jamaicans. They are not pitying those millions of human beings who are worse off than themselves, but envying the thousands who are better off. While they demand the equalization of incomes, they act by their trade unions and members of parliament to prevent poor foreigners from coming here to share in our comparative wealth, and to ensure that skilled workers shall be paid more than unskilled workers and men more than women. From him that hath more than me shall be taken; but to him that hath less than me shall not be given.

He who envies riches values them too much, or works for them too little. It is regrettable that a member of Parliament should be heard complaining that some people can lunch at the Savoy every day. There is too much envious luxury in our hearts; and the trade unions and the Labour Party are powerful organs to give effect to it.

Inequality of incomes, as Dr. Popper has pointed out to me, gives certain people a relatively harmless outlet for ambition and push. Had Hitler had an opportunity to make much money in business he might have settled down innocuously. The wish to excel must be given many different opportunities.

Envy under the banner of equality works against talent as well as against wealth. It works to prevent unusual talent from being encouraged and trained. It works to degrade universities, and other places where unusual talent is trained, into places where only average talent is required. It declares that the President of the United States should be a person whose family and education have not been better than average. It tends to attribute all avoidable evils of society to the talented and successful few, and to turn pity for the common man's distress into mean denunciation of those who can help him.

One should face the fact that some goods would cease to be goods of that kind if they were available to all. If everyone could join Oxford University, Oxford University would not be worth joining, because you would not meet in it a higher average of scholarship than you meet without joining it. The value of a university is that it gives you the society of better than average scholars; and it is impossible that everyone should be a better than average scholar. People had better face this fact, however hard they find it.

One should face also the fact that equalizing wealth involves lessening freedom. It means that people are not left free to acquire and enjoy and give and spend extra wealth. It is not true in general that 'the passion for equality makes vain the hope of freedom', to generalize a phrase of Acton's; but it is true that wealth can be kept equal only by a steady and considerable denial of certain freedoms. It is true also that the prohibitions necessitated by the equalization of wealth tend appreciably to discourage some useful forms of enterprise and responsibility. It is true, further, that, if we maintain equality of wealth by removing excesses as they occur, we thereby favour the lazy and the spendthrift at the expense of their opposites. It may well be, however, that these thrifty and industrious opposites will go on making and saving wealth as before, like the bees that go on working though most of their honey is always removed.

If these sentiments seem unfair to you, that is probably because you are aware that in the demand for economic equality there is much pity for human distress. I fully agree that men are often in distress, and that this requires the pity of us all, and that this emotion has recently operated largely under the flag of economic equality. I urge only that this is a bad flag for it to operate under, partly because it lets in also the bad emotion of envy, which then has a free sail under false colours. It is plenty for all that is desirable, not equal plenty for all. That each may have plenty we should if necessary tax and transfer any luxuries enjoyed by some, and we should ration scarce necessities. But, if we turn this care for a decent plenty for all into a demand for an equal plenty for all, we begin an endless envious bickering, since there always must be some good enjoyed by you that is not equally enjoyed by me, and the attempt to divide it between us will often cause its total disappearance. If you live by the sea and I do not, it will not improve matters to compel you to change houses with me once a year. If your parents are kind and mine are not, it will not improve matters to abolish family life. If you are able to administer a great enterprise and I am not, it will not improve matters to compel you to administer it jointly with me; I must just repress my envy and be content with other joys.

I am suggesting that the demand for economic equalization is a muddled and dangerous form of the demand that he who possesses luxuries shall yield them to him who lacks necessities. The latter demand is good; and, although the boundary between luxuries and necessities is a matter of opinion and shifts from year to year, yet there are plenty of clear cases; and, although the attempt to transfer part of the rich man's riches to the poor man sometimes results in the total disappearance of the riches, yet there are plenty of cases where it succeeds. To think of this as a demand for the equalization of wealth is to lose sight of many impossibilities and to entertain envy unawares. It is to lose sight, for example, of the fact that many men will not undertake extra work and responsibility unless they are given extra rewards for doing so.

Let us beware of supposing that to deprecate the demand for economic equality is to make a demand for economic inequality. We might as well think that to deny that the governors should aim at the prestige of the State is the same as to demand that they should aim at lowering the prestige of the State. There is a difference between saying 'do not seek equality' and saying 'seek inequality'. I am not saying 'seek inequality', but 'seek happiness for all, and take no account whether it makes us economically equal or not'. In economic matters the right to equality is only that each has a right for his necessities and reasonable comforts to be supplied by the State at the expense of whatever luxuries will supply them without a net loss of necessities. We want not equality but a good life for each; and the demand for equality often puts us on the whole farther from the good life. Equality is something to give to the less fortunate than ourselves, not something to take from the more fortunate.

3.24. *Equality in respect*

I come lastly to equality of respect. The first article of the Declaration of Human Rights asserts that 'all human beings are born free and equal in dignity and rights'. The word 'dignity' here suggests another kind of demand for equality, and one which is more justified. To be a human being is to have a dignity which requires respect from all persons. In virtue of this there ought to be a certain being on equal terms between any two men whatever, no matter how much one is above the other in some special way. A child is not the equal of his father in wisdom or experience or power or importance or authority. Nevertheless, in all good families the father is on equal terms with the child in a certain way in which in England he is sometimes not on equal terms with the cook.

Respect is opposed to contempt and humiliation. The demand that everyone is to be respected therefore involves that no one is to be fundamentally or utterly contemned or despised. However cruel or disgusting his crimes or his intentions, he is as a man to be respected. If contempt has any place in the emotions of a good man, it can only be contempt for some particular actions or characteristics of a man, not for his essential manhood.

Class snobbery is a powerful enemy of the equalization of men and women in respect. It makes it hard for me to invite my servant for a walk, harder still for him to invite me. It tempts me 'to flatter a blown up fool above, or crush the wretch beneath me' (Otway's *Venice Preserved*, i. 1). It makes men actually desire inequality, and feel injured when those below them in any way rise to their level. Class snobbery is not confined to certain classes. It often happens that a member of a lower class inhumanly despises or repulses members of an upper class, and a famous example of this is Aneurin Bevan's calling the Tories vermin. Nor is there any class whose members are all class snobs; in every class are found some men and women who give respect to all men and women.

Equalization in respect is fundamentally and greatly good in itself. It is included in 'le sentiment de la vie idéale, qui n'est autre que la vie normale telle que nous sommes appelés à la connaître', as Matthew Arnold quoted from George Sand (*Mixed Essays*, p. 320). But it is also good in its consequences, and may be recommended by them. 'To live in a society of equals tends in general to make a man's spirit expand, and his faculties work easily and actively; while, to live in a society of superiors, although it may occasionally be a very good discipline, yet in general tends to tame the spirits and to make the play of the faculties less secure and active.... To be heavily overshadowed, to be profoundly insignificant, has, on the whole, a depressing and benumbing effect on the character' (Matthew Arnold, *Mixed Essays*, pp. 10-11). 'The great inequality of classes and property, which came to us ⟨English⟩ from the Middle Age and which we maintain because we have the religion of inequality... has the... effect... of materialising our upper class, vulgarising our middle class, and brutalising our lower class' (ibid., p. 87).

Here then we find one sort of equality that really should be demanded. Yet this sort of equality is a moral rather than a political matter. It is not primarily a matter for governors or States, but a moral duty for each individual man. It is to be furthered not primarily by political devices but as all moral demands are furthered, by the training of our children and of our own wills. We are to preach and teach this demand, to think out its ramifications, to prepare ourselves by imagination to meet it in different forms. It is largely a matter of manners. As Matthew Arnold has written, 'it is by the humanity of their manners that men are made equal' (op. cit., p. 68). For the ideal of manners is not conformity to any taboo or convention as such, but precisely the achievement of universal dignity and happiness in so far as they depend on common communications.

Although the equalization of human dignity is not primarily a political matter, there are important possibilities of State action in the encouragement or discouragement of it. All passport and visa regulations are an indignity; and their increase in the twentieth century is one of several ways in which we have recently shown less respect for human dignity than our ancestors did. The segregation or subordination of races is another affront of the same kind and much greater degree. The most important part of equality before the law comes in here. Furthermore, the existence of government is by its nature a standing influence in the direction of humiliation. The governor's and administrator's power is a standing temptation to him to humiliate his subjects. We therefore demand whatever arrangements will so far as possible neutralize this bad tendency of all governments; and the outstanding device here is that the ruler holds power for a short period only, after which a new ruler is appointed by a general election. Thus democracy is a device for the equalization of human dignity as well as for the equalization of political power.

It is commonly held that the government can make a further great contribution to the equalization of human dignity by equalizing incomes. The moral basis of the demand for the equalization of wealth seems to be that it is an important means towards the equalization of dignity. But this is probably an error. Degrees of inequality in the respect of man for man do not correlate closely with degrees of inequality in income. For example, the equalization of human dignities is far more closely approached in the U.S.A. than in England; but the equalization of incomes is far less closely approached. It is not inequalities of income that maintain the terrible inhumanity of man to man in England. It is inequalities of class dignity that maintain themselves because they are a religion here, and strive to find inequalities of income in which to express themselves. There is a social disease in England, snobbery, which cannot be cured by levelling incomes.

3.25. *The basis of equality*

I have been speaking of the *demand* for equality, of the enterprise of *making* equal men who were unequal. A great deal of the discussion of political equality, however, has been expressed not as a demand but as a statement of fact. The Declaration of Human Rights declares that 'all human beings *are born* free and equal in dignity', and '*are* equal before the law'. Many defenders of equality have given the impression that they are describing what is so, not proposing what might be so. Their language has justified their opponents in taking them to be anthropologists rather than legislators.

Yet to say that all men are in fact equal in every way would be a stupidly false assertion, and would leave no further possible equality to be demanded in politics. That all men are equally valuable in every way appears to be also stupidly false, though something like it is implied whenever someone says 'I am as good as any man', or talks about 'the infinite value of the human soul'. It is also a plain falsehood that all men could, by some practicable arrangements, be brought to be in the future equal in all ways. We never shall be, and never could be, all equal in height and health and strength and longevity and charm and intelligence.

How is it then that thinkers have appeared to be asserting absurd falsehoods about actual equalities among men? Apparently in two ways. Demands are often made in the form of assertions. What looked like the indefensible assertion that all men are born free has often been in reality the defensible demand that no man be held in slavery. The verb 'is' does duty for the verb 'ought to be'. 'Cannot' does duty for 'ought not'. And so on.

That is one cause why political discussions of equality sometimes seem to be anthropological descriptions of the nature of man. But there is another and a more important one. We feel a need to state some basis of fact for any demand we make. We feel a need to base any demand for the future equalization of men on an assertion of some way in which they already are equal. What we have in mind is the hybrid doctrine that men should be *made* equal in one way because they inevitably *are* equal in another way.

What then is the equality in fact, on which we may base a demand for further equalization? It could be a different equality in fact for each different equalization that we demand. But in each case the basis, to be valid, ought to be something in which I am identical with every other human being; and it ought also to be something in which I differ from everything that is not a human being, unless we are prepared to extend the proposed equalization to monkeys and whales.

It is plausible to say that the factual equality on which our demands are based is just that we are all equally human beings, *homo sapiens*. But we may properly ask for further explanation of this. We may ask why we appeal to the equality of all humans as humans and base thereon a demand for further equalization, when we do not appeal to the equality of all mammals as mammals and base thereon a demand for the further equalization of all mammals.

There is the Christian answer: because men have immortal souls and no other animal does. This is wholly unsatisfactory, because 'soul' is a meaningless word. There is no way of teaching a person the meaning of this word, so that to tell him that he has a soul is to tell him nothing. Suppose we omit this word and say: 'because men are immortal and all other animals are mortal.' We have now a statement which is very unlikely on the evidence; the evidence certainly is that man is as mortal as any other animal. His spiritual life depends on his material body, and his material body dies. But suppose the statement were probable. Then it would weaken the demand for further equalization of men, not strengthen it. If man had a non-political eternity ahead of him, this would provide no good reason for the present equalization of political or legal power or rights or wealth or status. On the contrary, it would be a good reason for regarding all such earthly equalizations as trivial.

Another answer is: Reason. The equalization of men has been demanded on the ground that all men are rational. Whales are excluded because they are not rational. To be rational here means to be able to think, and not merely to think about the present in the bare sense of being prepared for one's prey to flee or for one's predator to spring, but to think abstractly and in concepts, about the absent and the past and the general, the good and the bad, the right and the wrong, the law and the case. To which perhaps we should add the power to send and receive communications of such thoughts.

This conception of man as the rational animal is Aristotelian, and perhaps even Platonic. Neither of those thinkers based upon it any demand for the political or social equalization of all men; but Aristotle does base his conception of political activity as such upon it. According to him City-States exist among men, and not among bees, because men and only men are rational in this sense (*Politics* A 2, 1253ᵃ 7-18). Furthermore, he thinks that 'probably every man has a duty towards everyone who can share in law and convention' δοκεῖ γὰρ εἶναί τι δίκαιον παντὶ ἀνθρώπῳ πρὸς πάντα τὸν δυνάμενον κοινωνῆσαι νόμου καὶ συνθήκης, *N.E.* viii. 11. 1161ᵇ6). If we had asked him whether a being must have reason in order to share in law and convention, he would have understood the question and he would have answered 'Yes'.

Reason gives an extraordinary responsibility and power of action and control, which make those who possess it inevitable controllers of whatever does not possess it. Reason must and will direct the course of events; and it is right that this should be as far as possible the reason of all rational beings. Therefore, the equality in fact of all rational beings as rational justifies a demand for their equalization as controllers of what is done, so far as this is not harmful in other ways. Thus we find a basis in fact for demanding the equalization of the vote and other political and legal rights.

Is reason also the basis for the demand for the equalization of respect? At first it seems to be so, because the possession of reason is a great dignity and worthy of respect. It is, indeed, a much better ground for demanding respect than the supposed immortality of the soul would be. Yet it does not seem to be good enough if we imagine a being who could think but not feel. If he feels no pleasure or pain or emotion, if he has no desire or aversion, then, however much and however abstractly he thinks, the demand for equality seems to have no point in his case. We should no more demand equal treatment of him than of a mountain, because neither of them suffers. The fact that all men are sufferers seems at least as important as the fact that they are all rational, as a ground for treating them equally. That dignity in every man which demands our respect seems to be mainly his capacity to suffer.

But now the whale and the monkey suffer too, and so do many other sorts of animal. We therefore look like having to say that all *vertebrates* are equal in dignity, and should be given equal respect, because they are all sufferers. This result would greatly sharpen our previous conclusion that the demand for equal respect is not primarily political. It would not be incompatible with man's killing cattle, if war or capital punishment is compatible with proper respect for the dignity of man.

If we wish to avoid this conclusion, the best apparent way to do so is to combine the capacity to suffer with the capacity to think, and say that we demand equal respect for all who are both sufferers and rational. For my part I do not care to put it like that, because when I do so I feel convinced that the suffering matters far more than the rationality. I demand respect for the cat and the rat and the jackal and the sheep, because I know they suffer and suffering is eminently respectable. All vertebrates ought equally to be respected by all men as fellow sufferers.

This does not entail that no man should ever kill a vertebrate. The right use of the power to kill is not to disuse it entirely. The lives of the other vertebrates are to some extent in our hands, both to take and to make. Competition is inevitable. Food is limited, but we can increase or decrease it. To choose never to kill any vertebrate would be, I suppose, to exterminate ourselves. I see nothing hypocritical in respecting the ox that I have bred and intend to kill for beef, or in respecting the rat while I recognize him as an inevitable enemy and intend to kill him.

Thus the only kind of equalization that I can unreservedly favour is so unpolitical that it starts from the individual person, not the State, and extends beyond humanity to all vertebrates. I think it is better called, not 'equality', but 'respect' or 'fraternity' or 'love'. Every being who suffers is my brother or sister. Equality is a political perversion of that fundamentally unpolitical thing, love.

3.3. FREEDOM

3.31. *Freedom is a good*

The word 'freedom', like the word 'equality', is a vague, abstract, and relative term which is offered to us as the name of a great political good. A stranger 'approaches you and says: "I am free." You are baffled. Has he just escaped from prison, from his debts, from his wife, from his sins?' This excellent illustration comes from the opening paragraph of Maurice Cranston's book on *Freedom*. His first chapter will teach you the meaning of the word better than I can do; and I wish it were proper for me to recite it instead of giving my own account.

'X is free' is an incomplete statement, like 'X is equal' or 'X is prepared'. X is prepared for what? X is equal to what and in what respect? X is free from what, and to do what? A piston can move about in any direction, so far as the laws of space and gravity go. But, when it is confined in a vertical cylinder, it is only free to move up and down, and not free to move sideways. This is an example of a very general type of situation which gives the word 'free' its use. The piston stands here for any thing or animal which in general can do some sort of action or suffer some sort of passion, so long as it is not prevented from that sort of action or passion by some particular cause. In any such case we say that the thing or animal is free to do the action or suffer the passion for which it has the capacity, when nothing prevents it; but when something does prevent it it is not free in that way. Thus for anything to be free or not free it must have the capacity, in the widest sense of the word 'capacity', to do or suffer something or other; and there must be some cause which does or might hinder it from realizing this capacity. Thus the idea of freedom is enormously general. Pistons can be freed as well as slaves. In fact, the idea finds applications in every field there is. Almost anything can be free or not free from an immense number of things. Some tomatoes are free from scale-insects. Some men are free from moral scruples.

Whenever we use the word 'free' or 'freedom' without mentioning any specific thing that is free, or any specific hindrance that it is free from, we leave open a vast area of undetermined possibilities. What, for instance, is a 'free school'? It might be a school free from control by the Church of England, or a school free from all religious control, or a school free from State control so that it is able to teach Roman Catholicism, or a school which children may attend without paying a fee, or many other things. To be 'absolutely free' would be to be capable of doing anything whatever, and free of every hindrance to the exercise of this unlimited capacity, that is, to be omnipotent, omniscient, omnicompetent, and totally unscrupulous, in a universe in which there was no other such being to hinder one's acts.

If, therefore, there is sense in the promulgation of freedom as a political ideal, certain specifications must be understood. The freedom meant must be freedom for certain specific entities from certain specific restraints. Down to the present, four specific political freedoms appear to have engaged our emotions more than any other. The earliest of these was the freedom of the individual man from arbitrary and unchallengeable control by his State and its officers, a freedom thought to be attained by democracy or by the rule of law, especially by subjecting the officers to law, and making them liable to prosecution in courts of law for illegal government. This is political freedom proper, by right of seniority, because it was already explicitly demanded in ancient Athens, and has been frequently demanded since. The other three kinds are much later, and were not effectively demanded until the nineteenth or twentieth centuries. The first to arrive of these was freedom as opposed to slavery, that is, freedom for every individual man from the restraints by another man involved in his being a legal chattel of that other. Later in the nineteenth century came the demand for freedom of States or would-be States from the restraints imposed by other States. Italy was thought of as a person already existing, although there was no State or government of Italy, but held in slavery by the various governments administering different parts of the peninsula. More obviously, Ireland was a State that required to be freed from England, and Poland a State that required to be freed from Russia. To hold this kind of freedom as an ideal is part of nationalism.

The latest of the great demands for political freedom is the demand for the welfare of all individuals to be achieved by the action of the State. This has been expressed by the phrase 'economic freedom', and by Roosevelt's 'freedom from want'. It is the least properly called 'freedom', and would be better called 'welfare' or 'State-maintained welfare'. However, it certainly involves the individual's being free from the experiences and sufferings of poverty and want. These four political freedoms seem to be the greatest yet demanded. Freedom of speech and freedom of worship, however, are also often demanded, and very important.

One man's freedom may conflict with another's. If the first man is free to flood a certain valley, the other man is not free to farm it. Freedom by its generality is full of conflicts. The four main political freedoms involve millions of conflicts great and small. If every man is free from slavery, no man is free to own a man. Above all, freedom as general welfare, the newest of the four, conflicts very much with the oldest, political freedom proper, because the maintenance of universal welfare by the State involves a lot of arbitrary decisions by the State's officers in taking away people's land and restricting their use of it and other matters.

Freedom is often harmful. Any kind of act will be harmful in some cases. Therefore freedom to do a certain kind of act will be harmful in some cases, no matter what kind of act you mention. Freedom of the press, for example, includes the freedoms to ignore important events, to keep silent about evil deeds committed by newspapers or journalists, and to pester suffering persons who are news. Freedom of religion includes freedom to sacrifice human beings, and to prevent them from amusing themselves on Sundays. Freedom is always conflicting with order and uniformity, which some people find a great good. Plato objected to the motley disorder which the principle of freedom produced in Athens. You can often hear a German justifying harsh or tyrannous government on the ground that there must be order, or at least you could before Hitler was put down. You can limit any given kind of freedom by specifying cases to which it shall not apply, but there will always be some harmful cases which you have not yet thought of. That is why governors find it much safer to abolish the freedom altogether.

Someone will object that this overlooks the difference between liberty and licence. Licence is harmful, he will say, but liberty never is. I believe this to be a mistake. I believe that liberty and licence are both equally freedom in the same sense of 'freedom'. The difference is only that we call a freedom licence when we think it ought to be taken away, and liberty when we think it ought to be allowed. Many people suppose that there is some further difference, but they cannot say what it is. They tend to assume that the consequences of liberty are always beneficial, and the consequences of licence always harmful; but any given freedom, whether liberty or licence, will be harmful in some cases and beneficial in some cases.

It follows that a freedom must not be condemned as a 'licence' merely because it is harmful in some cases, for it may do more good than harm. We have to judge of the effects and values on the whole. It follows also that a freedom must not be approved as a 'liberty' merely because it is beneficial in some ways, for it may do more harm than good. It follows also that, although freedom is good in itself, this by itself is not decisive in favour of any particular freedom. For example, the mere fact that freedom is good is inadequate ground for demanding a freedom for the motorist to go forty miles an hour on a public road; and the Automobile Association's argument, that a speed limit would be a 'serious interference with personal liberty', is an argument against all legal restraints whatever.

What are the values of the four main political freedoms, and are they liberties or licences?

In judging the latest one, freedom from want, we are not just asking ourselves the obvious question whether it is better for people to be happy or miserable, but whether it is better for the State to undertake the task of keeping all its subjects happy and free from want. Freedom in this fourth sense is not just the welfare of all the people, which is good by definition. It is the State taking measures to maintain the welfare of all the people. That is a very different matter, because it could be that State action to increase welfare succeeds only in diminishing welfare.

This question is hard to distinguish from the question of the value of States and governments in general. Why have them at all? Only because in some way or other they increase welfare. Thus it seems that every State is necessarily a welfare State; and yet we think of the welfare State as something new. It is no doubt a matter of degree. It is a great difference of degree whether the State is or is not a universal provider of education, of houses, of medical attendance. It cannot be right to say that the State should try to provide all the elements of welfare. It is certainly right to say that it should try to provide some of them. So we may say that State action towards general freedom from want is certainly desirable to some extent, but the question just what State action is always to be answered anew. I add that I think it is better to classify this matter under the head of freedom as little as possible.

What of nationalism, or freedom for States from States? Are we to adopt Woodrow Wilson's principle of selfdetermination, which seems to be that any area where most of the inhabitants declare themselves an independent State is an independent State? Wales is an independent State if the Welsh say so? And after that Pembrokeshire is a State that must be freed from the oppression of Wales if the men of Pembrokeshire say so? And after that the village of Newport is a State that must be freed from the oppression of Pembrokeshire if the Newporters say so? Wilson's principle seems to be the very one on which the Southern States relied in the War between the States, the very one that Abraham Lincoln rejected.

An opposite principle, which is also active in this century, is that all States should lose their freedom in subordination to a World-State.

If we give up worshipping States, and cease to regard them as ends in themselves, and come to regard them only as means to the good life of individuals, we shall settle the question of freedom for States purely by reference to its effects on the good of individuals. Every new State is a new governmental machine interfering with the liberty of individuals. Every additional State further restricts our freedom at frontiers and customs barriers. On the other hand, a State may be necessary to preserve and encourage a desirable culture, and that culture may be important to many individuals. We shall reach our decision in each case by balancing effects like these, all of them concerning individuals. We shall not demand freedom for a State without counting the cost to individuals, as has often been done. We shall not insist either on the principle of self-determination or on the principle that all States are subordinate to a World-State.

I need not linger on freedom from slavery. We are nearly all agreed now that slavery is bad and incompatible with human dignity, and that the ownership of slaves is a very corrupting form of power. It does not follow that we should do well to invade and control any parts of the world where slavery still lingers; and it does not follow that the abrupt abolition of slavery is always the best thing to do.

There remains the earliest and most properly so called form of political freedom, the freedom of the individual subject from his governors. Not his complete freedom therefrom, which could only be achieved at the price of anarchy, but the partial freedom consisting in the governors being themselves subjected to laws, being convictable before courts for breaking those laws, and being dismissible by popular vote. This freedom is a very good thing, although it is a negation. It consists in the negation or absence of State restrictions on our powers. At its base lies the positive good of life and power. It is the enhancement of this good by the consciousness that it might have been hindered by the action of officers but is not being so hindered, and this is a huge enhancement. Although we often like to be told what to do, yet all of us like to be free and dislike being restrained or compelled. All of us have experienced compulsion, at least the compulsion that grown-ups exercise on children; and that is no doubt part of what makes us all positively enjoy and approve this negative thing, freedom. Men must act freely if they are to develop energy and enterprise and judgement and originality. Coercion is bad, and permissible only when good consequences outweigh the badness of the thing itself.

Freedom is always in danger. There are very many of us who love to interfere, to boss, to get and exercise power over men. More dangerous, perhaps, than instinctive bossiness is the moralizing temper which believes that people must be made to behave in certain ways for purely moral reasons, which legislates, for example, that you may not do on Sundays anything that I think it morally wrong to do on Sundays. Most insidious is the fact that we often must sacrifice some freedom to some other good, and all legislation does so. Thus gradually arise, in unexpected ways, and for good reasons, many very serious gaps in our freedom.

There is no escaping the fact that the price of freedom is eternal vigilance. We must all be politicians all the time, restraining what Whitman called 'the never ending audacity of elected persons', and still more the never ending audacity of civil servants. We must be constantly reminding civil servants and representatives of their incompetence and our low opinion of them. But vigilance is not enough. We must also always be willing to suffer, that is at least to lose our jobs, and on rare occasions to lose our lives. The greatest safeguard against tyranny is the general knowledge that most people will rather kill or be killed than endure it.

The paradox of freedom is that freedom must be limited in order to be preserved, or that complete freedom is equivalent to no freedom. Complete freedom includes freedom for the bully to bully, for the bossy to interfere, for the unjust to steal or strike or kill. These freedoms must be removed in order to preserve the decent man's freedom to live decently.

The paradox of freedom is the essence of government. The first business of government is to promulgate and enforce laws. This is a restriction on freedom. But government is justifiable if the laws are so chosen that their reign increases the freedoms that all can have without damage to others, and decreases only those freedoms whose exercise destroys the freedoms of others. Freedom from arbitrary force and unjust interference can be obtained by submitting to just force and legal interference, and this can be far better. Laws and governments are like arsenic; they are poisons, but a little of them acts as a tonic.

In the village of my childhood there was a pub called 'The Live and Let Live'. 'Live and let live' is one of the best of all maxims, and suggests most of the right attitude towards freedom and tolerance. That village was in the county where of all counties freedom is most prized, the county of Nelson and Tom Paine, the county of Norfolk.

3.32. *Muddles about freedom*

The concept of freedom is very liable to muddles, because of its complicated and negative nature and its emotional importance. Let us now notice some of these.

First, freedom has often been confused with power, for example by John Locke (*Essay*, 2. 21. 8). It is easy to fall into the mistake of seeing in freedom only the less complicated and more positive idea of power which it presupposes. Freedom is in truth the absence of other men's interference with my exercise of the powers which I have by my nature. I *can* by my nature walk all over the land, but by the laws of property I am *free* to walk only over small parts of it. I *cannot* by my nature walk over the sea, and so the question of being *free* to walk over the sea does not arise if we use the word 'free' correctly. It does arise, however, if we simplify the word 'freedom' and make it mean merely natural power, as some people do. Then it makes sense to say that I am not free to walk on the sea but I am free to walk on all parts of the land. In this new sense of 'freedom' man is becoming freer and freer in that his powers are increasing. Though he still cannot walk on the sea, he can proceed across it in a vessel at more than twenty knots, and over it in a plane at more than 200 knots. This simplified sense of the word 'freedom', equivalent to the word 'power', could be in itself perfectly useful and good, since we really have powers to talk about. As things are, however, it is bad and to be rejected, for three reasons. First, we already have the word 'power' doing this job and doing it perfectly well; there is no need of a new word. Second, the word 'free' *is* needed, and very much needed, to do the job it has been doing for centuries (and, indeed, for millenniums, if we include its ancestors along with itself), namely to mean the absence of interference by other men or States with my exercise of my natural powers. Third, the new use is bound to be confused from time to time with the old use, and that brings the muddle of people talking about the extension of man's powers as if it were the prevention of one man from interfering with another. This is part of the origin of the sad spectacle, very common in this century, of men making proposals for the increase of our power and wealth in the form of mean invectives against other men, as if it were due to deliberate interference by other men that we are not infinitely wealthy and powerful. In this way freedom from interference comes to be confused with welfare, and welfare comes to be regarded as something we could all command if we were not being interfered with by wicked persons.

A certain fact has inflated this muddle to enormous size, namely the ambiguous status of the laws of economics. Are they laws of nature or laws of man? If they are laws of man they can be abrogated, and that would give us back a freedom in the enduring and proper sense of 'freedom'. But if they are laws of nature they cannot be abrogated, but at best circumvented or used to our advantage; and using them to our advantage would give us more freedom only in the new and improper sense of more power.

The laws of economics are not precisely either laws of nature or laws of man. They are not very like Newton's laws of motion; nor are they very like Napoleon's civil code. They are a middle thing. What sort of thing they are becomes most apparent when we immerse ourselves in social anthropology, the study of human culture. They have that partly intended but mainly unintended, that partly alterable but mainly unalterable, character which belongs to the enduring elements of any culture. Our powers over them are much the same as our powers over language. In any given culture a man must use pretty much the language that reigns in that culture at that time, or else lose greatly in effectiveness. He can be an eccentric speaker or writer; but he pays a price for being so, and even then he buys only a very slight divergence from the norm. As to those who can intentionally alter the reigning language, either by legislation or by example or by some other means, they are extremely rare. Alterations *are* all the time taking place; but *how* any given alteration occurs is nearly always unknown, and scarcely ever because someone intended it to occur. That is how the laws of economics are. They are like laws of man in that they arise out of man's activities, and that they do not reign for ever but only at certain times and in certain societies. On the other hand, they are like laws of nature in that they are not deliberately legislated by man, nor enforced by the judges and the police, and cannot be abolished by direct legislation. Sociology is a study to which the opposition between man and nature applies very badly. All the phenomena of society, including the laws of economics, are neither artificial nor natural in the ordinary sense of those words.

So much for the mistake of confusing freedom with power. Another mistake concerning freedom is that, from demanding the removal of all *interference* with our actions, we sometimes go on to demand the removal of all *influence* on our actions, and say that a man is not 'really free' if he has been influenced at all by another man's arguments or suggestions or wishes. Thus Queen Wilhelmina in abdicating the throne of the Netherlands declared that she was 'uninfluenced by anyone', presumably for fear that, if she admitted having listened to anybody's advice, it would be said that she had not abdicated of her own free will (*The Times*, 6 September 1949).

This extension of the meaning of the word 'free' is a mistake. It could never become the accepted meaning of the word, for the simple reason that if it did there would hardly ever be any occasion to use the word, since our actions hardly ever are uninfluenced by what others have done and said. To act 'of one's own free will' is not to act without being in any way influenced by others, but rather to act without being interfered with, that is forced or threatened or commanded. To say that you are not 'really free' unless you are totally uninfluenced is a muddle or a dishonesty, as is usual with the adverb 'really'.

Most muddles about freedom arise from being against certain freedoms and being afraid to say so. People who wish to recommend some large new legal restraint on our exercise of our powers, for perhaps a very good reason, often do not dare to admit that they are recommending a large diminution of freedom for the sake of some other good which they believe to be greater. Because of the strong and often thoughtless approval attached to the notion of freedom, they prefer to muddle our conceptions by declaring that 'true freedom' is not the absence of restraint at all but something quite different. But to muddle our conceptions is always a great pity; and it is needless in this case as in all, because every man can be brought to see, if he is reasonably approached, that there is sometimes good ground for abolishing some particular kind of freedom.

Among the more absurd of the current redefinitions of 'freedom', by people who are afraid to say that they are against certain freedoms, is the Marxist account of it, for which I quote from Professor J. D. Bernal in *The Social Function of Science*, 1939, pp. 381-2:

The freedom of the nineteenth century was a seeming thing. It was an absence of a knowledge of necessity. Its basis lay in social relations through a market. In liberal theory every man should be free to do what he liked with his own, buy or sell, work or idle. In fact he was tied by the iron laws of economics: laws socially produced but taken as laws of nature because they were not understood. In an integrated and conscious society this conception of freedom is bound to be replaced by another—*freedom as the understanding of necessity*. Each man will be free in so far as he realizes that he is taking a conscious and determinate part in a common enterprise. This kind of freedom is most difficult for us to understand and appreciate; indeed, it can only be appreciated to the full by living it.

There is nothing essentially difficult about understanding a necessity. For example, each of us understands easily enough that he must necessarily die. But it is difficult to appreciate the Marxist proposal that understanding a necessity shall in future be called 'freedom'. There is no good reason for this complete change in the use of the word. The Marxist makes the word 'free' mean something absolutely new, while pretending that he is explaining what it has meant all along and still means. I am afraid there is no doubt why he does this; it is because he is against freedom in the proper sense of the word but does not want to say so. To be free is in proper language to be not interfered with by other men or the State; but the Communist Party wishes to interfere with us all in a great many ways all the time.

The Marxist account of freedom gains plausibility in the following way. Getting to know about a law of nature or of society sometimes gives us more power than we had before. Thus not until the law of gravity was precisely known, perhaps, could we have built flying machines; and when you learn about anxiety-neuroses perhaps you are better able to avoid having one. In this way, then, the understanding of a necessity may give us more power; and the word 'freedom' is sometimes misused to mean power.

It is worth noting that one correct and important application of this is as follows. The better we understand the necessity which the Communists mean to impose on us, the more power we shall have to prevent them from doing it. Freedom from the Communist tyranny depends on understanding the necessity which the Communists wish to impose on us.

So much for muddles about freedom. The fulfilment of our political needs and ideals does not require any abuse of language.

We can and should continue to use the word 'freedom' in politics to mean only the absence of other men's and the State's interference with our exercise of our natural powers.

3.4. TOLERANCE

3.41. *The principle of tolerance*

Since the State is necessary but diminishes freedom, the question arises whether any good principles can be found to guide us in deciding how far the State should go in infringing individual liberty. John Stuart Mill's great essay *On Liberty* is an attempt to answer this question, a search for 'a principle by which the propriety or impropriety of government interference' may be tested (p. 72, Everyman).

Government interference may be divided into two great departments, interference with our freedom to do wrong and interference with the rest of our freedom. By 'wrong' here is meant something wrong independently of the State's laws, not just legally wrong in that it has in fact been forbidden by the State. A law against murder is an interference with our freedom to do the moral wrong of murder; but a law establishing income tax is an interference with our freedom to spend our own income in morally innocent ways. Only the last twentieth of Mill's *Essay* deals with the latter kind of government activity, where he takes an excessively individualistic view, while at the same time wrongly regarding socialism as not involving infringement of liberty (p. 164, Everyman). The bulk of the *Essay* deals with State interference with acts supposed to be wrong in some extralegal way. This is the sphere of tolerance, though Mill does not call it so. Tolerance is non-interference with wrong or harmful activities. It is not mere non-interference. Or, at any rate, the only kind of tolerance that needs to be defended and upheld is non-interference with the harmful. There is no need to argue that we ought not to interfere with the good and the harmless.

To demand toleration for someone is thus not merely to assert that we should leave him free. It is to reassert this, or very nearly this, after someone has interjected 'except to do evil'. To demand toleration is to demand that people shall be left free even to do evil in many cases. When *Pravda* countered Herbert Morrison's article by saying that 'there is free speech in Russia for everyone except enemies of the people', it betrayed that it does not understand what freedom and tolerance are. To demand toleration is nothing so obvious and selfevident as to demand free speech for friends of the people. It is precisely to demand free speech for enemies of the people.

Part of Mill's principle of toleration is that '⟨A man's⟩ own good, either physical or moral, is not a sufficient warrant ⟨for mankind to interfere with his liberty of action⟩. He cannot rightfully be compelled to do or forbear because it will be better for him to do so, because it will make him happier, because, in the opinions of others, to do so would be wise, or even right' (op. cit., p. 73, Everyman). I think Mill meant more than he wrote here. I think he meant that a man's own good is not merely not a *sufficient* warrant for interfering with him, but no warrant whatever, and does nothing to strengthen any case for interference, so that it ought never to be mentioned in any argument for interference. This, at any rate, is the form in which I myself hold this principle. A State, in other words, should not behave like a school, which compels each child for his own good much more than for the goods of the other children. In a school the child is compelled to learn mathematics for his own sake, and compelled to be peaceable for the sake of the other children. In the State the citizen should be compelled only for the sake of the other citizens, and not at all for his own sake. He may be compelled to avoid tuberculosis, because tuberculous persons are a danger to others; but he may not be compelled to avoid cancer, because this disease is no danger to others. It is wrong to say that 'no man has a right to anything save to that which is really good for him', and that 'the individual is often a very bad judge of his own happiness', if from this you are going to infer that the State is a good judge of the citizen's happiness and has a right to compel him for the sake of it (F. C. Montague, *The Limits of Individual Liberty*, pp. 183, 189).

It has been thought that Mill's principle fails because it depends on a distinction that cannot be made in practice, the distinction between harmful actions that harm only the agent and those that harm others too. But, even if this distinction never can be rightly made, many authorities do in fact appeal to it, for they claim to be restraining a person 'for his own good'; and Mill's principle says that this is an improper claim in any case. Mill's principle involves that, whether or not it is possible to find actions that harm the agent without harming anyone else, the claim that the action harms the agent is never a good reason for the State to forbid it.

Those who adopt the principle that the State may compel the individual for his own good probably feel it to be selfevident; but no practical principle is selfevident. The great reasons against it are, first, that compulsion is an evil which it takes much good to outweigh, and, second, that it is usually improbable that the State is a better judge of the man's good than he is himself. When you fill out a form of application for a passport, on which you are asked to say what is the purpose or good of your journey, you realize vividly how restricted and blind is the State's conception of possible individual goods. The State is not a god who knows my good better than I do; it is a tyrannical fool who cannot see most of the goods there are.

Another negative principle may be added: the State may not interfere with the individual merely on the ground that his action is morally wrong. That an act is contrary to the moral law is no good reason for suppressing it. Neither the government nor any other body or person has a right to enforce all moral rules all the time. Neither the State nor any church has a right to prevent men from doing what they ought not to do as such. The view that 'the State has a right to punish all moral delinquency' (Montague, op. cit., p. 192) is false; and is probably held only by confusion with the view that the State has a right to compel a man to be moral when by so doing it can prevent great harm to others. What gives the State a right here is the possible harm to others, not the immorality of the act. If all morally wrong acts were legally forbidden by the State, there would be no difference between morality and legality, and the duty to obey the government would be man's only duty, and no one could ever do the right thing in spite of there being no compulsion to do it. That is, no one could ever do right 'of his own free will' as we say.

A third true negative principle is that the State may not forbid acts on the ground that they are contrary to the will of a god. No one has ever produced, or ever will produce, good and reasonable evidence for any statement that the will of some god is so and so. But even if we did know what the will of some god was, we ought not to follow it unless we found that following it lessened human misery; and we ought to determine, whether following it did lessen human misery, by empirical investigation without reference to its being ordained by a god. We ought not to say: 'It is commanded by a god, and therefore it must make people less miserable, no matter what the appearances are.'

Mill intended to offer also a positive principle, embracing all cases where the State may rightly abridge the freedom of an individual to do wrong. He said that all cases where the State may interfere are cases of the 'selfprotection' of mankind, cases of 'preventing harm' to persons other than the agent interfered with, cases of conduct 'calculated to produce evil to someone else' (op. cit., p. 73, Everyman).

Did Mill intend to say the converse also, namely that whenever the individual does harm to others he should be restrained by the State? No, he said that, while 'damage, or probability of damage, to the interests of others, can alone justify the interference of society', it does not always do so (op. cit., p. 150, Everyman). Therefore his principle is not a complete positive guide to State action in this matter. However much we accepted it, we should still have to use other considerations also in deciding when the State should intervene. This incompleteness on the positive side is no doubt correct. Any true principle for the direction of State interference must be incomplete and leave a great deal to be decided by other principles or by judgement. No principle can relieve us from the need for continuous judgement here, because human circumstances alter and because different peoples may properly make different choices.

The best expression of the principle of tolerance seems to be this: we must not suppress the evil behaviour of other men until reasonable examination has made it very probable that trying to suppress the evil would greatly lessen human misery upon the whole. I will enlarge on each phrase of this principle in turn.

'Reasonable examination.' There must be careful and thorough examination, according to the best methods of inquiry and canons of evidence that reason recommends, of the question whether efforts to suppress the evil would in fact greatly lessen human misery. That is practically to say, whether it really is an evil or only seems so to its would-be suppressors. This is a question of natural science, of the prediction of future events; and it is to be determined as reason indicates that questions of predicting the future are to be determined. No person or government has a right to suppress any activity, if it has not taken reasonable care to ascertain that both the activity does cause much human misery, and efforts to suppress it would be successful and greatly lessen human misery on the whole.

'Very probable.' The great goodness of freedom, and the great fallibility of man, demand that the government shall not suppress any freedom until it has ascertained by the methods of reason that it is *very probable* that the attempt at suppression will greatly lessen human misery.

'Trying to suppress the evil.' For it is essential to take into account the possibility that one's activities of suppression may be ineffective, in which case one would merely have added a second evil to the existing one. It is no good predicting the consequences of the total disappearance of the evil without at the same time predicting to what extent one's proposed measures of suppression are going to succeed. That the suppression of the evil would enormously increase human happiness is perfectly irrelevant, and no ground at all for action, if also the measures proposed will not in fact suppress it.

'On the whole.' What has to be found is the net gain or loss, which depends on all the gains and all the losses; and therefore we must look for every significant result. For example, the act of suppression is itself an evil, since all loss of freedom is an evil; and this evil must be reckoned in the accounts on the debit side, instead of being omitted as it often is by the censorious and the tyrannous. 'On the whole' is a fundamental principle of all practical wisdom, all good judgement about what to do.

'Lessen human misery.' This is the only criterion by which men's freedom to do wrong may be taken away. All suppressions and interferences not justifiable by this criterion are wrong. I have earlier noticed and rejected the two other criteria which are often held to justify intolerance, namely the will of a god and the moral law. They are both wrong and to be abandoned.

The principle is, then, that we must not suppresss the evil behaviour of other men unless reasonable examination has made it very probable that our attempts to suppress it will greatly lessen human misery upon the whole. Lawmakers should be tolerant in making laws. Officers should be tolerant in exercising their powers under the laws. Electors should be tolerant in electing. Citizens should be tolerant in talking.

3.42. Free speech

The application of the principle of tolerance to speech and publication is as follows. Many publications are blasphemous; but this gives no one any right to suppress them, for the will of a god is not a proper criterion of what may be suppressed. Many publications are false; but falsehood also is not a proper criterion of what may be suppressed. Many publications are immoral; for example, lying is usually immoral, and many publications are lies. But this by itself gives no one any right to suppress or punish them, for the moral law is not a proper criterion of what may be suppressed. It is a true moral principle that no man has a moral right to publish what he himself believes to be false, and no man has a moral right to publish statements without taking reasonable care to ascertain that they are true. But these true moral principles do not by themselves give any right of suppression or punishment, for nobody has a right to enforce moral laws as such. A government may suppress a publication only if it has ascertained by reasonable methods that its attempt to suppress the publication would probably greatly decrease human misery or prevent its greatly increasing.

Above all, of course, it is essential for a government to tolerate criticism of itself. That criticisms of the government should freely circulate, including those which the government itself thinks to be mere abuse or grossly false or otherwise grossly unfair, is a very great safeguard indeed against those diminutions of human happiness which governments are liable to cause. In democracies the government is usually more tolerant of criticisms of itself than in autocracies; but it is by no means always tolerant enough. If, for example, you read Erskine May's account of the British Parliament's privilege rules, I think you will judge, as I have, that they amount to not tolerating reasonable criticism of the Parliament by the citizens who have to suffer from Parliament's doings. Fortunately, they are rarely applied. But there is nothing in the constitution to prevent their being applied; and the Parliament of 1945-50 contained a number of unusually selfrighteous and touchy politicians who invoked these rules against reasonable criticisms of their doings.

The greatest enemy of free speech in Britain is our laws about libel and slander, or rather the way in which our lawyers interpret whatever laws our Parliament makes about libel and slander. We have a great tenderness for people's reputation; and our lawyers make it very hard for us to publish the errors and shortcomings of living persons here. For this reason some important news about the United Kingdom is to be found only in foreign newspapers, and it is therefore wise to get the habit of reading some foreign newspaper regularly.

This doctrine about free speech is inconsistent with the doctrine expressed in Pope Leo XIII's encyclical letter of 20 June 1888, as translated by John A. Ryan and Francis J. Boland in *Catholic Principles of Politics* (New York, 1948, p. 174). Leo XIII there declared that public authorities ought diligently to repress the publication of 'lying opinions'. I propose to give reasons for free speech and against the doctrine of Leo XIII.

It is not a good reason for free speech to remark that 'people cannot help what they believe'. They can help publishing what they believe, for they can keep their thoughts to themselves. But, further, they *can* help what they believe to a large extent; for they can choose whether or not to seek and listen to evidence and argument on both sides of the question, whether or not to try to judge equally on the basis of all available evidence and argument, whether to be reasonable, in short. And their choice in this matter will largely determine what they believe.

There are two great and good reasons for free speech. One of them is simply that freedom is a great good, and any suppression of freedom is consequently an evil. And this is a very great and strong reason though it is short to say.

The other strong reason for free speech is that the toleration of free speech is far more likely to produce a general spread of true opinion than is the suppression of it; and truth and the general spread of truth are very great goods.

One of the premisses of this second argument, however, is disbelieved by many people. They hold that, if all views are allowed to be expressed, false views will be generally adopted and their true contradictories generally rejected. They hold that the false is more easily believed than the true, so that, if a man hears both a proposition and its contradictory freely asserted, he will usually adopt as true that one of the pair which is in fact false. Pope Leo XIII expressed this view in his encyclical already referred to, when he wrote:

If unbridled licence of speech and writing be granted to all, nothing will remain sacred and inviolate; even the highest and truest mandates of nature, justly held to be the common and noblest heritage of the human race, will not be spared. Thus, truth being gradually obscured by darkness, pernicious and manifold error, as too often happens, will easily prevail.

In these words the phrase 'mandates of nature' was probably intended to include moral rules; and it is probably a consideration of moral rules that chiefly leads people to adopt this view. They think that, if the contradictory of a moral rule is allowed to be preached as freely as the rule (e.g. 'you may have sexual intercourse with whomever you wish'), most people will adopt the contradictory and not the rule.

To me this proposition seems ridiculous on its face. Leo seems to be saying that a great truth has only to be contradicted by somebody in public to be generally disbelieved, and that seems absurdly improbable. But I shall not leave it at that. I shall develop an argument in favour of my premiss that the toleration of free speech is far more likely to produce a general spread of true opinion than is the suppression of it. My argument is that all men are fallible in their opinions and reasonings as in everything else, and therefore they need to take all available means of lessening the chance of their believing falsehoods, and the strongest means available to this end is to be and remain exposed to free criticism and argument and contradiction from all sides. To paraphrase and slightly weaken a statement by John Stuart Mill, the complete liberty of all men to contradict and disprove my opinion is a necessary condition of my being justified in assuming its truth. People go mad if they live in a world of their own; and governments and popes go mad if they hear no independent voices criticizing them. The habit of rational discussion, of listening to argument and searching for evidence, is of enormous value in increasing the spread of true instead of false opinions; and this habit is starved and discouraged by all intolerance of free speech. If you suppress the contradictions and arguments of others against you, you are not doing all you could to lessen the risk of your being wrong. If you are a governor this is immensely serious to those you govern, and a grave breach of your duty towards them.

This is true even of moral rules, the case where the intolerant have the strongest argument. Moral rules go against the flesh, and the reason for going against strong desires of the flesh is sometimes obscure. The reason for a moral rule is more obvious to the experienced than to the inexperienced. Hence there is a case for saying that moral rules may not be discussed, because the reasons for them cannot yet be properly appreciated by those who need them most.

Yet here, too, the case for intolerance is bad. Every moral rule either has a good reason, or ought to be abandoned as a useless restriction on liberty. A moral rule, like all laws, is a restriction on liberty; and a restriction on liberty is always improper unless it can reasonably be shown to be very probably the cause of a great diminution of human misery. While we should emphatically and solemnly preach to the young such moral rules as we believe to be important, we should also right from the beginning offer them the reason which in our eyes justifies these rules; and there is no good reason except the appeal against man's misery. When moral rules are not allowed to be criticized, bad ones creep in, and good ones are held in a stupid and immoral way. The man who suppresses the contradictors of his moral rules implies that either there is no good reason for his rules or at least he is incapable of giving it. It is unreasonable for a grown person to hold a moral rule for which he can give no good reason. To do so is to be still in the prison of taboo.

It is true that a powerful preacher will sometimes sway people to the side of bad action. But this is done by religious or moralizing persons more often than by others. It is true that sometimes, of a pair of contradictory statements, the false one obtains belief more easily than the true one. But the best precaution we can take against that happening is always to let both sides argue, never to suppress one side. For there is no good reason to believe that, if we suppress one side, we the suppressors are exempt from the human tendency to believe the false, or from the need of contradictors to keep us straight. Every man, however wise, needs all the criticism and argument and opposition he can get to keep him nearer truth than falsehood. As Mill put it in his great chapter on liberty of thought and discussion:

> Silencing the expression of an opinion is . . . robbing the human race; posterity as well as the existing generation; those who dissent from the opinion, still more than those who hold it. If the opinion is right, they are deprived of the opportunity of exchanging error for truth: if wrong, they lose, what is almost as great a benefit, the clearer perception and livelier impression of truth, produced by its collision with error (op. cit., p. 79, Everyman).

3.43. *All men are fallible*

I have based the demand for freedom of speech in part on the reason that freedom of speech is far more likely to produce a general spread of true opinion than is the suppression of any form of speech. And I have based this reason on the further reason that all men are fallible. I propose now to take the matter still another step further back, because many people deny or tend to deny the doctrine that all men are fallible. It is official Papist doctrine that the Pope, when speaking *ex cathedra* on faith or morals, is infallible; and many who are not Papists also feel that there is something wrong with the doctrine that all men are fallible.

First it is necessary to be clear what the word 'fallible' means. To say that anyone is fallible is simply to say that he sometimes makes a mistake. And to say that he is infallible is to say that, on the contradictory, he never makes a mistake. The notion is applicable not merely to persons, but to anything whatever that can in any sense habitually succeed or fail. For example, one could perfectly well call a cigarette-lighter infallible if it flamed every time one pressed the button, and never failed to flame. And this would be exactly the same sense of the word as when a Papist says that the Pope speaking *ex cathedra* on faith or morals is infallible.

Thus the notion of infallibility contains the notion of all or always or every time, and that of fallibility contains the notion of not all or not always or only sometimes. This involves that it makes nonsense to talk of infallibility or its contradictory in a context where no question of always arises. It is sense to say that the Pope speaking *ex cathedra* is infallible, but nonsense to say that when the Pope spoke at a certain moment he was infallible. It is sense to say that your lighter flames infallibly, but nonsense to say that it flamed infallibly when you used it just now. The words 'fallible' and 'infallible' have no application to particular cases and events. They apply only to a general class of cases or events. The Pope's utterances *ex cathedra* can in general be fallible or infallible; but one of them in particular cannot be either fallible or infallible; it can only be true or false. Anyone who calls some particular statement infallible is either talking nonsense or saying in an improper way that it is true.

Given that this statement made by this speaker is false, it follows that this speaker is fallible. But, given that this statement made by this speaker is true, nothing follows about whether this speaker is fallible or infallible. Given that a speaker is fallible, nothing follows about the truth or falsehood of any particular statement he makes. But, given that a speaker is infallible, it follows that any statement he makes is true. An infallible person would therefore never be required to give any reason or evidence for his statements. Or, rather, he would be able to give one and the same final reply to every challenge, no matter which of his statements he was challenged about. To the question How do you know that?, no matter which of his statements it referred to, he could always reply with truth and finality: 'It must be true because I say it and I am infallible.'

Thus to say that all men are fallible is to say that every man without exception makes at least one mistake in his life, and no man ever has gone or will go through his whole life without making a single mistake. And this is the proposition I wish to recommend now.

To say, or to deny, that all men are fallible, is to make an assertion about the course of events. The only justification for assertions about the course of events is experience. Direct or indirect experience, and experience extended or not extended by generalization and deduction; but in any case experience. Therefore this question whether all men are fallible is to be settled by nothing else but our experience of men.

I believe that all men are fallible on the ground of my experience. It seems to me an overwhelmingly probable induction from every day of my life. Every man with whom I have conversed for an hour or more has in my opinion evinced at least one error in that period. Every statement that I have read amounting to ten or more pages has appeared to me to contain at least one falsehood, if I was capable of judging it. My own past life, when I look back on it, appears to me full of mistaken opinions. Are *you* acquainted with any man who has in your opinion never made a mistake?

Ought I to go from the premiss, that all men I have met are fallible, to the conclusion that all men whatever are fallible? It seems to me that I ought, again on the ground of experience. The experience I have gathered of the general nature of man makes it immensely probable that all men will frequently entertain false opinions and utter false statements. That is, the fallibility which I have observed in all of my acquaintances and in myself seems clearly to depend on universal features of human nature. It depends in particular on the capacity of human language to make assertions about any matters whatever, whether we know anything about those matters or not, together with our frequent desire and need to know or believe propositions about all kinds of things, while at the same time our opportunities for really experiencing most things are extremely limited. Descartes was feeling for this when he explained human error as due to man's combining an infinite capacity to will with a finite capacity to judge. What he took for an infinite capacity to will is the capacity to construct a huge number of statements, which is inherent in human language owing to its huge and always extending vocabulary. The beasts, though also fallible, make far fewer mistakes than we do because they say far less.

Some persons tend to believe that the question whether all men are fallible is to be answered, not by experience and generalization, but by arguments from the Bible or some other book. A learned Papist once suggested to me that the infallibility of the Pope can perhaps be inferred from Matt. xxviii. 20 and Luke x. 16. But the question whether any man is infallible is not to be answered by pointing out that some book says that some man is infallible. For all books, including the Bible, are utterances by men; and our experience of men teaches us that their books, like their spoken words, are fallible. And therefore, if any book contains a sentence asserting that a certain man is infallible, it is extremely probable that the book shows its own fallibility by being false in this instance. The only respect in which the Bible is good evidence on the question whether all men are fallible is that, by the falsehoods which it contains, it enforces the generalization that all men are fallible. It would be just as unreasonable to believe that the Pope was infallible *ex cathedra* because the Bible said so (if it did) as it would be to believe that all men had blue eyes because the Bible said so (if it did). The statement that all men have blue eyes is disproved by looking at men until you see one whose eyes are not blue; and that is the end of that, no matter what any book may say. Similarly, the statement that the Pope's utterances *ex cathedra* are infallible is disproved by reading them until you come to one that is false; and that is the end of that, no matter what any book may say. In each case it is a question only of looking to see what happens.

'But', it is sometimes argued, 'the Bible and the Pope *ex cathedra* are not human utterances; they are utterances by God, and therefore infallible.' This is an assertion about what happens. Therefore the proper way to decide whether to accept or reject it is to appeal to experience. Experience overwhelmingly indicates that it is false and is to be rejected. We find the Bible and the Pope's pronouncements written or printed on ordinary human paper in ordinary human ways. We can observe a new papal pronouncement *ex cathedra* being composed with pen and paper by men in the Vatican. That they are fallible documents is abundantly shown by the falsehoods and horrors which they contain. Example of falsehood: Joshua made the sun stand still. Example of horror: thou shalt not suffer a witch to live. It is grossly bad judgement to claim for any document that it is true in every sentence because it is inspired by someone infallible.

The most serious and respectable objection to the doctrine that all men are fallible is the uneasy feeling that somehow or other this statement refutes itself. But it does not refute itself; and I will now try to remove the feeling that it does from the minds of any of you in which it may exist.

The most obvious kind of selfrefutation is selfcontradiction. To contradict oneself is to say and deny the same thing, or to entail one's own denial. Now 'all men are fallible' does not do this. It is not a selfcontradictory statement like 'all men have blue eyes but some do not', or like 'a father is not a parent'. It is a selfconsistent statement. It presents a possibility which, as far as logic tells us, could actually be realized in the world. Thus it is not selfrefuting in the obvious sense of selfcontradictory.

But there is another kind of selfrefutation besides selfcontradiction. If a man opens his mouth and says 'I am not speaking now', he makes a selfconsistent but false statement. The peculiarity of it is that the fact, to which one appeals to show that the statement is false, is the utterance of the statement itself. Precisely by uttering the statement he produces the state of affairs in virtue of which the statement is false. (Similarly, if a man says 'I am speaking now', he makes his statement true by uttering it.)

The statement that 'all men are fallible' is not selfrefuting in this way either, for you do not by uttering it produce an infallible man. (It would be remarkably convenient if you could make yourself infallible by declaring that 'all men are fallible'.)

These are the only two ways in which a statement can refute itself, so far as I can see. Either it contradicts itself, or by its utterance it provides a negative instance which disproves itself. Since 'all men are fallible' does neither of these, it is not selfrefuting.

In addition to selfrefutation there is perhaps such a thing as selfstultification. The statement that 'what I say is never worth saying' neither contradicts nor otherwise refutes itself; but it appears to stultify itself. A statement stultifies itself, we may define, if it entails that to assert it would be silly.

The statement that 'all men are fallible' does not stultify itself. On the contrary, if it is true it is very important, and a wise man will assert it from time to time.

I fear that, in spite of these explanations, the uneasy feeling may remain with some of you that the statement that 'all men are fallible' does after all somehow do away with itself. If that is so, I ask you to write down at your leisure exactly how it does this, and then to look for a flaw in what you have written. I think you will probably find a flaw; but, if you do not, bring it to me and I will try to find a flaw in it.

I will give now two examples of finding a flaw in such attempts. People sometimes say that 'those who argue against infallible authority claim infallibility for themselves'. The flaw here is that this is simply false. We do not claim infallibility for ourselves. Every man who utters a statement thereby implicitly claims that that statement is true. But he does not thereby claim that all the statements he ever utters are true. That is, he does not claim that he is infallible. Whenever a man makes a sincere statement he thinks it true; but no sensible man has ever thought that all the statements he had ever uttered or would ever utter were true. The statement that 'all men are fallible' is the same in this respect as the statement that 'all men are mortal'. The speaker of either of them claims to be telling a truth but does not claim to be infallible. Every statement equally claims truth for itself, and every statement equally refrains from claiming that its utterer is infallible.

This is a mistake that has been made by the assailants of infallibility as well as by its defenders. Mill wrote that 'all silencing of discussion is an assumption of infallibility' (op. cit., p. 79, Everyman). This, I regret to have to admit, is false. To silence a discussion is not to assume that one is infallible. The editor who declares that 'this correspondence must now cease', the chairman who forbids the raising of a certain topic, the headmaster who forbids the boys to debate birthcontrol, are none of them assuming themselves infallible. They are merely assuming themselves to be right in thinking that they ought to silence this particular discussion now. Silencing a discussion is an act of government. Are we to say that all acts of government assume the infallibility of the governor, or that only this special kind of act of government assumes the infallibility of the governor? Both are obviously false, but Mill's sentence implies that one of them is true. However, it is only Mill's expression that is wrong here. What he had in mind was the truth that only a belief in his own infallibility could morally justify a governor in permanently forbidding adult persons to express a certain view (cf. p. 85). But he failed to say clearly that it is a matter of moral justification, not of logical assumption.

Here is a second example of finding a flaw in an attempt to show that the doctrine that all men are fallible disposes of itself. People sometimes think that the proposition that 'we are fallible' entails its own contradictory in the following way: 'Assume that we are fallible; it follows that we may be wrong in saying that we are fallible; and from this in turn it follows that we are infallible.'

The flaw here is that it is false that the second consequence follows. From 'we may be wrong in saying that we are fallible' it does not follow that 'we are infallible'. 'Are' never follows from 'may be'. From possibilities alone one cannot rightly conclude to facts. We may call this fallacy the illicit process from possibility to actuality.

These two examples must suffice to illustrate the endless task of pointing out the flaw in fallacious arguments against the doctrine that all men are fallible. With them I conclude my recommendation of this doctrine, which is one of the premises for one of my arguments for free speech. But I want before leaving the topic to warn you against a certain misuse of this doctrine, a misuse which was perhaps committed by Oliver Cromwell on a famous occasion. In his letter of 3 August 1650 to the General Assembly of the Kirk of Scotland, Cromwell wrote: 'I beseech you, in the bowels of Christ, think it possible you may be mistaken.' What was his purpose in thus reminding his opponents of the fallibility of man? One good reason for doing this is to persuade your adversary not to suppress the publication of views opposed to his own; and that Cromwell had this purpose in mind is suggested by his mentioning, elsewhere in the letter, that the Kirk had been suppressing his papers whereas he had been publishing the Kirk's letters to him. On the other hand, the letter never unequivocally says that this is the purpose of the famous reminder; and some parts of it suggest that he was using it in another way, namely to insinuate that 'since you may be wrong, you are wrong and I am right'. One part of it implies that he knows he is right because he feels the grace of God upon him, and that way of thinking seems more typical of the man. Anyhow, the argument that 'since you may be wrong, you are wrong and I am right', whether or not Cromwell was guilty of it, is utterly fallacious and a damnable misuse of the doctrine of human fallibility. It is another case of the illicit process from the 'may be' to the 'are'. The undoubted fact that you *may be* wrong is an excellent reason for your allowing free speech to your opponents. But it is no reason for them to claim that you *are* wrong; for, from the truth that all men are fallible, nothing follows about who is in the right in any particular controversy. It would be better to say: 'I beseech Christ to make *me* think it possible that *I* am mistaken.' The fallibility principle should make us not merely patient of criticism, but eager for it.

This fallacy is often committed by lawyers crossexamining witnesses. 'But you could be mistaken, could you not?', they ask. Of course he could be mistaken, because he is fallible; but it does not follow that he *is* mistaken. It is a hard question to reply to. If you say 'No, I could not be mistaken', you appear to claim infallibility. But if you say 'Yes, I could be', you appear to withdraw your statement, or at least some of the force of it. Perhaps the best reply is 'One always *can* be mistaken, but one sometimes *is* not', or simply 'I could be, but I'm not'.

This completes my defence of my principle for the toleration of publication, against Leo XIII's position that authorities ought diligently to repress the publication of 'lying opinions'. Now that I have given the positive arguments for my principle, which are independent of any errors Leo XIII may have made in the statement of his view, I may remark that his letter makes his position more attractive by means of three confusions which are not detected by most of its readers. It confuses what is false with what the public authority thinks false, tacitly assuming that the public authority is infallibly right about what is false. It also confuses falsehood with lying, tacitly assuming that whoever utters a falsehood knows that it is a falsehood and so is guilty of the moral wrong of lying. And thirdly it confuses the true moral law, that men ought not to lie, with the false moral law, that public authorities ought to prevent men from lying.

3.44. *The limits of tolerance*

There are limits to tolerance; and this is implied by the principle of tolerance as I have formulated it. We may interfere with an evil where we have good reason to believe that our interference will greatly lessen human misery on the whole. I wish to point out certain departments in which the limits of tolerance come sooner than liberals have been inclined to think.

In the first place, a man's official position may diminish his right to free publication. For example, a teacher in a public institution has less right to publish his thoughts than a man who lives by mining. For it may be the case that the utterance of a certain opinion by a miner does not greatly increase human misery, but the utterance of the same opinion by a teacher does so. Perhaps it can be shown that a teacher who preaches suicide, or one who preaches communism, is probably greatly increasing human misery. If so, we are justified in depriving him of that job. But it is unlikely that it can be shown that a miner who preaches either of these things is doing much harm.

In the second place, the tolerance that should be extended to bad religions is a good deal less than is often claimed nowadays. While every religion should have freedom to publish and to preach, religion gives no right to disobey the ordinary civil laws made for the good of the people in this life. It gives no right to avoid military service, though a government is often wise to grant exemption from military service as a grace. A pastor's need to conduct a religious ceremony gives him no right to break a law that rations petrol or limits speed on the highway. Murder is still murder if someone holds a religion of human sacrifice. No civil crime becomes legal by being done out of religious beliefs or sentiments. Whatsoever is illegal in the commonwealth must be forbidden in the church. All religious practice must yield to, and be overruled by, the need to lessen the misery of man on earth, wherever there can reasonably be shown to be a conflict between the two. It is therefore too strong to say, as Locke did in his letter on toleration, that 'no man whatever ought . . . to be deprived of his terrestrial enjoyments upon account of his religion'. A man's religion has led him to kill prostitutes before now; and a man who kills prostitutes ought to be deprived of some or all of his terrestrial enjoyments.

Still less does religion confer any right to make and enforce special laws incumbent on the whole population regardless of its religion. Locke wrote truly that 'whatsoever is lawful in the commonwealth cannot be prohibited by the magistrate in the church'. The religion of the English Nonconformists gives them no right to force the Sunday Observance Law upon the people; and the existence of this law is a gross tyranny. Of the freedoms which religion should not have, the most fundamental is that it should not have the freedom to control those who do not wish to obey it. That is, it should have no legal force; and no law should be made or unmade for the sake of any religion. In practice, unfortunately, it is often easy for a religious group to take away other persons' freedom merely by saying that this freedom is 'offensive to their religious feelings'. As Max Beerbohm has put it, 'the Nonconformist conscience makes cowards of us all'. Nothing ought to be made illegal because it is a sin (sin being a religious notion), but only because it is injurious to the earthly life of man. Nothing ought to be punished because it is a sin, but only because it is illegal, that is, a contravention of the existing law of the land. For example, the following ought not to be a law in any State: 'He that sacrificeth unto any god, save unto the Lord only, he shall be utterly destroyed' (Exod. xxii. 20).

The most important limit to toleration is the limit to be placed on the freedom of those who wish to take away freedom. A government may interfere when reasonable examination of the evidence has made it very probable that the interference would greatly diminish human misery; and one kind of harm which may justify such an interference with someone's liberty is that harm which tends to overthrow the general reign of liberty. We may interfere with the liberty of persons who are likely to interfere with everyone's liberty. As Dr. Popper has well said, we have the right not to tolerate the intolerant. We should tolerate even them whenever we can do so without running a great risk; but the risk may become so great that we cannot allow ourselves the luxury.

The most essential thing not to tolerate is any move that is very likely to give power to uncriticizable and irremovable governors. At the present time this means mainly the Communists, a body of thoroughly intolerant and very active persons, whose fellows are already in tyrannical control of about a third of the human race. Since they are thoroughly intolerant, we have a good right not to tolerate them. For the sake of freedom we do tolerate them a great deal; but we should watch them always, and suppress them whenever reasonable examination makes it very probable that their activities threaten to end the reign of tolerance altogether, and that our suppression would stop this threat. Fortunately, we are well aware of this threat.

There is another great threat to freedom of which we are not well aware. The second most intolerant and active body in the world today is the Papist Church. It is the policy of this Church, long fixed and declared, that 'no State is justified in supporting error or in according to error the same recognition as to truth' (p. 314), and that 'the fact that the individual may in good faith think that his false religion is true gives ⟨him⟩ no right to propagate it' (p. 318), and that a Papist State 'could not permit ⟨members of a dissenting group⟩ to carry on general propaganda' (p. 320). Those are quotations from an official Papist book on politics, namely *Catholic Principles of Politics*, by John A. Ryan and Francis J. Boland, New York, 1948.

The danger of the Papist Church is not generally realized in England today. This is partly because the Communist Party is a greater danger, and the Papists are against the Communists. Partly also it is because most Papists do not know the political doctrines of their own Church. But mainly it is due to a third cause. It often happens that a body, which is fundamentally intolerant, turns tolerant while it is a minority among a tolerant majority. That is notably the case with the Papists in England now. They are tolerant men. But the doctrine of their Church is fundamentally and irretrievably intolerant; and whenever it comes into power in a particular place it turns intolerant in fact. The more liberal members, who often hold the higher places while the Church is a minority among a liberal majority, are now gradually replaced by illiberal leaders in greater harmony with the essential philosophy of the body. Hence the need to restrict the influence of Papists in England now is greater than it appears from the tolerant nature of the Papists with whom we are acquainted. Those are not the men who would be in power if the Church were in power. Englishmen have in the last 150 years gradually abolished their former safeguards against Papist control until there are almost none left, and no evil results have yet appeared, and so we are confident that all is well. But meanwhile the power, size, and prestige, of this body in the country have been steadily increasing, and its ancient principles of intolerance have been affirmed more explicitly than before. There are rocks ahead that must be seen to be avoided.

We have the right to see that neither of these intolerant bodies gets much influence in the government, or in any other powerful body, such as a trade union; and we ought to do so. We ought sometimes to see that individual members of these intolerant bodies are kept out of influential professions like the foreign service, the civil service, and the service of the elementary public schools. I do not say that you should never recommend a Papist for a post in the civil service; but I do say that you are to consider carefully that he is a member of a body which is always thoroughly intolerant when it has the power to be so, that he probably does not know himself how intolerant his church is, and that his presence in the civil service must tend to increase the influence of his church. I do say that you are to disregard all accusations that you are intolerant, or that you are persecuting religious minorities, or that you are unjust to an innocent man, in considering his religion; for your intolerance is only being intolerant of intolerant bodies; but the intolerance of his church is unlimited; and it is far more important that men in general should be shielded from that, than that this individual should be shielded from all disabilities arising out of his unfortunate allegiance.

Third on the list of dangerous intolerant bodies in England today come the trade unions. Their intentions are much less bad than those of either the Communist Party or the Papist Church; but their legal powers are much greater and much too great. The policy, to which they tend, that a man may not practice a trade without belonging to a union, is a great interference with freedom, and is protected by extraordinary legal exemption from accountability to the courts. Trade unions can break promises with impunity; and they can force a man to change his way of living with near impunity.

The principle of intolerance does not, however, indicate any denial of free publication to the intolerant. They should be allowed to publish their views as much as they please; and our defence against that should only be to publish our replies, never to suppress their publications. If we did otherwise we should offend against the principle that the free publication of all opinions is far more conducive to the general reign of truth than any suppression of any opinion whatever. If we judge that the voice of the intolerant is being heard too much and the voice of the tolerant too little, the right way to redress the balance is always to increase the voice of the tolerant. Government force and money may not be used to stifle the voice of the intolerant, but they may be used to increase the voice of the tolerant; and it is a pity that such use is sometimes condemned as 'propaganda'. It is not propaganda in the sense of lying libel, such as telling unproved stories of rape and murder about the enemy. It is propaganda only in the neutral sense in which all practical speech is propaganda, including these lectures of mine.

Censorship is not one of the legitimate forms of intolerance. That is, the government should not require proposed publications to be submitted beforehand to a censor for approval. By so doing it would prevent that clash of opinions from which truth is most likely to emerge. Freedom of expression should be absolute both in politics and in religion. Everyone should be allowed to express every opinion about gods and morality and ritual and man, whether blasphemous or pious, immoral or moral. Free speech in religion includes the freedom to preach and proselytize and try to make converts, which is denied to Protestants at the present time in Spain. It is a sad thing that one of our great defenders of toleration, John Locke, believed that atheism was not to be tolerated. It is a sad thing that atheists in U.S.A. and U.K. are still under serious disabilities in fact, though not I think by law. That is, the frank atheists are. But, in view of this intolerant attitude, there are probably many who conceal their atheism. As Disraeli made his characters say, 'Sensible men are all of the same religion'. 'And, pray, what is that?' 'Sensible men never tell.' There ought to be complete liberty of conscience, in the sense that anyone may say what he thinks true about gods and the moral law, as opposed to what any authority thinks true about them; and Leo XIII was grossly distorting this when he wrote that the only true liberty of conscience is liberty to follow the will of God. 'The moral decisions of others should be treated with respect, as long as such decisions do not conflict with the principle of tolerance' (K. R. Popper, *The Open Society*, U.S. ed., p. 508).

Some people give the name 'censorship' to all action whatever in restraint or punishment of publication. But that is a misuse of the word. A censor is an officer who examines each proposed publication because no publication may be made without his permission. In England now there are censors for the performance of plays and the showing of films, but not for the publication of books or periodicals or newspapers. It is not censorship if a publication is prosecuted after it has been made; and it can be prosecuted for other crimes besides not having obtained permission from an official censor. Nor is it censorship if some unofficial body declines to handle a publication because of its contents. It is not censorship if W. H. Smith & Son refuse to distribute the *New York Times* in this country. To condemn censorship is not to condemn all prosecutions for libel, nor is it to say that a newsagent is obliged to handle all publications however much he thereby exposes himself to prosecution for libel. Some libel law is certainly desirable. It is not good that an honest man should have no redress if a newspaper publicly calls him a 'hired liar'.

If any further restraint on newspapers were required, beyond the existing law of libel, it would not be to prevent them from publishing certain things, but to compel them to publish certain things. For instance, their constant refusal to publish the bad acts of newspapers is a serious harm to the community. I do not see, however, that any law could remedy it. A government office to decide what newspapers must publish would inevitably be staffed by men of bad judgement, and would do much more harm than good. All that a government can do in this respect is, apparently, to allow and encourage private enterprise in the publication of newspapers, in the hope that sometimes one newspaper will make known the wickednesses of another.

3.5. PEACE AND JUSTICE

3.51. *The uses of government*

So far in this survey of political goods the State and its government have not appeared advantageously. I have found that the State is not to be taken as itself a great good, that the good kind of equality is a personal rather than a political matter, and that freedom is to be obtained in spite of the government rather than through it.

Are there then no acceptable political goods that are secured primarily through the government? There must be; or else the right political philosophy is anarchism, the view that government is undesirable and should be abolished. This brings us to the questions: What are governments for? What is the use of them? Why have them at all, in view of their manifold disadvantages and unpleasantnesses? Why is anarchism wrong?

A great many ends have been put forward as being what

States are for. I have said earlier in these lectures that one of the purposes of a State may be to preserve a culture. Here is a list taken from a sentence by Acton: liberty, happiness, prosperity, power, the preservation of an historic inheritance, the adaptation of national law to national character, the progress of enlightenment, the promotion of virtue (Fasnacht, *Acton's Political Philosophy*, p. 89). This covers most of the obvious candidates; but it omits the God-State, for the State has often been regarded as its own end. And here are a few answers that have been given to the question what governments are for. Locke wrote that 'the great and chief end of men's uniting into commonwealths, and putting themselves under government, is the preservation of their property', and in property he included 'their lives, liberties, and estates' (*Second Treatise of Civil Government*, c. ix, §§ 123-4). Hume wrote that 'the principal object of government is to constrain men to observe the laws of nature' (*Treatise*, 3. 2. 8). Mill wrote that 'the most important point of excellence which any form of government can possess is to promote the virtue and intelligence of the people themselves' (*Representative Government*, c. ii). The constitution of Alabama states, or stated, that 'the sole and only legitimate end of government is to protect the citizen in the enjoyment of life, liberty, and property, and when the Government assumes other functions it is usurpation and oppression' (according to Lecky, *Democracy and Liberty*, i. 118). Lecky himself wrote that 'a Government can have no higher object than to raise the standard of national health' (i. 324). The word 'protection' covers two very different things; for the protection of a man against other men is very different from the protection of him against all the natural dangers to which he is subject. But even without this distinction there is plenty of variety in these statements.

This question what States and governments are for—is it a question of fact or a question of choice? It is not merely a question of fact, to be discussed like what is at the bottom of the sea. For governments are to some extent under our control, for us to do with them what we want. Our choice enters in, as in all questions of purpose and practice and goodness. On the other hand, it is partly a question of fact; for we need to know what things government can do and what things it cannot do, and what are the side consequences of the things it can do, in order to choose wisely what we will make it do. So our question can be put more precisely thus: What things *can* the government do, and, among all the things it *can* do, which do we *wish* it to do?

There is more than one right answer to each part of the question. As to the question of fact, What *can* a government do?, the powers of government differ in different times and places. Where telephones exist, for example, the government can do more than where they do not exist. And as to the question of choice, there is no reason why every wise nation must always make the same choice of what its government is to do, on pain of ceasing to be wise and becoming foolish. Many different choices might be equally wise, just as there are many different ways of earning his living that a person may choose without being a fool. It follows that no doctrine is acceptable which declares that '*the* purpose of government is so and so', assigning one and only one right purpose to all governments at all times.

Should the State promote virtue and intelligence? Certainly if it can. We cannot believe that the successful promotion of virtue and intelligence would be accompanied by side consequences that cancelled all the advantage. But can it? Not directly, because virtue and intelligence are essentially qualities of the independent man. The attempt to produce them directly produces instead at best a good breed of sheep; and this fact condemns much of the schoolmasterish politics of Plato and Aristotle. In the sentence I have quoted from Mill he writes of virtue and intelligence being promoted, not precisely by the State as such, but by the form of the State's constitution. He means that some constitutions by themselves have a much stronger tendency than others to promote these qualities in the citizens; and he is right. We have had recently, in Nazi and Communist governments, good opportunities to see how grossly those constitutions degrade the virtue of the citizens.

Besides the form of its constitution, the State has at least one other means of seeing to the virtue and intelligence of its citizens. That is to require all to be educated, and to provide education for those who cannot or will not buy it. I should say that the richer States have this means at their disposal; universal education is, however, so expensive that probably only industrial countries can afford it.

Attempts to increase the virtue and intelligence of the citizens by censorship, or by legal penalties for moral crimes as such, or by religious laws, have the opposite result. Religious faith being not a virtue but a vice, the State should not try to encourage it.

No doubt a State should do something to preserve and promote a good culture among its citizens. But it is hard to feel confidence in saying what in particular it should do. Questions of more than one language among the citizens of a single State are usually very difficult. Canada allowed French as well as English, but the United States insisted on English. You will not care to say that one is definitely the better thing to do. Every disappearance of a language is at least a sentimental loss; but every barrier to communication is a very great utilitarian loss. We sometimes find that those who insist on the preservation of a language are not supported by the majority of those who speak it. In Ireland, for example, the English-speaking teachers and politicians of Dublin insist on the preservation of Erse, and this makes the Erse-speakers in the west complain that they are being deprived of the opportunity to learn the English which they need.

3.52. *Socialism*

If there are useful and desired enterprises which cannot be performed except by concerted action of the whole town or people, and can be carried through by concerted action without the benefits being obliterated by the drawbacks, government should undertake them. Government should undertake such large enterprises as most members want done but cannot do individually or in private groups. Nearly everybody agrees that there are such enterprises. The most obvious of them are defence against attacking States, and the provision of roads.

There are also enterprises which can be done either by the government or by private groups. Thus at the present time the telephone service is provided by private groups in the U.S. but by the government in the U.K. Which of these enterprises the government should take over is an endless question of detail. The form of the question is always the same, namely, which will run it more conveniently, the government or private enterprise; but there is certainly not the same right answer for all enterprises at all times and places. For different governments at different times the right answer must vary, according to the varying wishes of the people, state of engineering, state of foreign politics, and many other factors. The extreme negative view, that the government should attempt no common enterprise at all, is certainly wrong almost everywhere, if not everywhere. It is possible to obtain very great material advantages by concerted action under the government, and that without serious risk of increasing the evil side of government. The extreme positive view, according to which nearly everything is better achieved by government and nothing should be left to private enterprise, is also certainly wrong. For example, the concentration of all literature and journalism in the hands of the State, as practised in Russia now, is very harmful to truth and freedom and beauty and political sagacity. Government planning is not the complete and only way to the good life; a certain kind of independence and selfhelp in the citizens is always necessary. Indeed, as Dr. Popper has well put it, the attempt to produce heaven on earth by government action invariably produces hell.

In Britain in the mid twentieth century there is much harmful ignorance of the side consequences of socialism, to use the word 'socialism' as a name for the situation where an enterprise that could be managed privately is being managed by the State. A dangerously large proportion of the people are quite unaware how helpless the individual is when the State is the only purveyor of a commodity, and do not see that to give the State a new function is usually to give more power over yourself to civil servants and city councillors and tax-gatherers and town-planners and other suspect persons. Many a man's thought on the matter is limited to the reflection that he can probably get higher wages out of the State than out of a private employer. In the present situation we can say that there must be very good reasons indeed to allow government action in any sphere in which it is new. Government activity in Britain now should be reduced, not increased.

What about the view that it is a function of the State to preserve a man's property? We find today both the old Lockean view that this is, indeed, the main or even sole function of the State, and the opposite view that property is theft. Tawney's book, *The Acquisitive Society*, in its indignation against landlords and shareholders, tends to suggest that all ownership requires a special justification, that thrift is not respectable and theft not condemnable, that you ought to be forbidden to make provision for your own old age or your children's helpless youth, and that as soon as you cannot work you may not eat except by grace of the State. To own no property is to be completely dependent on the State or some employer for living another month. That is a very bad position to be in. It is highly desirable that we should all be owners, enjoying the responsibilities and satisfactions and independences that ownership gives. What most Englishmen need now is not more doles from the State, such as cheaper rents in council houses, but more encouragement to be thrifty and save instead of buying television. About a third of the employees of the John Lewis Partnership immediately spend any shares they receive in the company. I believe, with regret, that that is typical of us British today. It is certainly not to be changed by Tawney's description of interest on savings as 'income unaccompanied by personal service'. Such language discourages all persons who, starting with no property, work hard and think of saving some of their income as they get it.

The State should encourage the citizen to own property. This makes it desirable to put as few difficulties and restrictions on to the small owner as possible, and to encourage saving. The greatest present discouragements of saving and ownership are inflation and the threat of confiscation. The former takes savings away gradually; the latter threatens to take them in a moment. The State can do much to lessen inflation and remove the threat of confiscation. That means that each of us should be prepared to forgo some present enjoyments for those ends, and instruct our politicians accordingly.

3.53. *The prime ends of government*

We cannot truly mention any end as being the one right purpose of government, but we can mention an end which is the primary and fundamental purpose of governments, both in fact and in right, namely peace. That peace is and ought to be the fundamental purpose of all governments is often forgotten, but never, I think, denied or disbelieved. It is often forgotten, nowadays, because it is nearly always achieved. There is an enormous preponderance of peace within the area controlled by each contemporary occidental government. Laws regulating and controlling the intercourse and transactions of all persons within the territory are made and known and nearly universally obeyed. Stealing and killing and private wars are reduced to very small proportions. So great is the measure of success achieved that many people do not realize that there was anything to achieve. They never contrast our peace and order and security with the conditions of disorder and banditry and feudalism and perpetual private war that still exist in some parts of the world, that have existed here at some former times, and that may exist here again if enough of us fail to realize what keeps them away. So little are the goodness and the precariousness of peace realized today that most people when they hear the word think not of peace in the primary sense, peace within the territory controlled by the State, 'the Queen's Peace', but of peace between one State and another, of the international area in which peace properly speaking has never yet existed, because there has never yet been an authority successfully enforcing a law. Yet all men are agreed, if they think of it, that the primary purpose of the State is the Queen's Peace, that is, that men do not assault or kill or force or bully each other, that it is possible to save and own goods without having them stolen. The primary purpose of the State's government over men is peace between men; and the primary purpose of a world-State over States, if there were one, would be peace between States. States secure peace by promulgating detailed laws (for example, what precisely constitutes assault), by providing officers for catching and trying apparent offenders against these laws, and by providing officers to punish convicted offenders; in other words, by providing legislators, policemen, judges, and jailers.

It is quite superfluous to give arguments that peace is a great good. But it is not quite superfluous today to remind ourselves that a State is doing a great deal if it only secures peace, and that it is easy for internal peace to disappear from an area, and that a revolution usually involves the disappearance of peace from the country for a time, giving freedom to most impulses towards theft or cruelty or murder or rape, as well as often causing famine by breaking down the means of production or distribution.

If there is an end of the State that comes directly after peace, and takes the second place, I think it is justice. But I am not confident what justice is, or how it is related to peace, to law, to rights, and to equality. I think that probably the word is used in several senses, closely related but different, and that most of these senses are closely connected with the notions of law or of rights or both.

I think that 'justice' means sometimes the maintenance of the Queen's peace, the going concern of judges examining accusations and the rest of it, the machinery, or the personnel, by which the peace is preserved; and that this is why certain judges are called 'justices of the peace'. Or else it means this machinery in so far as it works correctly, that is, punishes the true offenders and does not punish any innocents. And in this sense justice is obviously good.

It is true that we often find the whole judicial system condemned. We find it said that the judges are the only criminals, that truth does not look like truth in a court of law, and so on. But such statements can be accepted only as complaints against the actual administration of justice. We cannot believe that all possible judicial systems are worse than having no machinery at all to enforce peace. Jesus was wrong if by his 'Judge not!' he meant 'Have no courts of law!'

There is probably a second sense, in which we detach the notion of justice from that of peace in particular and attach it to the rule of law in general. Justice is that there should be law, and that it should be impartially and universally applied to all who fall under it; or it is the business of so applying the law which in fact rules. In this sense also justice is a great good. The rule of law is far better than the rule of a man or the absence of all rule.

Yet we can say that the law is unjust. That is because beyond the legal law there is the moral law or the natural law, and we sometimes appeal against the former to the latter. Justice now becomes the rule of the ideal law instead of the actual law. In demanding justice in this sense we are demanding morality and the right in politics and social relations, the opposite of Machiavellism. To demand justice in politics, in this sense, is to demand that men shall not forget their moral principles when they go into politics, that politicians and governments and States shall act within the moral law, that men shall not say that morality is for private matters only and has no application to affairs of State, just as they are not to say that in business we may break rules that we should keep among our friends. It is to demand that everyone's natural rights shall be recognized and preserved.

This use of the word 'justice' indicates the moralist's attitude towards politics. People apply it to political matters if they are moralists in politics. Godwin's *Enquiry concerning Political Justice* is so called because he believes in 'the propriety of applying moral justice as a criterion in the investigation of political truth' (II. ii). Plato makes justice the greatest virtue of the city for the same reason; and in so doing he is demanding the disappearance of the brutal, non-moral sort of political activity described by Thucydides.

It is evident that justice is a great good in this sense too. That there is sometimes a moral right and a wrong in politics, as well as in personal matters, is a statement that very few of us doubt; and nearly all of us demand that this right shall be pursued and this wrong avoided; and the few who deny this are definitely our enemies and to be overcome by force if necessary. We shall often leave the Machiavellian alone, because we decide that he is not very harmful or he is only play-acting; but we shall always consider that we have the right to use force against him.

On the other hand, it is also evident, unfortunately, that we are by no means clear or agreed as to which things are right and wrong in politics. Plato thought aristocracy to be just and democracy unjust; others think the reverse. Some think it just that business enterprises should pay interest to shareholders, and others think it unjust. Some think that when food is scarce it should be equally distributed among the population; but others think that a larger share should be given to the old, or to the young, or to the soldiers, or to the miners. And throughout a thousand spheres such disagreements constantly arise. We are nearly all agreed that justice should be done; but usually we are seriously divided as to what is just in the particular case. 'Wages in any occupation are fair when . . .' Any descriptive completion of this phrase will arouse objection from some quarter. (I have taken the phrase from Pigou's *Economics of Welfare*, 2nd ed., p. 520, where you can find a completion of it.)

For this reason justice, or morality in politics, which at first seems a grand thing, is liable later to appear empty and useless. In demanding justice we seem only to be demanding that political arrangements shall be what they should be, and that people shall get what they should get. The conception of justice seems even more unfinished than most ideals. Apart from keeping the peace, it seems hardly more than that each person should have his rights, whatever they are. And this reflection is liable to lead us to the cynical view that people are merely calling 'fair' or 'just' whatever they happen to want. Or, if we do not go so far as that, we may still come to think that justice is something inherently impossible, the mirage of a perfect distribution which should give everybody everything he wants and hurt nobody. The French may seem wise not to have included it in their famous triad.

The conception of justice *is* fragmentary and for ever unfinishable; and yet it is of very great value and importance. Disputes about whether so and so is fair or unfair are going to exist as long as man exists; but this is far better than that there should be no question of fair play in politics at all, and Machiavellism should be accepted. The idea of moral politics is part of our hope of dragging ourselves out of our predicament of conflicting interests; and, though we can never realize it perfectly, we can always be getting nearer to it.

3.6. DEMOCRACY

3.61. *The word 'democracy'*

The word 'democracy' is often used or defined in thoroughly muddling and harmful ways, even by persons of great education and responsibility and importance. For example, the word 'democracy' is definitely not the proper name for freedom of speech, and yet it was so defined by no less a person than Sir Stafford Cripps, when, in his book called *Democracy Up-to-Date*, he wrote: 'By democracy we mean a system of government in which every adult citizen is equally free to express his views and desires upon all subjects in whatever way he wishes and to influence the majority of his fellow citizens to decide according to those views and to implement those desires. To this there is a necessary corollary, that he must not use his own freedom of thought, speech or action so as to deprive others of a like freedom.' It is a great pity that a man of influence and good will should so muddle and confuse the public. The proper name for freedom of speech is 'freedom of speech', and 'democracy' is definitely not a proper name for it. Freedom of speech can exist in a non-democracy as well as in a democracy, while, on the other hand, it often fails to exist in a democracy.

Nor is the word 'democracy' a proper name for general good will, or benevolence, or the desire to lessen men's miseries, or the desire that men shall be able to realize themselves more than they now can. It was improper of Mr. R. H. S. Crossman to write, in his book called *Plato Today* (U.S. ed., 1939, p. 303), that 'the democratic faith is not tied to any political or social system. It regards all systems (including "democracy") as instruments for the self-realization of human nature; and if representative institutions are shown to be no longer useful for that purpose, then the democrat must look elsewhere for other instruments and better institutions.'

Nor is the word 'democracy' a proper name for good will on the part of rulers towards their subjects. A benevolent despotism is still a despotism, not a democracy. Communists are using the word in this way when they say that Russia is a democracy, and when they give the name 'people's democracies' to the nations which Russia is now oppressing.

The cause of most of these aberrations and muddles is that people know the word 'democracy' only as a term of strong political approval. It is a fact that nowadays the word suggests approval to most of those who know it, though there have been times when it usually suggested disapproval. The constitution which the word was invented to refer to has come to be widely approved of. Consequently, the word itself has come to suggest approval of that constitution as well as to refer to it. In many people's minds a further shift has occurred; the word to them now does nothing but suggest political approval, and no longer refers to anything specific. This is a very easy shift because, when we hear others using a strange word, we pick up their emotional intention much easier than their reference. These people, therefore, regarding the word as a mere instrument of political approval, apply it to anything whatever that they do approve of in the political or social sphere. In this way they come to talk about democratic handshakes, and to call a club democratic not on account of its government but because it is a club for both sexes, and other absurdities. I have even heard the ideal autocracy in Plato's *Republic* described as 'more democratic than anything we know'.

That is a plain degradation of language. It is unmitigated loss to take a word that once referred to a specific political constitution and make it a mere expression of political approval. To talk properly, and to keep in touch with the tradition of reason and classification which our intellectual ancestors have built up for us, we must use the word 'democracy' to refer to something. To what?

In the first place, the word should certainly be used to refer to a *constitution*, or at least to some specific constitutional arrangement. For it is clear that that is what it was invented to do, and what it is needed to do, and what it always has done except when it has been a mere expression of approval.

Secondly, the formation and history of the word both suggest that the constitution it shall refer to shall be that which consists in the people or *demos* being the government.

But here at least two difficulties arise. First, it seems that the government cannot be the people, and hence we have made the word 'democracy' a name for something that cannot happen, hence a name useless in practical politics. The government and the people physically cannot be identical unless the people are few enough to meet in one place where they can all hear each other. If they are too many to meet and hear each other, there inevitably arises a distinction between the people as a whole and one small part of it which for the time being is the government. Thus 'government by the people' strictly speaking never happens; and none of the States of the world can possibly be a democracy in this sense.

The nearest possible approach to strict government by the people is the referendum. A referendum occurs when the parliament or government, instead of itself deciding whether a Bill shall become law, refers the Bill to a vote of the whole people. Such a procedure makes a kind of momentary identity between the government and the whole people. For that moment, and on that one question, the people literally is the government.

A referendum is, however, an inefficient and usually harmful step, in my opinion; and in any case it can only be applied to a small part of the business of government. For practical purposes, therefore, it is necessary to alter our definition of 'democracy' a little. The phrase 'government by the people' can remain only as a very rough approximation to the meaning of the word. And we must find a definition which will stay close to our original intention but yet refer to something that can actually happen all the time.

The definition must continue to mention both the people and the government; but it must indicate some relation between them other than identity. John Stuart Mill chose the relation of representation. He wrote that 'it is essential to representative government that the practical supremacy in the State should reside in the representatives of the people' (*Representative Government*, p. 229, Everyman); and he generally made no difference between 'representative government', 'representative democracy', and 'democracy'.

I suggest that representation is not the essence, but only an inevitable means to the essence, of what we wish to indicate by the word 'democracy'; and that what we wish to indicate is the constitution in which the people can at regular intervals constitutionally dismiss the governors if they so choose. This is the sense in which I use the word; and I offer the following three considerations in favour of it. First, it is evidently close to, if not identical with, the sense in which the word has been employed by most good writers. Second, it refers to a very important question. When we examine the constitution of a State, we can hardly think of a more important question to ask about it than this: Can the governors be peaceably dismissed by the people, without revolution, or not? And this question becomes, on my definition, the question: Is it a democracy? Thirdly, this definition divides existing States into two groups. There are today States in which the people do in fact regularly choose between two or more possible governments, and the one which they choose becomes in fact the government, and, if they reject the one that was governing before, it in fact ceases to be the government. Thus the United Kingdom is today a democracy in this sense, because every five years or oftener the people have a choice between at least two possible governments, and, if the people reject the men who have been governing, these men do in fact leave the government offices and hand over the power to the new men. They do not stay in 10 Downing Street and order the police to arrest the leaders of the party that has received the popular vote; and if they did the police would disobey them. There are other States in which this does not occur, though in some of them it is pretended to occur. Russia, for example, is and always has been a non-democracy in this sense, because the people are never offered a choice of rulers, and no Russian government ever withdraws because the people have voted another government into power. In the last four decades a pretence of democracy in this sense has been made in Russia; but it has been only a pretence, because the people have had only one party to vote for.

The word 'people' gives rise to further difficulties in the definition of 'democracy'. Who are the people? What is the *demos*?

When Aristotle undertakes to distinguish the kinds of constitution, he writes: 'The sovereign must be either one or few or the many' (*Politics* iii. 7. 1279^a 27). He does not write: 'The sovereign must be either one or few or *all*.' By his phrase 'the many, *hoi polloi*' does he mean all the citizens or not? If the many are not all the citizens, how are they distinguished from all the citizens? Are they the poor, or the largest social class?

When we raise these questions, our first thought may be that by 'the many' he must have intended all the citizens, because otherwise he would have had to add all the citizens as a fourth kind of sovereignty. Since he did not write 'the sovereign must be either one or few or many or all', he surely meant all the citizens by his phrase 'the many'. But no. He goes on explicitly to define 'democracy' as the sovereignty of the poor (1279^b 19, 40). Thus we are confronted with the unpleasant idea that Aristotle defined 'democracy' in a Communist rather than a Liberal sense, as being the dictatorship of the proletariat rather than the sovereignty of all the citizens. And this is largely true, including the notion that the proletariat rules exclusively for its own benefit and is merciless towards the smaller classes; for, if the many rule with an eye to the common advantage, Aristotle calls the constitution by another name, to wit 'polity'. 'Democracy' is an essentially bad constitution in Aristotle's language, because its sovereign power is essentially selfish.

The only mitigations of this disappointing discovery are, first, that Aristotle in his great political charity is willing to make the best of all constitutions including democracy, and, second, that he is not as clear as he should be about the distinction between the rule of the largest class and the rule of all, so that some of his remarks may, in spite of his definition, be about the rule of all.

You may think that this distinction has no importance, on the ground that, if the constitution gives the power to all the citizens, then in practice the largest class will be the ruler. But the largest class may be divided against itself on some questions, leaving the matter to be determined by the votes of a smaller class. Or the constitution may provide proportional representation in order to give more influence to the smaller classes. And however much the largest class may have the power in fact I cannot recommend that it should have all the power in theory. In my view the distinction between the rule of all the citizens, and the rule of the largest class of them, is vital to good politics; and democratic theory has suffered much from its being overlooked. I therefore choose the definition that makes it easiest to express this value-judgement, and mean by 'the people' not the largest class but all of the citizens.

There is still one awkward question of definition left: Who are the citizens? Who is to have the vote? No State has ever yet given a vote to every human being on the ground. So far they have all excluded minors and foreigners. Many have excluded the whole female population and still been called democracies. How large a proportion of the population must, in our opinion, have the vote, for us to call it a democracy?

On this question our definition had better be framed so as to allow the suffrage law to vary greatly within the democratic constitution. It would not be expedient to say, for example, that no State is a democracy if its women have no vote. I think the idea of democracy is that the suffrage belongs at any time to everyone who at that time is generally recognized as being a fully responsible person. So long as it is the general opinion, shared by women as well as men, that women are not fully responsible, a State can be a democracy without giving votes to women. But it must give them votes, or cease to be classified as a democracy, as soon as its subjects mostly believe that women are as responsible as men. The United Kingdom now is a democracy although we do not give the vote to schoolboys, because we genuinely believe that schoolboys are not fully responsible. If we came to believe that schoolboys are just as responsible as men of fifty, we should have to give them the vote or cease to call ourselves a democracy. Thus it is essential to democracy, I suggest, that the State contains no member who is considered to be fully rational, and reasonably educated, and yet is forbidden to vote.

The inconvenience of this definition is that it makes it possible for a State to change from democracy to non-democracy in virtue of nothing but a shift in the citizens' opinions about the responsibility of schoolboys. Yet this seems better than including some specific franchise law in the definition of 'democracy'.

There is no word that is clearly recognized as meaning the precise contradictory of democracy. The words 'absolutism', 'dictatorship', 'authoritarianism', 'totalitarianism', 'tyranny', 'despotism', 'monarchy', and 'oligarchy', all refer to some species of the contradictory of democracy rather than to the contradictory itself. We might coin the words 'demoduly' or 'ademocracy' or 'non-democracy', of which the first two are more purely constructed but the last is more generally understandable.

I see no use for the phrase 'democratic principles'. There is only one democratic principle, and that is that the State should be a democracy, that is, that by the constitution there shall be, every few years, a vote of all responsible members to determine whether the present governors are to continue or be replaced. To talk of further democratic principles is to import too much into the meaning of the word 'democracy', to begin the mistake of using the word 'democracy' as a portmanteau for everything you approve of in politics.

People are particularly fond of introducing freedom and equality into the definition or the principles of democracy. But it is better to call each of those by its own name, because then you can see more clearly what in fact are the relations between freedom and equality and democracy in the proper sense. Democracy entails that every responsible citizen is equal with every other in that each has at least one vote. It does not entail any other equality. Whether democratic States have a tendency to produce or aim at other equalities among their members is a question for empirical investigation, not a part of the definition of the word. Democracy also entails that every responsible citizen is free to cast a vote for or against the governors every few years. It does not entail any further freedom; and whether actual democracies have in fact displayed, on the average, more tendencies to produce further freedoms than have non-democracies is a question for empirical investigation, not part of the definition of the word.

Still less does democracy entail anything about socialism or capitalism. A democracy may or may not have the great enterprises in public hands; and a State where they are all publicly owned may perfectly well be a despotism.

The phrase 'economic democracy' is employed mostly by people who are confusing two different things. For an economic enterprise, such as a factory, to be in itself a democracy, would mean that the managers or governors of the factory were dismissed and rechosen at short intervals by the whole body of persons engaged in the factory in any capacity; and for this to be a reality and not a sham there would have to be an alternative body of managers, an opposition party, willing to take over the management of the factory. That is one of the two things people are confusing when they talk of 'economic democracy'. The other is legislation by the State to control the management and activities of the factory for the benefit of the workers in the factory, or perhaps for the benefit of the whole country. The two things are quite distinct and do not necessarily go together. On the contrary, State control of the factory must necessarily limit and interfere with the democratic control of the factory by its own members. The factory cannot at one and the same time be completely controlled both by its own members and by the State. A part of the bewilderment and disappointment of the Labour Party in Britain in the 1950's was that their own nationalization laws in the previous decade had caused them to realize this distinction for the first time. They were bewildered and upset to discover that governmental control of an industry is not the same thing as the control of an industry by the whole body of its workers.

Another muddle about the word 'democracy' was introduced by

POLITICAL GOODS 235

Sidney and Beatrice Webb. In 1902 the Webbs published a book called *Industrial Democracy*, which was read for decades thereafter. They did not define the title; but the book is about trade unions, and until the last chapter the impression given is that the British trade unions are democracies and this is the fact referred to by the title. In the last chapter, however, they often use the phrase 'in the democratic State ⟨so-and-so⟩ will be ⟨the case⟩', thus giving the impression that they think that no democratic State as yet exists, and therefore that the United Kingdom is not a democracy. Thus the trade unions are democracies in the body of the book; but in the last chapter the United Kingdom is not a democracy. This is not because they saw a significant difference between the constitution of the United Kingdom and the constitutions of the British trade unions. It is because they use a new meaning of the word 'democracy' in the last chapter. Without saying so, they now use the phrase 'democratic State' to mean a State where not merely the State itself but also every body within the State is democratically constituted. At least this is the tendency of their language, though no doubt they would have been disconcerted if asked whether the army should be democratically organized. They imply that it is desirable that no organization whatever should be non-democratically constituted, and the absurdity escapes them because they have their eyes on industry only.

To define 'democracy' as the constitution in which both the State itself, and also every body within the State, is democratically organized, is to make the logical mistake of defining a word through itself. Apart from that, and even if we understand what is meant because we use our knowledge of the ordinary meaning in order to construct this new meaning, the definition is useless and impractical, because it gives us a concept that will never apply to anything actual, and deprives us of a concept we need.

So much on the definition of the word.

3.62. *Democracy is a great good*

I come now to appraise democracy. That is, to attempt the apparently rash enterprise of doing better than Mill did in the third chapter of his essay on *Representative Government*. I shall consider in order the material, the moral, and the political, values of democracy. First, then what is the material value of democracy?

It used to be said that democracy is inefficient compared with non-democracy. To call a constitution efficient or inefficient is much vaguer than calling a vacuum-cleaner efficient, because we know perfectly well what a vacuum-cleaner is supposed to be efficient at, whereas it is by no means clear or agreed what a constitution is supposed to be efficient at. The most obvious candidates are war and prosperity. It is no longer plausible to say that democracies are inefficient at war. The twentieth century has seen two wars greater than any previous war; and each of them has been won by a combination of mainly democratic States, and lost by a combination of nothing but undemocratic States. Autocracies are more apt to start wars, but democracies are more apt to win them.

Is democracy more efficient than non-democracy at producing prosperity, that is, a satisfactory average level of health, happiness, comfort, and security? It is not wise to answer this question by examining merely the correlations of democracy and prosperity in the past. The United States is now the most prosperous State in the world. It would certainly have been much less prosperous if it had had a very bad constitution; but that does not tell us how much of its prosperity is due to its democracy. Evidently much of it is due to factors that have nothing to do with democracy, notably its having possessed a vast virgin territory in the temperate zone, its having been able to avoid the handicap of frontiers and customs barriers throughout this great space, and its having been colonized by Protestants. I hesitate to follow Mill's opinion that we can see clearly in history that people are more prosperous when they are under democratic constitutions (op. cit., p. 210, Everyman). If there is such a correlation, I think democracy may be the effect and prosperity the cause. The Germans seem to be a people who can achieve prosperity without democracy.

Mill thought that a democratic constitution makes the citizens more selfdependent, and their selfdependence in turn makes them more prosperous. I think this is a mistake, due to confusing democracy with individualism, as Mill tended to do. Individualism involves selfdependence; but democracy may produce socialism as easily as individualism.

There are more likely paths than this from democracy to prosperity. One of them is indicated by the following argument in favour of democracy. Changes of governor will come to every State from time to time. In a non-democracy they involve the brutalities and miseries of revolution; but in a democracy they do not. Democracy is, from this point of view, a device for allowing revolutions to occur without misery. It is, in fact, the only truly 'revolutionary' constitution; and the claim of the Communist tyrants to represent 'the revolution' is, as usual, muddled logic and bad science. There is no such thing as *the* revolution. But there is *a* revolution every time one set of governors is replaced by another. And *a* revolution occurs much more frequently where there is a democracy than where there is a Communist tyranny. In this way I think I do see a distinct connexion between democracy and prosperity. Democracy is much less liable to devastating forms of revolution.

It is not in the least true that democracy is less stable than other constitutions. The stability meant here is stability of law and order, namely that violence and theft are steadily repressed, and one always knows who is the governor. Or at least this is the only kind of stability that is desirable and can properly be put forward as an advantage in a constitution. But this kind of stability is much commoner in democracies than in non-democracies, precisely because in non-democracies every change of governors is a lawless revolution.

There is one other well known path by which democracy tends towards prosperity. In a non-democracy it is bound to occur from time to time that the rulers are ignorant of or apathetic about some grave and remediable misery that some of the people are suffering. The miseries of the English factories in the early decades of the nineteenth century continued as long as they did because the rulers were assured by their economists that these miseries were inevitable, while the sufferers had no vote by which to dismiss a set of rulers who believed them inevitable. The sufferer knows that the shoe pinches more often than the ruler or expert knows it. As Dr. Popper has well put it, 'democracy, the right of the people to judge and to dismiss their government, is the only known device by which we can try to protect ourselves against the misuse of political power' (*The Open Society*, U.S. ed., p. 316).

On the other side there is a character of democracy which makes against prosperity, namely its tendency to improvidence. People often vote according to their wealth. Hence in democracies the poorer 70 per cent. of the electors tend to vote together. And when they do so they tend to vote improvidently and not to face unpleasant facts, partly because the poor are more improvident than the rich, and partly because the expenditures which they vote will not fall directly on themselves. An outstanding example of this was the United Kingdom in the 1920's and 30's. Disgusted and disheartened by the horrors of the recent war, the British shut their eyes to the realities of power and practically refused to have an army. If they had been provident and realistic they could have prevented Hitler and the horrors of the Second World War. All democratic States tend to be wholly occupied in progress and the construction of a better world, whereas the real political problem, unfortunately, is very often how to prevent regress and the destruction of what we have now. In the two great wars all the democracies somehow managed to overlook the obvious fact that they were fighting to defend the prosperities of the nineteenth century, not to improve on them. In a democracy statesmen are confronted by the anxious topic of 'honesty with the electorate'. In other words, how can one tell one's electors the unpleasant truth and yet get elected?

When I try to judge these various considerations, I incline to think that democracy does on the whole tend to prosperity more than non-democracy does, but that this tendency is in general by no means great enough to form a very strong reason in favour of democracy.

At the present time, however, the situation is unusual. There is now only one alternative to democracy, namely rule by the Communist Party. And it is quite obvious that wherever the Communist Party rules it spreads a degree of misery, poverty, fear, and degradation, by contrast to which every democracy is very prosperous. In our present special situation, therefore, democracy does very definitely make for prosperity.

What are the moral advantages and disadvantages of democracy? That is, how does it improve or disimprove character?

Let me take separately the character of the governors and the character of the whole people. As to the character of the governors, a strong argument for democracy is contained in Acton's famous phrase that 'power tends to corrupt, and absolute power corrupts absolutely'. Government requires, or is, a use of force. When men possess force they are tempted to misuse it. No person or group or office is likely to resist for long the temptation to misuse absolute power, whether executive, military, judicial, or police. Acton wrote that 'the possession of unlimited power corrodes the conscience, hardens the heart, and confounds the understanding'; and he quoted Leibniz's statement that 'those who have more power are liable to sin more; no theorem in geometry is more certain than this' (G. E. Fasnacht, *Acton's Political Philosophy*, p. 134). The possession by a man of power over others tends to make him morally worse, and tends to make suffering for those over whom he has power. We can hardly be saved from moral corruption without the moral judgements and penalties imposed on us by our fellows. The democratic constitution checks this dangerous tendency of the ruler's power, by making him responsible to the people, because he can always be dismissed by them.

That power corrupts, and that without the control of our fellows we tend to become immoral beasts, is a fundamental hard fact of human nature which it is immensely important to realize. The chief fault of the inventors of Callipolis and Utopia, and their lesser competitors, is that they insist on imagining a human nature which should be good although free from control by other men. Such imaginings are vain and dangerous.

This important argument was belittled by T. D. Weldon in his book, *States and Morals*, p. 252. But his belittlement rested upon a quibble, on giving to the word 'power' an arbitrary sense which Acton did not intend. 'Power', Weldon wrote (p. 203), 'is quite a different thing from strength or force. It is not even legalised force, though legality is an element in it. Power is more accurately the control of force authorised by consent.' In Weldon's language, then, power does not corrupt because power is by definition force kept straight by resting on the people's consent. But we may add, and he should have added, that force corrupts, and this is what people meant when they said that power corrupts. Here then is a way in which the democratic constitution strongly tends to improve the character of the rulers. It is not without its drawback, however. Since the ruler depends for his place on the choice of the people, he is tempted to flatter the people, to appeal to their passion rather than their judgement, or, worse still, to appeal to the sectional passion of some small part of the people on whom his election depends. Democracy is liable to bring the demagogue; and the art of oratory is liable to command the art of government. The rulers will be as bad as the people's passions demand and their consciences allow. When the majority of the voters are base, as they sometimes are, the rulers will be base.

The drawback is less than the advantage. Upon the whole, democracy distinctly tends to produce better rulers than does non-democracy. The best ruler is not the cleverest ruler, nor is he the most aggressive for his State or the most successful in war.

As to the character of the whole people, Mill's chapter in favour of democracy is mainly a claim that democracy greatly improves the character of a people, making them much more intelligent, large-minded, active, selfdependent, and practical, and much less envious.

Democracy tends, as non-democracy does not, to raise the political maturity and responsibility of every voter, to encourage his public spirit, and to make him contribute his deliberations to the common good. It becomes every man's opportunity and duty to take part in discussions concerning the public good, and to form his judgement thereon. By thus involving discussion, democracy moralizes politics, both internal and external, because in public discussion it is necessary to take the moral point of view to persuade others. Acton remarked that 'Machiavelli's teaching would hardly have stood the test of Parliamentary government, for public discussion demands at least the profession of good faith' (Fasnacht, *Acton's Political Philosophy*, p. 138).

There is, however, much to be said on the other side. Mill expects selfdependence because he confuses democracy with individualism. Tocqueville contradicts Mill's view about envy when he writes (*Democracy in America*, I. xiii): 'Democratic institutions have a very strong tendency to promote the feeling of envy in the human heart; not so much because they afford to everyone the means of rising to the level of any of his fellow-citizens, as because those means perpetually disappoint the persons who employ them. Democratic institutions awaken and foster a passion for equality which they can never entirely satisfy.' And he remarks that this is why the most notable men in a democratic nation are usually not placed at the head of affairs. This is still, 130 years later, a salient defect of the country about which Tocqueville was writing. One of the dominant themes in the propaganda for a candidate for the presidency of the U.S. is usually the assertion that he is no better than the average citizen, that his home and education were mediocre, that his present tastes and companions are very ordinary, that he is, in one of their favourite phrases, 'as common as an old shoe'. Democracy has a definite tendency to discourage recognition and reverence for all the better kinds of superiority, as Mill himself recognizes later (op. cit., pp. 319-20). As E. M. Forster wrote in his *Two Cheers for*

Democracy, democracy encourages the cult of mediocrity, and fosters vulgarity by making mass approval the supreme arbiter.

Democracy has a tendency to encourage an improvident or selfish attitude to public affairs in the electorate. Politicians, in trying to get themselves elected by a group of electors, are permanently tempted to appeal to the interests peculiar to that group; and thus each group of electors is permanently tempted to consider its own interests as the aim of its political activity. Thus the general spread of public spirit, which is very necessary to the good working of a democracy, is opposed by a mechanism inherent in the nature of democracy. One can sometimes see, in the faces of a crowd listening to an election speech, a disgusting and terrifying illustration of this evil tendency.

Furthermore, the law that power corrupts acts on the people as well as on the rulers. Democracy by limiting the powers of the rulers saves them from corruption; but at the same time it has a tendency to corrupt the largest class among the people by giving it unlimited power. A democratic State is liable to become a corrupt tyranny of the largest class over the other classes, disguised by referring to the largest class as 'the people' or 'the workers', as if physicians were not people and did not work. The Labour Party in the United Kingdom has a strong tendency to be a tyrannical class party of this kind. Such a tyranny of the majority is often unconscious, because the majority believe they have a right to the goods of the minority, or believe that it is not they but the august State who is getting the benefit. It makes for unconscious selfishness in the majority, conscious hatred in the minority, and improvidence in the finances of the State. It makes, as Mill said, for 'government intended for . . . the immediate benefit of the dominant class, to the lasting detriment of the whole' (op. cit., p. 254, Everyman).

What is the resultant of these forces? Does democracy on the whole improve or disimprove the character of the people? I do not know. Very probably it does the one in some situations and the other in others. Sometimes it seems to me that, as we grow more democratic, so we all grow more demanding for ourselves and more indignant or contemptuous of others. James Fitzjames Stephen, an enemy of democracy, wrote that 'the fact is that we all more or less condemn and blame each other, and this truth is so unpleasant that oceans of sophistry have been poured out for the purpose of evading or concealing it' (*Liberty, Equality, Fraternity*, London, 1874,

p. 86). On the whole, however, I hesitantly judge that democracy does improve the nation's character; and I hope that democratic selfishness and hate are only a short stage of transition from the abject respect of the peasant for his king to the equal respect of all men for all men. So much for the moral effects of democracy.

I come lastly to the political value of democracy. The greatest value of democracy is that it is a fundamental part of the great good of freedom. It gives to every individual, managed by the State as he is, the greatest possible share in being himself the managing State. It mitigates to the greatest possible degree the inevitable subjection of us all to the State. It is thus a good in itself, not merely a device for obtaining other goods.

It is also a powerful device for safeguarding other forms of freedom. To be free to dismiss one's rulers is a powerful means of securing that one's rulers do not without very good reason take away other freedoms. Only a people that can dismiss its governors can compel its governors either to withdraw a law, or to make a law to curb the activity of some other body that is interfering with the life of the people. It was thus a grave mistake in the 1930's when men said that political freedom did not matter, and only economic freedom was important. Whether by 'economic freedom' they meant more opportunity to consume, or laws to control business enterprises for the benefit of their employees, in either case the power to dismiss one's governors is by far the most likely tool to produce economic freedom. Political freedom is the key to economic freedom, as Dr. Popper has well pointed out (*The Open Society*, c. xvii).

I do not attach much value, however, to the power of democracy as a tool for non-political freedom, because it can also be used against non-political freedoms, and often is. Democracies have in practice a strong tendency towards the unjustifiable restriction of various liberties, when we contrast them with aristocracies. This is because the largest class tends to be more censorious than the nobles, more given to moral indignation, more likely to regard as wicked or dangerous anything unfamiliar. There is always in a democracy the danger of the insane frenzy or terror or lust of the mob. Demos tends to be in social matters indiscriminately tyrannous, and Mill's essay *On Liberty* is largely about this danger. It is the cause of the curious fact that some democracies resemble dictatorships far more than they resemble aristocracies. Democracies and dictatorships equally involve the suppression of the nobles, and often the destruction of them; for in dictatorships only those succeed who adopt the popular vulgarities. This is beautifully realized and described in the eighth book of Plato's *Republic*; and in our own days it has been well illustrated by the dictatorship in Germany in the 1930's and that in Argentina in the 1940's.

The sure political good of democracy is therefore not the consequential freedoms that it may produce, but the essential freedom that it is. Political freedom is very good in itself. 'Ne me demandez pas d'analyser ce goût sublime, il faut l'éprouver' (Tocqueville, *Ancien Régime*, III. iii). You need not value it yourself if you do not wish to; but you ought to allow it to us who do value it.

It is another facet of the same thing that democracy is the political embodiment of the good kind of equality, which consists in the equal dignity and consideration of man. It removes the humiliation of the subject's permanent and absolute subordination to the rulers in a non-democracy. Democracy is political freedom and political equality, however much it may in practice interfere with various other freedoms and equalities; and that is its essential goodness.

There is one great political good with which democracy appears to have no connexion, and that is the maintenance of law and justice and rights. The rule of all may be conducted with or without law and justice. There must, indeed, be the minimum of constitutional law that enables us to say the State is a democracy; but beyond that the democratic State may respect law or contemn it, and may be slow or fast to destroy the legal and the customary rights of inconvenient persons, and may be patient or impatient of an independent judiciary that stands up for individual rights and the reign of law.

3.63. *Plato's argument against democracy*

I can bring out further what I take to be the essential goodness of democracy by considering Plato's famous argument against it in his *Republic* (488). He there compares the democratic State to a ship whose captain, though goodhearted, is stupid and imperceptive, and whose crew spend their time besieging the captain with requests to be allowed to navigate the ship, each urging his own suitability for the work. We are to suppose that neither the captain nor any of his crew knows anything about the stars or the winds, or admits that there is such a thing as an art of navigation dependent on knowledge of these; and there is no competent navigator on the ship at all.

And we are to imagine what kind of voyage this ship will make. Now, says Plato, the captain in this image represents the people of a democratic city, in control of affairs in that city. They are good-hearted enough; but they are stupid and ignorant, and they have no conception of the art of government, or of the science of the good on which this art should be based. They are all the time being harangued and advised by demagogues, the crew of the image, telling them how to navigate the ship of State and asking to be put in charge; but none of these demagogues has learnt the true art of government or even admits that there is such a thing. True government, however, is a serious and difficult art based on obscure but certain knowledge of the essence of the good and the bad and the just and the unjust and so on.

Thus Plato by this image of the ship clearly means to say that government is a high art based on a high science, and the people as a whole can never be in possession of this science, and therefore the people as a whole ought not to be in charge of affairs; that is, democracy is bad. As he goes on, he adds many less important points to his judgements. Thus he finds that democracy corrupts the science and character of any potentially good statesman, because it compels him to truckle to the mob. He finds also that democracy tends to produce an improper disorderliness and amateurishness and variety among the citizens, and an improper equality among unequals. Slaves act as if they were free, and dogs decline to get out of the way of men.

The democrat need not be worried by Plato's arguments that democracy tends to disorderliness and to equality; for the democrat likes equality, and dislikes the order that Plato thinks important. But it is otherwise with Plato's main argument, that government is a science, and no science is the possession of the whole people, and therefore democracy is fundamentally mistaken. This is a very serious objection, and it appears that the defenders of democracy have not yet faced it, although it has been before them for more than two millenniums.

To meet this objection we may begin by pointing out that no art is as sure as the science on which it is based. The calculator practising mental arithmetic makes mistakes more often than the mathematician stating the theorems of the science. The life-history of a medical practice contains more errors than the textbook of pathology on which it was based. Plato himself saw this, in another connexion, when he wrote that practice attains truth less than theory does (*Rp*. 473 A). Hence, even if there were a sure science of politics, it would not follow that the practitioners of the art of government always acted rightly. The art and practice of government must always be more imperfect than the science on which they are based.

But the fundamental answer to Plato's argument must be to deny the premiss that government is a science. I say that government neither is nor ever can be a science in the sense intended by Plato. That is to say, no man is or ever will be in possession of certain knowledge as to what it is best for the State to do in all matters at all times.

I urge that our experience of politics is massively in favour of this view. When we cast our minds over the recent history of politics as far back as we have experienced it, we see that it has been full of surprises and bewilderments. Unexpected events and situations have kept on occurring, and our measures to deal with them have often had unexpected and unwanted results. It is true that almost everything that happened had been predicted by someone; but it is also true that this was mainly because almost everything possible had been predicted by someone, and amid the wild welter of predictions one was bound to come true and the rest were bound to be falsified; and the man who predicted one event truly predicted others wrongly. In 1953, for example, practically no one foresaw the big French strike in August. In 1956 practically no one foresaw the Suez affair; and probably no one at all expected it to come out as it did, or the results of his State's acts to be what they were. Surely anyone who will consent to look at actual politics, whether in his own experience or in history, will admit that they are a welter of largely unforeseeable and uncontrollable events, and that to talk of controlling them by a sure and magisterial science is wide of the mark. New factors may arise at any time in politics. No one can guarantee to foresee them, or to know how to deal with them. All that can be guaranteed is that those whom the new factor hurts will complain if speech is free, and will press their representatives to find a remedy in a democracy.

One of the so called 'sciences' that have much to do with government is economics. The history of the intervention of this science in politics, so far, is a history of gropings and errors and a few successes. The economists are evidently not agreed among themselves as the mathematicians are. It is clear that many of them have given bad advice to governments in the past. Surely it is very probable that they will do so in the future also. Surely it is very probable that the same is true of every other set of persons who offer us a so called 'science' to apply to government.

Predicting political events, and predicting the consequences of a given act by a given State, will never become like predicting eclipses of the sun and moon. There are two differences to make that impossible, the complexity and the alterability of human affairs.

Eclipses depend on the motions of only three bodies, and those motions are known. Political events depend on billions of factors, and most of them are necessarily unknown to any predictor. Neither have we the data, nor could we do the calculation if we had. Men's feelings do not admit of computation even if you know them. That is the complexity which prevents prediction in politics.

The other eternal barrier is that men can predict with certainty only events that no man can influence. If some man by his actions can influence the outcome, then no man can with certainty predict that outcome. To put it more pregnantly and yet without serious loss of accuracy, whatever one man can alter no man can predict, and whatever one man can predict no man can alter. What we predict is always at best what will happen if nothing which we have failed to take account of intervenes. Where persons are capable of intervening to change the result this is a very big IF.

One thing that never affects eclipses is our predictions of eclipses. In discovering when the sun will be eclipsed we do not have to think: 'The astronomer royal has predicted that the sun will be eclipsed on such and such a day. Now how will the sun react to that? Will it be annoyed and decide to disappoint the astronomer?' Such questions do not arise because the sun is not a thinking being. If it were a thinking being we could not predict its movements with such completeness as we do. But men *are* thinking beings, and such questions do arise when we try to predict their acts; and this by itself makes it for ever impossible to turn politics into physics. For this reason the Platonic science of politics, and the Marxian science of politics, and any other science of politics, are impossible will-o'-the-wisps that will never be realized. Faith in them does much harm, turning men away from the fruitful effort to make judicious little adjustments here and there, and giving unconscious tyrants confidence in their wild schemes. The remark that 'the masses are not the wisest statesman', though true in what it primarily asserts, is profoundly false in insinuating that there is or ever could be such a man as a perfectly wise autocrat to whom the government of ourselves might wisely be abandoned, and in persuading us to forget that the masses *are* the statesman least likely to bully or neglect the masses.

If we look at the particular science on which Plato proposed to base government, namely his Dialectic or science of Essences, we find that it was not a genuine science, but a confusion of two genuine activities one of which is a science. There can be a real science of the meanings of words. It includes lexicography and semantics and philosophical analysis. Plato's science of Essences was in part the practice of this, for its key question was What is x?; and the question What is x? is the request for a definition; and definition rightly understood is about a word. Such a science is, indeed, very important for practical politics. Politics is largely talk, and those talk much better who thoroughly understand the nature of the words they are using. But such a science cannot provide, either alone or in combination with anything else, a basis for absolutely certain and expert government.

The other genuine activity, which Plato in his Dialectic of Essences was misapprehending and confusing with the science of words, is not a science but the choice of values. The Essences which he actually studied were nearly all values, as Justice, Goodness, Beauty; and his activity consisted largely, though unconsciously, in making and recommending his choices as to what things are beautiful and what things are good. In this aspect also his Dialectic was a genuine and important part of politics, for politics is in fact largely choosing. What do you value in the social sphere? Do you prefer the peasant culture of the Cévennes or the industrial culture of St. Étienne, and which do you wish France predominantly to be? Is national prestige all important to you, so that you will sacrifice to it your fellows' lives and your country's honesty, or is it not? These are pre-eminently political questions, and they are pre-eminently questions of choice; questions of what you will do, not questions of what the facts are.

But it is just because they are questions of choice, that they are not questions for experts, and no scientist has a right to decide them for us over our heads, however greater his knowledge is than ours. And this is the most important part of the answer to Plato's argument against democracy. Government is a choice, a choice of the social life we are to lead; and nobody else has the right to make that choice for us. Everyone of us, howsoever stupid and uninformed, has a right to his share in this grave choice that vitally concerns him. The public discussion, which is essential to good politics, is largely the formation and approximation of our choices.

This is implied in Plato's own analogy of the ship, though he did not realize it. In fact we do not let the expert navigator choose our destination for us. We tell him where to take us. The fact that he knows the art of navigation, while we do not, gives him no right to take us to Valparaiso when we wish to go to Buenos Aires. He is the servant in voyaging, not the master; and so must the expert be in politics.

The same is true of the physician, on whose analogy Plato relied for political arguments in his later work *The Statesman*. It is for your physician to tell you that if you live vigorously you will probably die within a year, while if you stay in bed you will probably live for ten years more. But it is not for him to decide which of the possibilities you are to realize; that is your choice. This fact is concealed from some of us by the unconscious assumption that it is of paramount importance to live as long as possible, no matter what sort of life it is. But this should neither be an unconscious assumption nor be decided for us by our physicians. It should be consciously decided by ourselves. It is in fact a common defect of physicians to try to dictate our ends to us. They usually insist on regarding the prolongation of life as more important than the avoidance of pain. The recent discovery of a connexion between cancer and tobacco has revealed a tendency in some of them to try to force our choice in this dilemma, by demanding legislation.

That is my rebuttal of Plato's argument against democracy. I think it constitutes the only possible rebuttal of it. You cannot defend democracy if you agree with Plato that government is or could be a science. In showing that government is not a science but a choice, we show why democracy is an essential feature of the best political society.

3.64. *The maintenance of democracy*

We sometimes hear it said that liberals and democrats have no faith to set against the Communist faith. Is this a proper complaint, and does it indicate any action?

We must make a distinction. In one sense it is true that the democrat has no faith to set against the Communist faith, but a matter for congratulation not complaint. For in one sense of the word 'faith', and the most common sense of it, faith is unreasonable devotion, belief or action contrary to the probabilities. In this sense the reasonable man never has a faith, either in democracy or in anything else; and the Communist has faith in the doctrines of Marx or Lenin precisely in that no evidence or argument could make him abandon them. To desiderate a democratic faith, in this sense, would be to long to enjoy the delights of fanaticism and cease being a reasonable person, to desire to be dispensed from the duty of weighing evidence and holding oneself always prepared to change one's view in case of new considerations altering the balance of probability. Communism is indeed a faith, a religion, in a very large part of the sense of those words. It shares the counter-rational character of what is usually called 'religion', though not its theism; and the threat of Communism against reason today is a little like the threat of primitive Christianity against the reasonableness of the Greeks and Romans. But it is not necessary for modern reason to succumb to faith as much as ancient reason did. The gloomy view that only another fanaticism can beat a fanaticism is false. It is not reason and love that need fear a Communist victory, for they are the most efficient instruments in the world when energetically applied. It is laziness and selfishness that need to fear it; for the Communists are neither selfish nor lazy.

This suggests another way of taking the complaint that we democrats have no faith to set against the Communist faith. Perhaps it means that we are lazy and selfish, and unwilling to fight for the preservation of democracy. In this sense it is a very different matter, and clearly to some extent justified. Certainly it would be wrong to be selfish and lazy in the defence of democracy, and certainly we are all of us sometimes less energetic and selfless in this cause than we ought to be. Let us therefore review what is required of us as upholders of the democracy in which we reasonably believe.

Part of this is the question what is required of us abroad. Evidently a democratic State should, other things being equal, be active in promoting and preserving and encouraging democracies elsewhere. In our present situation it is very bad to be in serious opposition to another democratic State, and desirable to swallow a great many wrongs and griefs and humiliations rather than divide the democratic world. About the only thing that could justify grave opposition to another democratic State at the present time would be very good evidence that such opposition was necessary and sufficient to preserve democracy on the whole, because the policy of the other democracy was very dangerous to all the democracies. It is certainly essential for the democracies to be prepared for war for an indefinite time in the future. The dreary and impoverishing business of keeping the democracies militarily formidable must be kept up for farther ahead than we can foresee. Vague talk of 'law not war', or of 'outlawing the bomb', weakens resistance to the Communist tyranny and tends to destroy democracy.

The maintenance of democracy at home has both a personal and an institutional side. The question of the institutional means of maintaining democracy is one I shall not touch. It includes the questions: Is proportional representation likely to help or hinder the maintenance of a democracy? And what about the compulsory vote, as in Australia? And would it be useful to have an initiation ceremony, to be gone through by each citizen on coming of voting age? There is an enormous deal to be studied here, and it is a proper study for persons calling themselves political scientists, because it is a question of fact not choice, of whether this particular institution in this sort of circumstances does in fact help or hinder the maintenance of democracy. All that I leave aside, and conclude with some remarks on our personal duties as defenders of democracy.

First and foremost among our personal duties is that we shall be reasonably and not unreasonably convinced that democracy is a better constitution than non-democracy. That is, we must know and weigh the arguments for and against democracy, and remain prepared to abandon our advocacy should considerations ever point on the whole the other way. We must never let our reasonable adoption of democracy degenerate into faith and fanaticism. We must never succumb to the delights of absolute certainty and the refusal to reconsider.

Next, we must hand on and teach the tradition of these matters. We must explain them to our children, and to whomever else it is our duty to explain them. There is a tendency today to neglect to hand on traditions and at the same time complain that nobody is handing them on. We even find parents who expect their children to know right from wrong by some innate intuition, and blame the poor creatures for not knowing what they have never been taught. The modern emphasis on thinking things out for oneself, excellent though it is, has tended to have this bad result, that things that must just be taught have not been taught. Moral and political instruction have tended to go the same way as rote-learning, into oblivion. This omission we ought to make good. And that involves two things that come hard to many people. One is the utterance of platitudes. Many parents today find it difficult to utter platitudes to their children; we are in undue dread of being Poloniuses. The other thing that comes hard to many people is the art of teaching, the skill to give the lesson when the learner is ripe for it and so that he can use it. All parents at least ought to acquire this skill, in order to give their children the principles of politics and morality. They ought not to leave it to the schools, for the schools can never do it. It requires individual attention and the right moment, and the right moment is liable to come in the bath or on a walk, when the schoolteacher is not there.

Thirdly, we may perfectly well have to die for democracy, either as soldiers in war or as conspirators in revolution. The opposition between faith and reason is not that only the former ever tells a man to die for his cause. The difference between democracy and non-democracy today makes, it appears to me, so great a difference to human happiness and dignity that we ought sometimes to risk death for it. We should all be soldiers of democracy. That is, we should already have accepted the principle that we may have to die for it. And in death are here included all those sufferings which, while they are commonly reckoned less dreadful than death, feel more dreadful to many hearts, namely outlawry, the disapproval of one's neighbours, the agonized incomprehension of one's wife, and torture. It seems clear that, if it were well known in a country that large numbers of the citizens would abandon their comfort and go underground to conspire for the restoration of democratic practice if they thought it had in fact been abrogated, this would be a great influence at all times against any such abrogation. I think, therefore, that it is probably the duty of all of us democrats living under a democratic constitution to make this decision, and to let others know on suitable occasions that we have made it.

This trenches on the question of revolution. When, if ever, is there a moral duty or right to attempt the illegal overthrow of the governors? Certainly there could sometimes be such a moral duty. There could be a monstrously harmful governor who could not be legally removed but could by illegal means be replaced with someone much less harmful; and if this happened revolution would evidently be a moral duty. Can we then write any principle bearing on the matter? Dr. Popper has written that 'the use of violence is justified only under a tyranny which makes reforms without violence impossible, and should have only one aim, that is, to bring about a state of affairs which makes reforms without violence possible' (*The Open Society*, U.S. ed., p. 340). This implies both that violence may be right under a tyranny and that violence is never right under a democracy. I have found by writing to him that Dr. Popper allows one case where violence may be right even under a democracy, namely where the country is about to cease to be a democracy and some illegal action might prevent this. The disappearance of the Czechoslovak democracy in the 1940's suggests this. By legal means the Communist Party gained control and ended democracy. It seems that this could not have been prevented by any legal means, but could have been prevented by some illegal action. So perhaps it is not a right liberalism always to abstain from violence in a democracy. The use of violence is justified even under a democracy if it is necessary and sufficient to prevent the democracy from turning into a non-democracy. But we must add, as before, that the aim of this violence must be only to uphold and preserve the democracy.

I seem to see a second situation in which violence may be right under a democracy, though I have not obtained Dr. Popper's agreement to this one. It was made clear by Mill that in a democracy a majority can tyrannize over a minority. It seems to me that if this minority is geographically separable from the majority, and if it is permanently thwarted by the majority, it may in some cases have the right to secede; and that, if the majority refuses to allow this right peaceably, the minority may have the right to secede by force if it can. I dare say that Abraham Lincoln was justified in refusing secession to the Old South. But he did not produce a good reason; he merely asserted that 'the union of these States is perpetual'.

There ends my digression on revolution; and I return for a last minute to our personal duties concerning the maintenance of democracy. I have only two more to urge. The first is that we ought to remember, and be on guard against, those defects to which, as we have seen, democracy is liable, such as public improvidence, majority tyranny, and private selfishness and envy and disrespect. A wise man will bear the defects and dangers of democracy in mind, and consider how they are to be avoided.

Only an unwise man, however, will say that in view of these defects democracy ought to be abolished. The idea that, since democracy is defective, it ought to be abolished, is an example of the commonest error in political philosophy, which I call 'utopianism'. By 'utopianism' I mean the idea that there is a perfect constitution, and politics could be perfect. The last of our democratic duties which I shall mention is to avoid utopianism. Politics are and always will be a creaking, groaning, lumbering, tottering wagon of wretched makeshifts and sad compromises and anxious guesses; and political maturity consists in knowing this in your bones.

Koestler tells of a Communist discussion in which, after the coming Communist Utopia had been dwelt on with enthusiasm by several speakers, André Malraux put the question: 'And what about the child who gets run over by a tramcar?' There was a painful silence. At last someone said: 'In the planned society there will be no accidents'; and this was gratefully accepted. Utopianism is so prevalent and so unrealistic that it can convince a roomful of people that one day there will be no more sudden deaths of children.

There is plenty of Utopianism in democratic countries too. It was well illustrated by an advertisement once written by the eminent publicist Dorothy Thompson and placed in the *New York Times*. She wrote in the person of the people, who addressed the politicians and complained of them for not having achieved perfect happiness and peace. 'We said [it ran] . . . Soon there will be victory over the forces of evil. . . . All these families in all the nations . . . have identical needs, hopes, and yearnings.'

Alas, yes! Each of those families yearns to have lots of beefsteak, though there is not enough beefsteak in the world to go round. And each of those families yearns for its own nation to be top dog, though only one nation can be.

Utopianism often leads to excessive moralizing and indignation in politics. He who believes that society could be perfect easily becomes indignant at politicians who effect compromises. Hence the New Statesman type of politics, consisting in moralistic abuse of everything that is done. Let our politics consist in specific proposals for the future, not in abuse of the past. Let us spread the convictions that evil is always with us, that politics is always a choice of evils, and that democracy, for the reasons I have recited, is the best of the very imperfect constitutions which alone are possible.

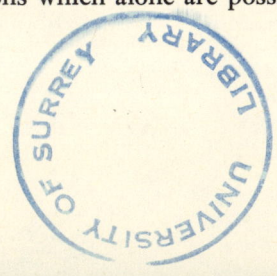

INDEX

Topics mentioned in the list of Contents are not mentioned here

'Absolute', 18
Acton, 160, 174, 180, 220, 238 f., 240
Analytic synthetic, 39, 81 ff., 90
Anscombe, G. E., 43
Aquinas, 68, 71, 118 f.
Argument from ignorance, 88 f., 118
Aristotle, 14, 17, 24, 29, 33-34, 53, 67, 69, 70 f., 112, 154, 158, 160, 186, 221, 231 f.
Arnold, Matthew, 72, 111, 139, 144, 178, 182, 183
Arnold, Thomas, 109, 112
Atheism, 218
Augustine, 59, 68, 69, 111, 119
Authority, 97 f., 133

Bacon, Francis, 83
Barker, Ernest, 33
B.B.C., 10, 117, 130, 138
Beerbohm, 215
Belief, 74-77, 151
Benda, 67
Benson, Stella, 106
Bentham, 97
Berenson, Bernard, 60, 61
Bergson, 114
Berkeley, 79
Berlin, Isaiah, 159, 178
Bernal, J. D., 196 f.
Bernard, 68
Bevan, Aneurin, 182
Bible, 150, 209, 210, 215. *See also* New Testament
Boland, Francis J., 138, 204, 216
Bosanquet, Bernard, 36
Boswell, 135
Bradley, F. H., 111
British Labour Party, 17, 30, 160, 178, 179, 234, 241
Buliard, Roger P., 165
Burden of proof, 87
Burke, 114
Butler, Joseph, 88
Butterfield, Herbert, 138

Cambridge Journal, 9
Campbell, C. A., 93, 95
Cary, Joyce, 10
Castlereagh, 120
Catholicism, *see* Roman Church
Censorship, 218 f., 221
Christian Evidence Society, 115

Civil servants, 175, 193, 223
Classes, 182, 184, 241, 242
Clifford, W. K., 94
Cohen, Morris, 94
Communism, 68 f., 159, 196 f., 215, 221, 228 f., 232, 237, 238, 249, 253
Conscience, 108-13, 128, 215
Consensus of mankind, 127
Conservatism, 159
Contempt, 182
Contradictories, 76, 210
Cranston, Maurice, 188
Cripps, 228
Croce, 159
Cromwell, 212 f.
Crossman, 228
Culture, 164 f., 192, 222

Descartes, 72, 84, 86, 94, 209
Design, 127 f.
Dewey, John, 29, 34
Dialectic, 247
Dignity, 70, 92, 105, 134, 157
Disraeli, 218

Economics, 195, 227, 234, 237, 242, 245 f.
Envy, 179 ff., 240
Euclid, 11, 84, 85, 94
Ewing, A. C., 162, 172
'Exception proves rule', 78

Faculties, 72 f., 101 ff.
Faith, 101, 103, 115, 118 ff.
Fallacies, 88 f., 212 f.
False question, 15-16
Fasnacht, G. E., 160, 220, 239, 240
Flaubert, 62
Forster, E. M., 240
Franklin, 139
Freedom, definition of, 194
Fry, Roger, 62

Gifford Lectures, 114
Godwin, 226
Gollancz, Victor, 10
Gore, 79, 92

Hare, R. M., 131
Harrod, R. F., 29, 103
Helvetius, 108
History, 170

INDEX

Homosexuality, 113
Housman, A. E., 52, 107, 156
'How can . . . ?', 89
Hume, 73, 79, 86, 128, 220
Humility, 104, 147, 151, 153 f.
Humphrey, 73
Huxley, Aldous, 40

Ignorance, 88 f.
Improvidence, 9, 141, 152, 237 f.
Interpretation, 141 ff.
Intuition, 22, 92, 101, 103, 140
Irvingites, 127

Jesus, 111, 112, 226
Justice, 225 ff., 243

Kant, 56 f., 101, 109, 110
Ker, W. P., 54
Killing, 56, 187
Koestler, 253

Langford, 76
Laver, James, 110
Law, 174, 176 ff., 186, 189, 193, 226, 243
Lawrence, D. H., 104
Lawyers, 63, 203, 213
Lecky, 220
Leibniz, 238
Leo XIII, 204-13, 218
Lewis, H. D., 116
Lewis, John Lewis Partnership, 224
Liberalism, 159
Licence, 190
Lincoln, Abraham, 191, 252
Linton, 72
Listener, The, 10, 138
Locke, 74, 94, 194, 214 f., 218, 220, 223
Logic, 93 f.
Logical, 79
Lord, A. R., 163

Maitland, F. W., 171 f.
Malraux, 253
Manson, T. W., 142, 144, 146 f.
Mathematics, 58, 83 ff., 94, 123 f.
May, Erskine, 203
'May be', 88, 212 f.
Meineke, 161
Mill, John Stuart, 18, 50 f., 94, 111, 198 f., 201, 205, 206, 211 f., 220, 221, 230, 235 f., 240, 241-3, 252
Miracles, 127
Misology, 72, 80, 105
Montague, F. C., 199 f.
Moore, G. E., 21-23, 25, 29, 30, 32-33, 71, 77, 109, 110, 111, 158
Moral anarchy, 132 f.
Morality, 60, 100, 110, 111, 112, 130-8, 200, 203, 205 f., 226 f.

Nagel, Ernest, 94
Nationalism, 160 ff., 189, 191 f.
Nations, 165
Nelson, E. J., 76
Newman, J. H., 68, 86, 92, 96, 115, 120, 121, 150 f.
Newspapers, 219
New Testament, 59, 68, 74 f., 105 ff., 108, 115, 118, 119, 140 ff., 158, 209, 226
Newton, 84
Nonresistance, 146, 152, 159
Norfolk, 194

Old Testament, 150, 209, 210, 215
Orwell, George, 163
Otway, 182

Pascal, 68, 69, 74 f., 85, 93 f., 116
Paton, H. J., 26
Patriotism, 167
Peace, 224 f.
Persons, 171
Philosophy, 10-11, 247
Physicians, 247
Pigou, 227
Plato, 11, 14-20, 29, 32, 34, 52, 58, 59, 66 f., 71, 72, 80 f., 87, 93, 94, 104, 105, 111, 122, 139, 158, 160, 162, 186, 190, 221, 227, 229, 243-8
Pope, The, 103
Popper, K. R., 50 f., 162, 179, 215, 218, 223, 237, 242, 252
Port-Royal Logic, 94
Possibility, 88, 212 f.
Post, Laurens Van der, 168
Pravda, 198
Prayer Book, The, 63 f., 149
Prediction, 246
Prichard, H. A., 130
Pride, 103 f., 163
Principles, 37-40, 48-53, 118, 172, 200, 201, 233
Propaganda, 218
Property, 178 ff., 223 f.
Purity, 65, 147, 153

Race, 164 f., 183
Radio Times, 117
Ragg, Lonsdale, 141
Rationalist Annual, 10
Referendum, 230
Respect, 181-4
Revolution, 237, 251 f.
Roman Church, 138, 188, 204 f., 207, 209, 216 f.
Ross, W. D., 59, 74, 109
Rousseau, 96
Russell, Bertrand, 26
Ryan, John A., 138, 204, 216

Sand, George, 182
Scepticism, 77
Schopenhauer, 54, 55
Scott, Douglas, 161
Selfrefutation, 210
Sex, 61 ff., 149
Sherrington, 114
Sidgwick, Henry, 100
Sin, 215
Skeaping, John, 55
Slavery, 189, 192
Smith, P. Nowell, 28
Snobbery, 181-4
'Social', 166
Society, 166
Society for Psychical Research, 95, 129
Sociology, 134
Soul, 185
Spinoza, 84, 108
Standards, 37 ff.
Steno, 84
Stephen, James Fitzjames, 107, 241
Stevenson, C. L., 37-38
Strachey, Lytton, 109
Suicide, 56 f.
Sunday Times, 9

Tawney, R. H., 178, 223 f.
Teachers, 214, 250 f.
'The', 16-17
Theology, 116
Thompson, Dorothy, 253
Thucydides, 226

Times, The, 89, 110, 115, 161, 175, 196
Tocqueville, 240, 243
Tolstoy, 53, 114 ·
Tomas, V., 38
Toulmin, Stephen, 38
Trade unions, 179, 217, 235
Truth, 28, 65-70, 134; Criteria of, 28, 90 f.

Ultimacy, 38-41, 65 f.
Unbelief, 74-77, 151
United Nations, 176, 184
United States, 179, 183, 222, 236, 240
Urmson, J. O., 37, 169, 170
Utilitarianism, 50 f.
Utopianism, 253

Validity, 86 f.
Values, 9-14, 18
Voltaire, 53

Wages, 227
Webb, Sidney and Beatrice, 235
Weldon, T. D., 166, 239
Welfare, 189, 191, 195, 227
Wellington, 120
Whitehead, 104, 110
Whitman, 193
Wilhelmina, Queen, 196
Wilson, Woodrow, 164, 191
Wittgenstein, Ludwig, 26, 43
Wolf children, 128
World-State, 192, 225

Yeats, W. B., 62, 96